the way to eat now

The Library of Congress has catalogued the earlier edition as follows:

Names: Hart, Alice, author.
Title: Good veg : ebullient vegetables, global flavors : a modern vegetarian
   cookbook / Alice Hart.
Description: New York, NY : Experiment, [2017] | Series: New vegetarian
   Includes index.
Identifiers: LCCN 2016045768 (print) | LCCN 2016048592 (ebook) | ISBN
   9781615192861 (cloth) | ISBN 9781615192878 (ebook)
Subjects: LCSH: Vegetarian cooking. | LCGFT: Cookbooks.
Classification: LCC TX837 .H3738 2017 (print) | LCC TX837 (ebook) | DDC
   641.5/636--dc23
LC record available at https://lccn.loc.gov/2016045768

ISBN 978-1-61519-573-2
Ebook ISBN 978-1-61519-574-9

Cover design by Beth Bugler | Text design by Sarah Smith
Prop styling by Tabitha Hawkins
Food styling by Alice Hart
Cover and author photographs by Emma Lee

Manufactured in China

First paperback printing April 2019
10 9 8 7 6 5 4 3 2 1

the way to eat now

MODERN VEGETARIAN FOOD

ALICE HART

THE EXPERIMENT

NEW YORK

Contents

Chapter 3: Quick 79

Chapter 4: Thrifty 111

Chapter 5: Gatherings 145

Chapter 6: Grains 185

Chapter 7: Raw-ish 215

Chapter 8: Afters 259

Chapter 9: Pantry 291

Introduction

THIS IS MY SECOND BOOK on vegetarian cooking, and the culinary climate has indisputably changed for the better in the five or so years that have passed since I wrote the first. Rather than being relegated to the sidelines or dismissed as problematic, vegetarian food is now, rightly, widely celebrated for its diversity and myriad benefits, whether for health or in terms of cost or the environment. The time is right for a book packed to the rafters with ideas and a rainbow of colors, so you never need wonder what to cook for any occasion.

You might be looking for inspiration after a lifetime of vegetarianism, or seeking ideas for new meat-free meals; there will be recipes here for you, almost all based on our sheer and fabulous variety of fresh produce. There are chapters on Grazing and Gatherings to cover the sociable, convivial way we eat on weekends. Many of these recipes are slower projects: gnocchi made with purple potatoes and baked with goat cheese and kale, or vegetable-filled pot sticker dumplings with a black vinegar and chile dipping sauce. The Afters chapter was written with entertaining in mind, too; many of the recipes are made without common allergens such as dairy, eggs or gluten, or are simply vegan, to make it easier when cooking dessert for a crowd. Hopefully, a single recipe—such as the Blood Orange and Olive Oil Cake with Almonds, or the Roasted Pineapple, Coconut and Makrut Lime Sorbet—should suit all.

Both the Quick and the Thrifty chapters cover midweek eating, with faster cooking and, usually, fewer ingredients, to get supper on the table without much fuss or expense. A note on "quick cooking": I want you to feel inspired and happy to be in the kitchen, rather than coaxed there with broken dreams of supper-in-six-minutes-using-only-three-ingredients. Quick, for me, means a good supper in thirty minutes or so . . . and time to unwind as I cook. Based on this premise, I hope you will forgive me for failing to hit the frenzied fifteen-minute mark in most cases. . . .

Mornings, one of the larger chapters in the book, is intended to straddle both weekday and weekend eating, from brunches to snacks, juices to smoothies, nut milks to butters, providing balanced ideas that aren't full of sugar. Many of the recipes (Sweet Potato Cakes with Lime and Avocado, or Overnight Smoky Baked Beans, for example) will also do just as well later in the day.

I feel that the key to satisfying vegetarian cooking is in contrast. This is most evident in East Asian recipes—you will find many here—where the balance of hot versus cool, crisp versus soft, sweet versus sour, chile heat versus refreshing herb, is all. The theory has legs beyond East Asia though and, if you bear it in mind, will add so much to your cooking, even if it is simply in making a perfectly balanced salad dressing or adding hot toasted nuts to a cool dish as a final flourish of texture and temperature. Consider texture and temperature as much as taste; it will elevate your cooking. So will putting effort into the basics: A patient and wise cook will tease out extravagant base flavors as, say, a chopped onion slowly caramelizes in oil or butter, adding revolutionary flavor to their finished supper. Never trust a recipe that tells you to soften an onion in three minutes!

Any food writer has to pick a level at which to aim, from three-ingredient, five-minute cheats for novice cooks right through to high-end, restaurant-style projects for the ambitious and highly skilled reader. The level of this book, if you will, is that of keen and interested home cook, as I find many vegetarians to be. I assume you have a good array of spices in your pantry and won't mind being generous with fresh herbs. The sheer variety of fresh produce available to many of us is astonishing and inspiring, and this forms the basis of this book, so you will have to forgive the odd weird and wonderful vegetable or less common herb creeping in. You will find advice on where to find them, and I have always tried to bear the fraught supermarket shopper in mind, suggesting good alternatives to any unusual additions.

Thoughtful eating—by which I mean "healthy with a good dose of common sense"—shouldn't be tricky and needn't be patronizing. I find the popular practice of demonizing certain foods an utterly joyless experience; far better, I think, to eat natural and unprocessed most of the time and let life take its enjoyable course for the rest. In a nutshell: Eat a rainbow of vegetables (most of the time) with real ingredients rather than processed (most of the time) . . . which is where the Raw-ish chapter comes in. Here, you will find recipes that give a particular nod to vibrancy without compromising on taste, via, for instance, a simple (but wonderful) Grated Brassica and Date Salad, or Almond-Stuffed Vine Leaves.

Still considering raw foods, I run through sprouting for beginners, achievable ways to ferment and how to incorporate seaweed in your cooking— all incredibly nutritious habits, and enjoyable and delicious rather than worthy. It makes sense to me, for example, to soak nuts and seeds when the idea strikes and I have a spare minute. Put simply, the soaked nut or seed (or, indeed, grain) gets ready to sprout. Slowly dried out or not, the texture and taste improve, too; almonds, for example, plump up and taste fresh and true with a milky "snap." Even undried soaked nuts are delicious and make an interesting texture tossed through a salad or steamed grain.

I use whole grains often—nearly always, in fact—favoring their rustic character and ability to keep us feeling satisfied for longer . . . but if a recipe would be made clumsy by their inclusion, I see no problem in using the refined equivalent. See the ingenious Malaysian fresh spring rolls known as *popiah* in this book: I tried making the delicate wrappers with whole-grain flour, but it lacked the elasticity needed for such a thin spring roll skin. Surely eating a wide range of colorful, natural ingredients and enjoying them is more important than the odd handful of white flour in the mix?

Grains, unrefined or not, are not always in fashion, as they are rich in energy-giving carbohydrates. . . . But this isn't a diet book, it's a cookbook full of recipes for giving pleasure, sometimes wholesome, sometimes less so, and grains are invaluable for balance. In their dedicated chapter, they add interest as well as welcome bolster, in light, crunchy Quinoa and Fava Bean Falafel with Lemon, or a resonant Very Green Spelt "Risotto."

As for sugar, that other ready carbohydrate source, I try to use naturally sweet vegetables and fruits and just enough unrefined sugar in lieu of refined versions. Unrefined sugars—from maple syrup to natural raw cane— contribute nuanced flavor and trace minerals without such a sharp spike in energy. They are still sugars, though (not a bad thing, just a reminder). Concentrating and caramelizing the sugars in vegetables and roots through a roast in the oven or a flash in a griddle pan is a technique I use often, to add all-important zing and balance. Relishes, sambals and fresh chutneys, such as Sweet Pepper and Chile Jam or Roasted Tomato and Pickled Lemon Relish, sing with flavor as they aren't packed with sugar.

Assuming you eat enough vegetables, I find the nutritional trick with vegetarian food is to give thought to protein . . . with the caveat that most of us don't need vast slabs of it to make it through the day. A sensible amount—nuts or seeds, pulses, eggs, dairy yogurt or cheese, whole grains or soy products—will suffice. You'll find myriad ways of using them here, often championing nuts and seeds (underused, well-priced protein and invaluable for interest). Combine a couple of proteins for extra boost and more variety; for instance, a handful of cooked freekeh grains add substance to a lima bean–rich tabbouleh with a good dusting of Sesame Seed Za'atar (page 299) in the Grains chapter.

And it's worth noting that cheese can be an issue for vegetarians. Rennet, an enzyme used to coagulate many cheeses, is traditionally derived from bovine stomachs. It's easy, however, to find vegetarian cheeses made with nonanimal rennet. In this book I have only used cheeses exclusively or commonly found in vegetarian form. If you are a nonvegetarian trying to eat more meat-free food, this is unlikely to concern you. The choice is entirely yours and cheeses can be swapped to suit. You will also find recipes for rudimentary rennet-free fresh cheeses in these pages, in the form of ricotta and labneh.

Protein is, perhaps, an even more important issue for vegans. The protein in nonanimal foods does not contain the full quota of amino acids the body needs, but combining certain foods—such as dried beans, peas or lentils with whole grains—completes the essential amino acid quota. In practice, this could be as simple as baked beans on whole-grain toast, but a grain bowl with a tahini dressing or a tofu and noodle stir-fry has the same effect. (I found it easier to avoid honey in any otherwise-vegan recipes, as it can be a contentious ingredient, and maple or date syrups are an easy swap.)

Predominantly, this is a book to celebrate fresh produce. I hope the emphasis on ebullient vegetables and bold flavors will inspire you through the seasons and occasions. There is certainly an interest in health and vitality threaded through it, but hopefully a measured and realistic strand. Above all, my intention is that you will cook these recipes for yourself and for loved ones, vegetarian or not, and that they will bring you joy.

chapter one

mornings

"**B**RUNCH PUTS YOU IN A good temper, it makes you satisfied with yourself and your fellow beings, it sweeps away the worries and cobwebs of the week." Guy Beringer, 1895.

Before chancing on this quote, apparently taken from an article entitled "Brunch: A Plea," written by a British man in *Hunter's Weekly*, I had wrongly assumed brunch to be an American invention, so strong is the pancake-and-coffee culture there now.

Mr. Beringer was clearly onto something, but, though I include suitably distinguished brunch-worthy recipes in this chapter in the form of spiced waffles and parsnip pancakes, homemade labneh and sprightly sweet potato cakes, very few of us can afford the luxury of leisurely brunches or breakfasts on a daily—or even weekly—basis.

I don't think there's much to be done, in a cookbook at least, about the pace of most of our mornings, but if you have an interest in good food and eating well, I suspect you'll be eager to start the day off on a positive note with some proper fuel. This is tricky at breakfast time. Certainly in the UK, where I'm based, there is still a widespread reliance on packaged breakfast cereals, many of them sugary and refined, in spite of the manufacturers' hard sell to the contrary. Children and adults so often start the day by opening a package for a life-giving jolt of sugar.

There's no easy solution to this in terms of time pressure, but the fact is that homemade hot cereals will contain only the sweetness you add and afford you some control over their cost. My vegan Winter Baked Chia and Berry Oatmeal (page 6) is easily adapted to suit any seasonal berry mix, nut or seed. It will gently satiate a sweet tooth without causing blood sugar spikes and subsequent crashes. The energy in the oats is released slowly, tempered by the good fats and vital protein in the nuts and seeds. More to the point, baked oatmeal, and, in the warmer months, Bircher Muesli (page 8), can be swiftly prepared the night before they are needed. A batch of Bircher Muesli will last for a few days in the fridge, ready for portions to be topped with fresh juice and/or your favorite milk and fruits. Overnight Smoky Baked Beans (page 38) can also be made well ahead and even frozen in portions, if sweet breakfasts are not to your taste.

Waffle batters can be made well ahead and are especially popular with small people, who invariably love to help make them. The Spiced Buckwheat Waffles with Mango (page 16) don't have to be sweet. Drop the fruit and swap in snipped chives for the sweet spices, if you prefer. Make the crisp-edged waffles following the same method (they will also work as little drop scones if you don't have a waffle iron), but serve them with fresh ricotta cheese, a few drops of balsamic vinegar and roasted peppers; or a poached egg, sliced scallion, avocado and cherry tomatoes; or seared tempeh slices, toasted pumpkin seeds, arugula and squash cubes you have roasted the day before.

Likewise, eggy bread works well in a savory incarnation. Use your favorite bread—a stale sourdough or seeded loaf is ideal—dipped into a bowl of beaten egg, a touch of milk and a spoon of chopped herbs, until just shy of sodden. You can add a whisper of crushed garlic, finely grated vegetarian Parmesan or spices such as paprika, too. Fry the doused bread in oil or butter until lacy and golden on both sides, then top with roasted tomatoes, sautéed mushrooms or wilted spinach and goat cheese.

Using whole-grain and unrefined ingredients wherever possible has become second nature in my home cooking. If you can choose ingredients with a lower glycemic index and more fiber (which, invariably, whole-grain and unrefined versions possess), your body will take longer to break them down, ensuring blood sugars remain steady. This means selecting whole-grain flour instead of refined white, or reaching for old-fashioned rolled oats instead of instant. You will also be adding natural flavor and character to your food in the process.

If eating, or even sitting down, first thing simply isn't an option, nut- or seed-packed protein snacks, such as my Cashew and Coconut Bites (page 17), offer more sustenance than a midmorning Pop-Tart. Health food shops and even supermarkets sell variations on this theme, but they are expensive; besides, they're very easy to make at home. You will be able to adapt the flavors and, if they suit your lifestyle, mix up bulk batches to freeze, saving money on ingredients. They make an excellent snack to have on hand when traveling, as they keep very well, boost flagging energy levels and are easy to eat.

Use quiet moments to stock up for the week ahead. Blend soaked nuts and seeds into dairy-free milks, or make your own indulgent nut butters, ready for toast and smoothies (see pages 20 to 25). Almost-instant jams can be whipped up from seasonal fruit, chia seeds and not much more (see page 18). It takes some effort and forethought, but prioritizing good, nutritious food doesn't just set you up for the day, it lays down the tone for your daily eating and can help to form better habits in everything you cook.

Many-Grain Porridge with Brown Butter Squash and Apple

Serves 4

- 1¼ cups (250 g) mixed whole grains (in groat form, if applicable) such as amaranth, barley, buckwheat, freekeh, kasha, millet, oats, quinoa, rye, spelt and/or teff . . .
- Pinch of sea salt, or more, to taste
- 2 tablespoons salted butter
- 2 cups (250 g) peeled, deseeded and finely chopped dense and firm winter squash
- 1 firm eating apple, such as a Cox, Gala, Pink Lady or Jonagold, cored and finely chopped
- 1 small cinnamon stick
- 2 tablespoons coconut sugar
- 1¼ cups (300 ml) whole milk

'm sure you don't need a recipe for basic hot cereal. But this is a rugged incarnation and warrants a recipe of sorts for the longer simmer and the sheer amount of liquid involved. To cook the grains—use whatever varieties you have or prefer—in relatively little time, steep them in water before you go to bed. You can make the porridge a day or two before and reheat servings with extra water or whole milk. You could serve this porridge with any fruit compote, honey or syrup, but sweet, buttery winter squash, softened with apple and warming spices, makes a welcome change.

To make this vegan, swap almond milk for the dairy milk and use coconut butter in place of the butter (but forget about browning it first).

1 Put the grains in a large mixing bowl and cover generously with cool water. Leave to soak overnight, or for at least a couple of hours if time is short.

2 Drain the grains and transfer to a large saucepan with a pinch or so of salt and 3¼ cups (750 ml) of fresh water. Bring to a boil, then reduce the heat and simmer gently for 20 to 30 minutes, stirring often, until the porridge is thick and the most stubborn grain in the mix is tender. This isn't an exact science . . . keep tasting and adding water to loosen as needed until the grains are softened to your liking and the mixture is very thick. Plan on a minimum of 20 minutes' simmering time for the tiny grains and grasses, more for stubborn groats.

3 When the porridge is almost cooked, melt the butter in a large frying pan set over medium heat and cook, stirring with a wooden spoon, for a few minutes, until it turns a couple of shades darker and begins to smell toasty. Add the squash and apple with the cinnamon and cook, stirring occasionally, for 15 minutes, until tender and browned, but still holding its shape. Stir in the sugar and cook for 5 minutes more, until caramelized.

4 Add the milk to the cooked hot cereal and cook gently for about 5 minutes, until thickened to an oatmeal-like consistency. Divide between bowls and top with the spiced squash and apple.

Winter Baked Chia and Berry Oatmeal

Serves 4 to 6

- 3 cups (700 ml) almond or coconut milk, or other milk of your choice, plus more to serve, optional
- 2½ cups (200 g) old-fashioned rolled oats
- ⅔ cup (100 g) pumpkin seeds
- 2 tablespoons chia seeds
- ⅔ cup (100 g) frozen or fresh raspberries

A hands-off and nourishing oatmeal for cold, busy mornings. I have kept this version vegan, but you can use any milk—dairy or otherwise—and add other grains such as quinoa, barley or rye flakes for up to half the weight of the oats. To my taste, this doesn't need any added sweetener, but a dash of maple or date syrup—or just a handful of dried fruit—will tailor the recipe to the sweeter toothed.

1 Preheat the oven to 375°F (190°C), if you are making the oatmeal immediately.

2 Combine the milk, oats, pumpkin seeds and chia seeds in a 12 × 8-inch (30 × 20 cm) ovenproof dish and stir in 1½ cups (350 ml) of boiling water. Set aside to swell for 5 minutes. At this point you can also cover the dish and leave until the next morning, if you like. Even if it appears set, I usually find that it sorts itself out in the oven.

3 Add the berries, stir well and bake in the oven for 25 minutes, until bubbling gently and browning at the very edges. Remove from the oven and rest for 5 minutes, to allow the liquid to settle.

4 Eat as it is, or pour milk over each serving at the table.

Coconut-Chia Strawberry Bowls

Serves 4 to 6

- One 13.5-ounce (400 ml) can coconut milk or coconut drink (see recipe introduction)
- ½ cup (90 g) chia seeds
- Finely grated zest of 1 unwaxed lemon, plus a small squeeze of juice
- 2 teaspoons vanilla extract, or the seeds from 1 vanilla pod, split, seeds scraped out
- 1½ pounds (700 g) very ripe and sweet strawberries, hulled
- 2 to 3 teaspoons sweetener of your choice, such as honey, maple syrup or any sugar
- ¼ cup (15 g) toasted coconut flakes

Bowls, pots, cups . . . serve this summery breakfast however you wish. The chia seeds swell to thicken the coconut milk and crushed strawberries into a delicate dessert, something akin to chilled tapioca pudding in texture. If you want to lighten this up, swap in any coconut drink with no added nasties for all or half of the richer canned coconut milk.

1 Put the coconut milk in a mixing bowl with the chia seeds. Stir well and set aside for 20 to 30 minutes, stirring now and then, until the chia has swelled and thickened the liquid.

2 Add the lemon zest and juice, vanilla and 1 pound (400 g) of the strawberries to the bowl and crush with a potato masher until no whole berries remain (but you want a bit of texture here, so leave a good few strawberry pieces in the mix). Now stir in your choice of sweetener to taste and divide the mixture between small bowls. At this stage you can chill the bowls for 30 minutes to firm up the mixture. It can actually be chilled for up to a day but—personally—I dislike the firm, gelled texture that forms.

3 Top with the remaining strawberries, halved or sliced according to size, and the toasted coconut flakes.

Bircher
Muesli

Each serves 2

ircher muesli, that versatile bowlful of oats and nuts, softened in milk or juice for a few hours while you sleep, then combined with seasonal fruit and perhaps some yogurt in the morning, has entered common breakfast parlance. Many winter porridge eaters switch to a sprightly Bircher muesli (or "overnight oats") in the warmer months.

Vary the milks, using dairy or plant milks, and don't feel you have to stick to oats: Rye, quinoa, spelt, barley or buckwheat flakes can replace some or all of them. If you choose to add chia seeds, as we did for the photo, compensate for their thickening nature with extra fruit juice or milk. Hopefully, the following ideas will inspire as the seasons change.

- 2 apples, cored and coarsely grated, plus more sliced apple to serve
- Squeeze of lemon juice
- ¾ cup (70 g) old-fashioned rolled oats
- ½ cup (50 g) quinoa flakes
- ⅓ cup (30 g) chopped pecans
- ½ cup (100 ml) apple juice
- ½ cup (120 ml) milk (any sort)
- ¼ cup (60 g) Greek or coconut yogurt

APPLE, QUINOA AND PECAN

1 Toss the grated apples with the lemon juice to keep them from browning, then mix with the oats, quinoa flakes and pecans in a bowl. Add the apple juice and milk. Stir well, cover and chill overnight.

2 The next morning, stir in a bulging spoonful of the yogurt, divide between 2 bowls and top with the remaining yogurt and some sliced apple. Sweeten with a little honey, if you wish, though I usually find it doesn't really need anything else.

- 1 apple, coarsely grated
- Squeeze of lemon juice
- 1 cup (80 g) old-fashioned rolled oats
- ⅔ cup (50 g) rye flakes
- ½ cup plus 1 tablespoon (130 ml) apple juice
- ½ cup (120 ml) almond milk
- 3 ripe plums
- 2 ripe figs
- 1 tablespoon ground flaxseeds

PLUM, FIG AND RYE WITH FLAXSEEDS

1 Toss the grated apple with the lemon juice to keep it from browning. Put the oats and rye flakes in a bowl, add the apple, apple juice and almond milk and toss well to combine. Cover and chill overnight.

2 The next morning, halve, pit and chop the plums, then quarter the figs. Divide the oats between 2 bowls and top with the fruit and flaxseeds.

- 1½ cups (120 g) old-fashioned rolled oats
- 2 tablespoons unsweetened desiccated coconut
- ½ cup (100 ml) coconut milk (the drink, not the canned milk)
- ½ cup (100 ml) fresh peach juice
- 3 ripe nectarines
- ¼ cup (60 g) Greek or coconut yogurt

NECTARINE AND COCONUT

1 Stir the oats and desiccated coconut with the coconut milk and peach juice in a bowl. Cover and chill overnight.

2 The next morning, halve, pit and chop the nectarines. Fold half the fruit through the oats with 1 tablespoon of the yogurt. Divide between 2 bowls. Serve the rest of the fruit on top of the oats with the remaining yogurt.

Teff, Banana and Maple Loaf

Serves 8 to 10

- ¼ cup plus 1 tablespoon (75 g) coconut butter, plus more for the pan
- 1 cup (125 g) whole-grain spelt flour
- ⅔ cup (100 g) teff flour
- 2 teaspoons baking powder
- 1 teaspoon baking soda
- ¾ cup (175 ml) almond milk
- 2 tablespoons white wine vinegar
- ¼ cup (50 g) coconut sugar or dark brown sugar
- ⅓ cup (75 ml) maple syrup (dark color, robust taste, if possible)
- ¼ teaspoon fine salt
- 3 large, blackened bananas, peeled and mashed, plus 1 large banana, peeled and sliced lengthwise to decorate
- ½ cup (50 g) finely chopped pecans
- 1 teaspoon ground cinnamon
- 1 teaspoon vanilla extract

For anyone nervous about baking without eggs, forgiving banana breads are an excellent place to start. Mashed banana is a natural egg replacement as well as a sweetener, meaning the batter doesn't need much in the way of sugar (maple syrup and coconut sugar in this case). Teff is a natural whole grain; find it at health food shops or online. Combined with whole-grain spelt flour, the flavor is nutty and sweet.

1 Preheat the oven to 375°F (190°C). Lightly grease a 6-inch (15 cm) square pan with coconut butter and line with nonstick parchment paper.

2 Combine the flours, baking powder and baking soda in a large bowl and mix well. In a container, mix the almond milk with the vinegar. (It will curdle slightly. Don't worry at all.)

3 Melt the coconut butter in a saucepan with the sugar, 3 tablespoons (50 ml) of the maple syrup and the salt. Remove from the heat and stir in the mashed bananas, pecans, cinnamon, vanilla extract and soured almond milk. Pour into the flour bowl and mix well.

4 Spoon the mixture into the pan and overlap long slices of banana on top to decorate. Slide into the center of the oven and cook for 20 minutes. Cover with foil if the cake is browning too quickly and bake for a further 20 to 30 minutes until well risen, firm and golden.

5 Let cool in the pan for 15 minutes, then spoon the remaining maple syrup over the top to glaze. Let cool for at least 30 minutes more before cutting into squares if you can't wait, but I'd really recommend letting it cool completely first. In fact, I think this is even better eaten a day or so later, once it has become stickier and fudgier.

Tisanes and Teas

The caffeine addicts among us occasionally need a little encouragement to put the coffee pot down in the morning. Teas and tisanes—the very word stemming from early barley water concoctions—can have powerful, invigorating or comforting effects, depending on their character.

Simmering pot barley (aka Scotch barley) in water and adding lemon—plus a little honey if you wish—makes an incredibly delicious and nostalgic drink, rich in B vitamins, iron and magnesium, among other trace minerals. Double the recipe to make a large pitcherful in the summer, to keep in the fridge and drink over ice, or warm it through gently in the winter as an alternative to tea.

The Matcha Coconut Cup will energize as much as an espresso. Fine, green matcha powder doesn't come cheap, but a little goes a long way and, because it is made from the entire green tea leaf, contains about ten times the nutrients of standard, steeped green tea.

Cleansing teas can be a real weapon, especially in the colder months; there is nothing like turmeric, ginger and lemon for fighting off a cold, while the peppercorns in the hibiscus infusion are warming.

Serves 1

- 1 teaspoon matcha (green tea powder)
- ⅓ cup (75 ml) coconut milk (the drink, not the canned milk)

MATCHA COCONUT CUP

To make a frothy, short morning drink to put a skip in your step, put the matcha powder in a cup. Warm the coconut milk in a saucepan with ⅓ cup (75 ml) of water over medium heat until hot, but not boiling. Have a small whisk ready and, as you pour the liquid onto the matcha, whisk briskly and keep whisking for about 30 seconds until you have a frothy and comforting, pale green cupful.

- 5 black peppercorns
- 1 tablespoon dried hibiscus flowers or petals
- 2 to 3 teaspoons honey, or to taste

HIBISCUS HONEY TEA

Lightly crush the black peppercorns with the base of a jar or with a mortar and pestle. Put them in a heatproof pitcher with the dried hibiscus flowers or petals. Pour over 1 cup (250 ml) of boiling water, or enough to cover, stir well, then set aside to steep and cool for 10 minutes. Strain into a large mug and sweeten with honey to taste. This makes a slightly peppery and warming drink with a tart, black currant flavor from the hibiscus.

Serves 4 to 5

- ⅓ cup (50 g) pot or Scotch barley or pearl barley
- 1 unwaxed lemon
- 1 tablespoon honey, or to taste

BARLEY WATER

1 Put the barley in a saucepan with 1 quart (1 L) of water and bring to a boil. Once boiling, reduce the heat and let the water simmer very gently for 25 minutes. Meanwhile, pare the zest from the lemon using a vegetable peeler and taking care to avoid the bitter white pith. Add the pared zest to the barley water and set aside to steep for at least 20 minutes or until completely cool.

2 Strain the barley water (pick out the lemon zest, then use the simmered barley left behind in a salad) and add the juice from the pared lemon and the honey. Serve as is, gently warmed through, or chilled and over ice.

Serves 1 generously

- ½-inch (1.5 cm) piece fresh ginger root, sliced
- ¼-inch (6 mm) piece turmeric, sliced
- 1 unwaxed lemon slice
- 2 green cardamom pods

SPICED TURMERIC TEA

1 Put the ginger, turmeric, lemon slice and cardamom pods in a large mug. Use the end of a rolling pin to bruise everything lightly, aiming to crush the cardamom in particular. Fill up to the top with 1 cup (250 ml) of just-boiled water and set aside to steep for 10 minutes, or until cool enough to drink.

2 Strain, or drink straight from the cup avoiding the aromatics, and steep with more hot water from the kettle for a second cupful.

Parsnip-Millet Pancakes with Bramble Compote

Serves 3 to 4

- 2⅓ cups (275 g) millet flakes
- 2 tablespoons coconut sugar or brown sugar
- ½ teaspoon sea salt
- 2 eggs
- 1 parsnip (4 ounces/120 g), scrubbed and grated
- 1 teaspoon vanilla extract
- 2½ cups (600 ml) unsweetened coconut or almond milk, plus ¾ cup (200 ml) to loosen the batter
- 10.5 ounces (about 1 dry pint/300 g) blackberries, fresh or frozen
- 3 tablespoons maple syrup, plus more to serve
- 1 heaping teaspoon baking powder
- 2 tablespoons peanut oil, plus more if needed

Grated parsnip adds a wholesome sweetness and structure to these gluten-free millet pancakes. I like them made with coconut milk for the flavor, but almond milk or a combination of both works, too, or you could just as well use dairy milk if you prefer. Begin this recipe at least a couple of hours (or the night) before it's needed, to give the millet time to swell and form a batter.

1 Put the millet flakes in a food processor and pulse-blend until quite finely ground (a bit of texture is fine). Combine this textured millet flour with the sugar and salt in a large bowl and set aside. In a separate bowl, beat the eggs lightly. Add the parsnip, vanilla and the 2½ cups (600 ml) of milk and stir to combine.

2 Combine the bowl of wet ingredients with the dry, cover and set aside for at least 2 hours (or chill overnight), to allow the millet to swell.

3 Once the pancake batter has rested, put the blackberries in a small saucepan with the maple syrup and a splash of water. Bring to a boil and simmer for 5 minutes or so, until the berry juice begins to thicken. Keep warm.

4 Just before cooking the pancakes, stir the baking powder into the batter with the extra ¾ cup (200 ml) of milk and up to ¾ cup (200 ml) of water as well, to loosen the mixture to the texture of thick heavy cream.

5 Heat a cast-iron or heavy-based frying pan over medium heat. Wipe the surface with paper towels dipped in the oil. Space out spoons of the batter in the pan to make round-ish pancakes, cooking for 1 to 2 minutes on each side, flipping only once the batter begins to bubble on the surface and the pancake has turned golden brown beneath.

6 Repeat until the batter is used up, to make 10 to 12 pancakes in all, trying to serve them as you cook, as they're definitely best hot from the pan. Stack the pancakes up on each serving plate and drench with the warm, maple-y blackberries, offering more maple syrup at the table for those who want it.

Spiced Buckwheat Waffles with Mango

Makes 6 to 8 (depending on the size of your waffle iron)

- 2 large, ripe mangos
- 3 green cardamom pods
- 1½ cups (360 ml) buttermilk (or see recipe introduction)
- 1 egg
- 1 teaspoon peeled and finely grated fresh ginger root
- 1 teaspoon vanilla extract
- ½ teaspoon fine salt
- ¾ cup (100 g) buckwheat flour
- ½ cup (75 g) whole-grain or white spelt flour
- ¼ cup (25 g) almond meal
- 1 tablespoon ground flaxseeds, optional
- 2 teaspoons baking powder
- Squeeze of lemon juice
- 3 tablespoons unsalted butter or coconut butter, melted
- Greek yogurt or coconut yogurt, to serve, optional
- Maple syrup or honey, to serve, optional

Nutty and mild buckwheat flour is the perfect choice for a relatively wholesome waffle batter. If you don't have buttermilk, sour 1½ cups (350 ml) milk (any type, even plant-based) with 2 teaspoons lemon juice.

How many waffles this makes depends on the size of your waffle iron; plan on 6 to 8 as a guide. This batter can be used to make Scotch-style drop scones in a frying pan, if you don't own a waffle iron.

1 Slice the cheeks from both mangos, cutting as close to the pit as you can. Cut any remaining flesh and skin away from the pit and pare the skin off, chopping the flesh. Scoop out the cheeks and chop or slice as you wish, saving all the juice. Set aside.

2 Crush the cardamom pods with the base of a jar to release their little black seeds. Crush these finely with the jar base or with a mortar and pestle, discarding the green pods.

3 Beat the buttermilk, egg, ginger, vanilla and salt together in a bowl with the crushed cardamom seeds. Combine the buckwheat and spelt flours, almond meal, ground flaxseeds, if using, and baking powder in a large container. Make a well in the center and gradually whisk the wet mixture into the dry to make a smooth batter. Stir in the lemon juice and 2 tablespoons of the melted butter.

4 Heat a waffle iron according to the manufacturer's instructions. Wipe a little of the reserved melted butter over the iron with paper towels and spoon in enough batter to make a layer less than ½ inch (1 cm) thick, almost to the edge of the molds (the waffles will spread a little). Close the iron and cook until the waffle is pale brown all over with a crisp shell.

5 Ideally, serve these as you cook them. Failing that, keep the waffles warm in a low oven while you cook the rest. Serve with the chopped mango and spoonfuls of yogurt, if you like. You can add maple syrup or honey, too, if you have a sweet tooth, but they are honestly sweet enough without.

Cashew and Coconut Bites

Makes about 12

- 1 cup (80 g) unsweetened desiccated coconut
- 1¼ cups (100 g) old-fashioned rolled oats
- Large pinch of sea salt
- ¾ cup (130 g) pitted Medjool dates
- ⅓ cup (150 g) unsweetened cashew butter
- 1 teaspoon vanilla extract

These little snacks, a homemade and far cheaper version of those sold in health food shops, hardly constitute a good breakfast, but they are very handy to have about as an energy booster when rushing or traveling. The recipe is easily doubled.

1 Put the coconut in a frying pan set over medium heat and toast, stirring often, for 1 minute or so, until it turns a very pale, even brown. Let cool.

2 Put the oats, ¾ cup (60 g) of the toasted desiccated coconut and the salt in a food processor and pulse-blend until quite finely ground. Add the dates and pulse again to finely chop. Transfer into a mixing bowl and stir in the cashew butter and vanilla extract with a wooden spoon, gradually working the mixture together until it holds when pressed.

3 Roll into spheres, each about the size of a walnut. Spread the remaining desiccated coconut out on a plate and roll the bites in it to coat lightly. Keep chilled in an airtight container for up to 1 month.

Chia Jams

All make 1 large jar

These fresh jams are thickened with fiber-rich chia seeds instead of pectin and are kept in the fridge for up to two weeks, so you aren't bound to the high sugar levels required for traditional preserves. As a guide, when varying quantities, simmer 14 ounces (about 1 dry pint/400 g) of berries until they begin to break down, then stir in 2 tablespoons chia and any dry flavorings (such as vanilla seeds, spices or grated ginger) and simmer for a minute, adding up to 3 tablespoons of sweetener, such as honey or maple syrup, as demanded by the berry and your sweet tooth (or lack of it). Set aside to thicken.

It's true that the recipes here use different quantities, but stick to the base formula above and you can make a simple jam from any berry.

- 14 ounces (400 g) rhubarb (Champagne, aka early or forced, if possible), trimmed and cut into roughly 1-inch (2 to 3 cm) pieces
- 1 tablespoon peeled and finely grated fresh ginger root
- ¼ cup (50 g) coconut sugar, plus 1 tablespoon if necessary
- 3 tablespoons chia seeds

RHUBARB AND GINGER

1 Put the rhubarb and ginger in a saucepan with the ¼ cup (50 g) of coconut sugar and ¼ cup (50 ml) of water. Bring to a boil, then cover with a lid, reduce the heat and simmer gently for 10 minutes, until the rhubarb begins to break down. Taste and add the final 1 tablespoon of sugar if the rhubarb tastes too sour.

2 Stir in the chia seeds, simmer for a further minute, then remove from the heat. Set aside for 10 minutes, then stir well. Cover and cool completely.

- 14 ounces (400 g; about 10) very ripe and sweet apricots, pitted and roughly chopped
- 1 vanilla pod, split, seeds scraped out
- 2 to 3 tablespoons acacia honey or other light-flavored honey, optional
- 3 tablespoons chia seeds

APRICOT AND VANILLA

1 Put the apricots, vanilla seeds and pod in a saucepan with 2 tablespoons of water over medium heat. Heat through and simmer gently for 10 minutes, stirring near constantly, until the apricots soften and begin to break down. Taste and add as much honey as you like, if the apricots taste sour to you (if they are extremely ripe, they might not need any).

2 Stir in the chia seeds, simmer for a further minute, then remove from the heat. Set aside for 10 minutes, then stir well. Cover and cool completely.

- ⅓ cup (15 g) dried hibiscus flowers
- 14 ounces (about 1¼ dry pints/400 g) ripe raspberries or mulberries
- 3 tablespoons chia seeds
- 3 to 5 tablespoons acacia honey or other light-flavored honey (or light-colored maple or agave syrup for a vegan jam)

RASPBERRY (OR MULBERRY) AND HIBISCUS

1 Put the dried hibiscus flowers in a heatproof bowl or cup and cover with ½ cup (100 ml) of boiling water. Set aside for 10 minutes, stirring occasionally. Strain to remove the dried flowers, pressing down to release as much of their flavor as possible.

2 Put the raspberries in a saucepan and slowly heat through, crushing the berries as much as you wish with a potato masher or the back of a spoon. Bring to a boil, reduce the heat and simmer gently for 8 to 10 minutes, until the juices have run. Stir in the chia seeds and hibiscus water, then cook for a further minute. Taste and add as much sweetener as you feel it needs. Remove from the heat and set aside to thicken for 10 minutes. Stir well, cover and cool completely.

Nut and Seed Milk

Makes about 2 cups (450 ml)

- ⅔ cup (100 g) nuts or seeds, or a mixture, as fresh as possible
- 1 tablespoon ground flaxseeds, optional (though they help the milk to emulsify)
- Tiny pinch of sea salt
- Maple syrup, honey or coconut sugar, optional

Delicate and nutritious, these homemade milks rely wholly on the quality of the ingredients; the fresher the nuts, the better the milk. Buy them from shops with a high turnover, such as bustling health food and Asian shops. I keep mine in the freezer, which is probably why the drawers don't open. You'll need two 12-inch (30 cm) squares of muslin or cheesecloth (or buy nut milk bags online).

1 Start with a large mixing bowl, because the nuts or seeds will swell. Cover the nuts or seeds with plenty of cool water and leave to soak in a cool place overnight, or for at least 8 hours. They should swell and soften all the way through to their centers, though particularly large nuts such as Brazils may need as long as 24 hours to soften up.

2 Drain them and put in a powerful blender with 2 cups (500 ml) warm water, the flaxseeds, if using, and a stingy pinch of salt. Blend on a high speed for 1 to 2 minutes until the milk looks satiny-smooth.

3 Set a large sieve over your original mixing bowl, line it with both squares of muslin or cheesecloth and pour the milk in slowly. Leave it to filter through for a few minutes. Gather the corners of the fabric up, twist to make a "money bag" shape and squeeze out over the bowl. The remaining milk will eventually be forced out, leaving the dried-out pulp behind.

4 Now you can choose to leave the milk unsweetened—it's ready to drink or blend into smoothies, sauces or cereals as it is—or add maple syrup, honey or coconut sugar to taste. You can blend in dates to the same end, or add flavorings such as nutmeg, vanilla, cinnamon or cocoa.

5 The ground pulp left in the muslin or cheesecloth doesn't have to be composted or go to waste; you can stir it into cooked grains or cold cereals, blend it into soups, or add it to bread dough before cooking, to name but a few uses. Keep the fresh milk covered in the fridge for up to 5 days. It also freezes well.

VARIATIONS

OAT MILK

Makes about 2 cups (450 ml)

Soak 2½ cups (200 g) whole or old-fashioned rolled oats in 2 cups (450 ml) cool water for at least 8 hours or overnight. Add a tiny pinch of sea salt, blend until very smooth and strain the milk through a fine sieve or, for a really fine result, a sieve lined with a double layer of muslin or cheesecloth. As with nut milks, 1 tablespoon of ground flaxseeds can be added before blending to help the mixture emulsify. Dilute as you wish and use as is, or sweeten to taste, as for the Nut and Seed Milk. Keep chilled for up to 5 days.

RICE MILK

Makes about 2½ cups (600 ml)

Soak ¾ cup (150 g) white or brown rice in 2½ cups (600 ml) water and leave in a cool place for 12 to 24 hours. Add a tiny pinch of sea salt and blend thoroughly for at least 2 minutes, until very smooth. As with nut milks, 1 tablespoon of ground flaxseeds can be added before blending to help the mixture emulsify. Leave to settle for 10 minutes, then blend thoroughly again (rice is tricky and needs a thorough blending to pummel all the grains into submission). Strain through a fine sieve or, for a finer result, a sieve lined with a double layer of muslin or cheesecloth. Sweeten to taste with maple syrup, coconut sugar or mild honey, as for the Nut and Seed Milk. Adding vanilla extract or seeds enhances the flavor of rice milk, while blending it with a little almond milk or coconut milk gives it more body. Keep chilled for up to 5 days.

Nut Butters: Their Many Variations and Uses

Makes 1 medium jar

- 2¼ cups (300 g) unsalted, shelled nuts or seeds
- 1 tablespoon coconut butter or flavorless nut oil
- Good pinch of sea salt
- 3 Medjool dates, pitted, or maple syrup or honey to taste, optional

These days, nut and seed butters can be bought in every guise and variety, from sugar-laden and smooth to wholesome and textured, running the whole gamut of nuts and seeds. I urge you to make your own because it is worth it, if only occasionally, for reasons of taste and cost. Ideally, you need a powerful blender with a tamper to move around the ingredients and get them pushed into the turning blades. However, making nut butter in the small bowl of a powerful food processor does work, though it takes a lot longer and gives coarser results. I have also found that a good hand blender and a bit of elbow grease give impressive, smooth nut butters in very little time.

I have given you three options in the following recipe:

1 Make nut butter with raw nuts
2 Soak and dry the nuts before making the butter
3 Roast the nuts before blending

Obviously, the first option yields the easiest and quickest nut butter.

The second option is by far the most time-consuming, but is also the most nutritious, while the difference in flavor and texture is astounding. As well as turning pure, sweet and strong in taste, the soaked nuts retain their plumpness, even after drying. Though a dehydrator is probably ideal, it is perfectly possible to dry nuts out in an extremely low oven or in a warming drawer.

The soaking and gentle drying process also makes the nuts far more digestible, while preserving their enzyme levels and beneficial oils.

If nut enzymes aren't your bag, choose option three: Roast the nuts or seeds, ramping up their flavor and darkening their color in the process. The roasting process denatures enzymes and breaks down some of the oils in the nuts or seeds, meaning some of their nutritional benefits are lost.

Pouring a little coconut butter or oil into the mix while blending helps the nuts or seeds to emulsify and blend freely. Add dates, or another natural sweetener such as maple syrup or honey, to sweeten if you wish. Use any combination of nuts and seeds; you can even add spices in the form of vanilla, cinnamon, ground ginger, or cocoa.

If soaking and drying your nuts or seeds:

1 Place the nuts in a large bowl, cover with cold water and set aside in a cool place for 6 to 12 hours, depending on size. Walnuts, pecans and seeds will take less time; almonds and hazelnuts will take more. If you are using cashews, pine nuts or macadamia nuts, soak them for 2 to 4 hours only, as they tend to get a bit slimy if left for too long; that would be fine for making nut milks, but not so desirable when dehydrating afterward.

2 When ready to dry out, either use a dehydrator if you have one, or preheat the oven to as low as the dial will go; set the dial at barely halfway to 225°F (110°C). Spread the well-drained nuts or seeds out on a baking sheet in as near to a single layer as possible. Slide into the oven or dehydrator. Stir now and then as they dry. Different sizes will take different times to dry out and become crisp; plan on seeds taking 4 to 6 hours and nuts taking anything from 4 to 9 hours. When done, they should be light, very dry and crisp.

If roasting your nuts or seeds:

Preheat the oven to 375°F (190°C). Spread the nuts or seeds out on a large baking sheet in a single layer. Roast for 5 to 7 minutes, stirring after 3 minutes to check their progress, until golden and fragrant. Let cool.

Now to the nut or seed butter itself:

1 Put your nuts or seeds, whether soaked and dried, or roasted, or just as they came, into a high-speed blender with a tamper stick to muddle the ingredients as they blend; or into a large measuring cup, ready to blend with a powerful hand blender; or into the small bowl of a powerful food processor. Add the coconut butter, salt and dates, if using. Blend until the mixture is as smooth as you want. In the case of the food processor, you must use a small bowl or a mini processor for this to work and you will need to keep stopping to push the nuts down toward the blades with a spatula. It will take up to 8 minutes to liquefy and blend. The high-speed blender and hand blender methods will only take 2 to 4 minutes.

2 Spoon into a clean jar and seal with a lid. The nut or seed butter will keep in the fridge for up to 2 months.

Labneh

Each serves 4

- 1¾ cups (400 g) Greek yogurt

Labneh is strained yogurt that can be eaten sweet or savory, as a dip or spread with bread and crackers, or added to dishes in place of sour cream or soft cheese. In the Middle East, it is often served for breakfast with a drizzle of olive oil. The slightly acidic, highly nutritious whey (the thin draining liquid), has endless uses: Add it to bread doughs instead of water; simmer vegetables in it; or blend it into soups.

1 Line a sieve (or colander) with muslin or cheesecloth. Spoon in the yogurt, set it over a bowl and chill for 12 to 24 hours. Give it a squeeze now and then to encourage it to drain. The longer it drains, the firmer and richer the labneh will be. It can be sweetened with maple syrup, honey, sugar or jam, or rendered savory . . . think chopped herbs, garlic, chile, spices, citrus zests, chopped nuts or seeds, either stirred into the labneh or used to coat spoonfuls of it.

2 To keep the savory incarnations for more than a few days, cover with olive oil, adding extra aromatics if you like, seal and chill for up to 3 weeks.

BREAKFAST IDEAS

To make a light breakfast or brunch, divide a batch of plain labneh between 4 smallish serving plates and top with your choice of the extras below.

HONEYCOMB, PEACH AND TOASTED SESAME OATS

To make toasted sesame oats, melt 1 tablespoon salted butter in a frying pan over medium heat. Add ⅔ cup (50 g) rolled oats and 2 tablespoons sesame seeds and cook, stirring, until golden. Add 1 tablespoon honey and cook for a minute until the mixture caramelizes. Set aside to cool slightly, then spoon a little over each portion of labneh, with sliced peaches and spoonfuls of honeycomb (honey from the comb, rather than the confectionery sort!).

PASSION FRUIT AND COCONUT

Spoon the insides of 3 large and wrinkled passion fruits and 1 tablespoon toasted coconut flakes over each portion of labneh. Add coconut sugar or honey to taste, if you like.

POMEGRANATE SEED AND CHIA

Slice off the hard ends of a pomegranate, then score the skin from top to base and pull the fruit apart to release the seeds, pulling the pith away and discarding it. If you open a pomegranate in this way, not many of the seeds break open. Divide most of the seeds between 4 portions of labneh with 1 tablespoon chia seeds per portion. Crush the remaining seeds with your (clean) hand to finish each bowl with a little fresh pomegranate juice.

Fresh Juices and Smoothies

Juicing is an enormous subject, covered exclusively and exhaustively in many books and websites, so what I offer here is general, commonsense advice for those simply wishing to boost their intake of fruits and vegetables. This shouldn't be torture. If you still dislike green or pure vegetable juices after experimenting, but a fruit-based blend (perhaps with vegetables thrown in undercover) tastes good to you and gives you needed energy, then drink the latter. (It is useful to know that passing blended vegetable smoothies through a fine sieve, muslin or cheesecloth can render them more pleasurable to drink than unstrained vegetable smoothies.) However, I would argue that eating with health in mind is as much about boosting mood and enjoyment as it is about kale intake. This is a cookbook, after all, and the ideas on its pages are intended to make you, the reader, happier! (Along those lines, don't forget that fresh juices make superb cocktail bases. . . .)

Juicers and high-speed blenders are different beasts: The former extract, leaving fibrous pulp behind; the latter often need extra liquid to get things moving as they blend ingredients together finely, making them a versatile tool in the kitchen. Both enable the drinker to absorb significant quantities of fruits and vegetables in one glass.

Juices are more nutrient-dense, but lacking in fiber, meaning they are quickly and easily assimilated by the body; fresh smoothies are less concentrated, but contain all the fiber in the ingredients used, so they will keep you fuller for longer. They can easily be boosted or flavored with added ingredients, such as nut milks and butters (pages 220 to 225), or sprouted seeds. In the simplest terms, think of a smoothie as a potential meal replacement and of a juice as a highly concentrated supplement.

When it comes to equipment, centrifugal juicers, with their high-speed spinning discs, are the most common and often the cheapest option. They are best used for juicing watery vegetables and fruits, but usually fall down on getting the most out of leafy and stalky greens. Masticating juicers literally mash and grind at low speeds, making them more suitable for green vegetable juices (they can also be used to make nut butters and fruit sorbet bases). Triturating juicers are the investing evangelist's double-gear version of masticators, with even slower speeds and even more power. Whichever kind you go for, I'm afraid I have yet to find any juicer that doesn't take a bit of time to rinse out and clean after using.

High-speed blenders—I'm talking Vitamix and NutriBullet here, to name a couple—can be used to blend far more than fruits and vegetables, so they are arguably the more useful purchase if versatility is key for you. Sustaining breakfast smoothies, based on energy-rich

ingredients such as bananas, yogurt, cereals and berries, can be whipped up in seconds. I use my NutriBullet (the pro one for extra oomph) to blend everything from dips and smooth salsas, to nut butters and milks, to ice cream bases, to milkshakes, to cold soups. . . .

But I have also invested in a decent juicer and use both regularly and exclusively because they are so different.

If using a juicer, you'll get through a far greater volume of ingredients per serving. If using a high-speed blender, you'll use less by weight—guided by the lines inside the blender container—and will need a bit of water to get the blades moving, but you can throw in nutritious additions from the Boosters list on page 33 to sustain and add bulk. Some of the Boosters, such as cold-pressed oils and spices, can be stirred into juicer-made juices to good effect, but juices are often most delicious when left pure.

Either way, rinse and roughly chop your ingredients beforehand, leaving thin skins on and including cores. I pare the zest and pith from citrus fruits and throw the flesh in whole, whether using a juicer or blender. (You can do this prep the night before and keep everything chilled overnight for a speedy morning juice.) Focus on seasonal, ripe produce and buy local as much you can. Organic fruits and vegetables will contain fewer pesticides than nonorganic if buying everything from a supermarket, but I would always choose home-grown or local farm produce over supermarket organic.

When it comes to getting flavors right, trust your taste and your instincts, rather than throwing a load of ingredients together and hoping for the best. The chart on page 33 of suitable produce is intended to inspire, rather than dictate, and is by no means an exhaustive list. To make a vegetable or a vegetable and fruit blend, choose from the bases, either Mildly Sweet or Light—or simply pure Sweet Fruit—and add concentrated Accents and/or Zing ingredients to tweak the flavor. Fresh herbs are a game-changer. Experiment, but go cautiously so as not to create waste if you don't like the results; you can always add more next time.

For example, if I want a vegetable juice gently sweetened with fruit, I might choose one or two Mildly Sweet bases, let's say beet and pear, their sweetness tempered with cleansing notes of fennel from the Light group and the iron-rich hit of kale as an Accent. Lemon juice and mint from the Zing group would brighten. If I wanted it sweeter and without green additions, the beet and pear base could be increased in volume and lifted with the Zing of ginger and Sweet Fruit of blackberry.

For those on a less-sweet bent, choose only one Mildly Sweet base—say, honeydew melon (or forgo it all together) and add two Light bases—let's opt for celery and cucumber—to make a gentle and refreshing glass. Add a Zing of fresh herbs and/or turmeric to the juicer at the end or, if blending these in a high-speed blender, change the texture to silky with a Booster of avocado (which isn't terribly suitable for a juicer due to its low water content; the same goes for mango, coconut flesh and banana—if you do add these, always balance their richness with a squeeze of citrus juice).

Another way to combine ingredients confidently is to group them by color. Oranges and yellows tend to go together, as do reds and purples, or pale greens and whites. Apart from kale, I have generally stayed away from brassicas in the lists, as they can be overpowering and hard to digest, but if they work for you, throw in broccoli, cabbage or spring greens.

Try to drink any juice or smoothie immediately to get the most out of it. If that isn't feasible, pour into a sealed container with as little air as possible, keep chilled and consume within 24 hours.

*All make 1 large glass
or 2 smaller glasses*

- All ingredients are roughly chopped, unless indicated

CALM AND SOOTHING

JUICE: 3 pears + 2 fennel bulbs + 2 kiwis + 1 lemon

SMOOTHIE: 1 small pear + ½ fennel bulb + 1 kiwi + 1 lemon + water up to the fill line

CLASSIC GREEN

JUICE: 2 green apples + 3 celery stalks + 4 or 5 kale leaves + large handful of mint + 1 large lime

SMOOTHIE: 1 green apple + 1 celery stalk + 1 or 2 kale leaves + 3 sprigs of mint + 1 lime + water up to the fill line

DEEP PURPLE

JUICE: 2 beets + 1 pomegranate, seeds only + large handful of blackberries + 1-inch (2.5 cm) piece peeled fresh ginger root

SMOOTHIE: 1 grated beet + ¼ pomegranate, seeds only + small handful of blackberries + ½-inch (1.5 cm) piece peeled fresh ginger root + water up to the fill line

SWEET TROPICAL

JUICE: 2 carrots + ¼ large pineapple + ½ papaya + 2 oranges + 1-inch (2.5 cm) piece peeled turmeric

SMOOTHIE: 1 grated carrot + 1 slice pineapple + ¼ papaya + 1 small orange + ¼-inch (6 mm) piece peeled turmeric + water up to the fill line

MILDLY SWEET

Apple

Beet

Carrot

Gooseberry

Kiwi

Melon

Parsnip

Pear

Pineapple (add last to centrifugal juicers due to the fibers clogging the blades)

Sweet pepper

Sweet potato

LIGHT

Celery

Cucumber

Fennel

Lettuce

Tomato

SWEET FRUIT

Apricot

Blackberry

Blueberry

Cherry

Fig

Grape

Orange

Papaya

Peach and nectarine

Pomegranate

Raspberry

Strawberry

ACCENTS

Arugula

Asparagus

Black currant

Kale

Mustard greens

Nettle

Pak or bok choy

Spinach or chard

Watercress

ZING

Ginger (root)

Grapefruit

Herbs and vegetable leaves (such as fennel tops and celery leaves)

Lemon

Lime

Turmeric (the fresh root, not the ground spice)

BOOSTERS
(to stir in or blend)

Avocado

Banana

Bee pollen

Booster powders such as spirulina, wheatgrass or protein

Chia seeds

Chili powder or cayenne pepper

Cider vinegar (raw)

Cinnamon

Coconut (fresh)

Cold-pressed oils

Mango

Nut and/or seed butters

Oats or oat bran

Soaked nuts or seeds (such as hemp and flaxseed)

Sprouted seeds

Wheat germ

Paneer Corn Cakes with Charred Chile Salsa

Serves 4

For the charred chile salsa
- 3 large red peppers
- 1 red chile, roughly chopped
- 2 tablespoons extra virgin olive oil
- Squeeze of lemon juice
- Small handful of parsley, finely chopped
- Sea salt and freshly ground black pepper

For the corn cakes
- 2 ears sweet corn
- ½ cup (75 g) fine cornmeal or polenta
- 3 tablespoons (20 g) cornstarch or unbleached all-purpose flour
- ½ teaspoon baking soda
- ½ cup (120 ml) buttermilk
- 1 tablespoon salted butter, melted
- 1 egg, lightly beaten
- ¾ cup (120 g) coarsely grated paneer
- 2 scallions, finely chopped
- Peanut oil, to fry

Brunch food is often just as good at lunch or supper, and these natty, sizzling fritters are no exception. Spice them with nigella and cumin and eat with mango chutney instead of the salsa, or top the version below with poached or fried eggs. Replace the paneer with halloumi or cheddar if you like your cheese to have more clout and, when sweet corn isn't in season, use ¾ cup (100 g) frozen kernels, defrosted.

1 To make the salsa, preheat the broiler to medium. Slice the peppers into cheeks from top to base, leaving the cores and stems behind. Spread the pepper cheeks out on a baking sheet, skin-sides up, and broil for 7 to 10 minutes, flipping them halfway so that they char evenly. The skins should blister and blacken. Transfer the peppers into a bowl, cover with a plate and set aside to steam for 10 minutes.

2 Peel as much skin as you can from the peppers, though a little left behind will do no harm. Now, either finely chop the peppers and chile, then combine with the extra virgin olive oil, lemon juice and half the parsley, to give a coarser salsa, or put them in a mini food processor, pressing the pulse button until finely chopped and a bit saucy. Either way, season to taste. Set aside.

3 Strip the kernels from each ear of corn with a sharp knife. Discard the corncobs.

4 Combine the cornmeal, cornstarch, baking soda and a good seasoning of salt and pepper in a large mixing bowl. Make a well in the center and add the remaining parsley, the buttermilk, melted butter and egg. Use a balloon whisk to bring everything together, making a smooth and thick batter. Stir in the corn, paneer and scallions.

5 Place a large frying pan over medium heat and add a good glug of oil (don't be stingy, or the fritters won't turn out lacy-edged and crisp). Fry generous tablespoons of batter for 2 to 3 minutes, until bubbles appear on the top and the bases turn golden, then turn and cook for 2 to 3 minutes more, until golden on the second side.

6 Serve the fritters hot and sizzling from the pan, with the salsa spooned over, or alongside.

No-Knead Seeded Breakfast Loaf

Makes 1 medium loaf

- 1⅓ cups (200 g) whole wheat bread flour, plus more to dust
- 1⅓ cups (200 g) white bread flour
- ½ cup (60 g) rye flour
- ⅔ cup (100 g) mixed seeds (flax, pumpkin, sesame, sunflower seeds . . .)
- ¼ teaspoon instant yeast
- 1½ teaspoons fine salt
- A little flavorless oil

A handsome loaf to have on hand at breakfast time, either fresh from the oven or toasted over the course of the week. Making bread over a day or two is about as easy as real bread is ever going to get, without using mechanical help. The dough here is left to rise very slowly, developing the gluten in the flour—and, importantly, improving the flavor—without kneading.

1 Combine all the dry ingredients in a large bowl and add 1½ to 1¾ cups (350 to 375 ml) warm water. The water needs to be at body temperature: A good trick is to measure your water out, then close your eyes and dip a finger in . . . if you find it hard to tell if your finger is in the water, you have hit the right temperature range. Stir the mixture first with a wooden spoon, then with your hands, to form a soft, sticky dough. It will look shaggy, but that's fine; you don't need to overmix it, just make sure there are no remaining floury bits in the bowl. Cover with plastic wrap and leave in a warm place for 15 to 18 hours.

2 Lightly dust a work surface with flour and flour your hands; you only need a little. Fold the dough over on itself, cover with oiled plastic wrap and leave for 15 minutes.

3 Line a baking sheet with parchment paper and sprinkle it lightly with whole wheat flour.

4 Using a minimal amount of flour and contact, shape the dough into a spreading round and slide it onto the baking sheet. Cover with a clean kitchen towel and leave in a warm place for 2 hours, until doubled in size.

5 Before the dough has finished rising, place a large, lidded Dutch oven in the oven and preheat to 425°F (220°C). When the oven is ready, carefully take the hot Dutch oven out, very gently transfer the dough in, then replace the lid. Bake for 30 minutes, then remove the lid and cook for a further 15 minutes or so, until golden on top. Transfer out of the Dutch oven and cool on a wire rack.

Sweet Potato Cakes with Lime and Avocado

Serves 4

- 3 medium sweet potatoes, peeled and coarsely grated (about 4 cups/600 g)
- 1 small red onion, finely chopped
- 2 garlic cloves, crushed
- 1-inch (2.5 cm) piece fresh ginger root, peeled and finely grated
- 2 tablespoons brown rice flour
- 2 tablespoons cornstarch
- 2 red chiles, 1 finely chopped and 1 finely sliced
- Sea salt and freshly ground black pepper
- Large handful of cilantro leaves, roughly chopped
- ¼ cup plus 2 tablespoons (90 ml) olive oil or coconut butter, melted
- 2 ripe avocados, halved and pitted
- 2 limes, 1 juiced and 1 quartered

A beautiful little recipe, as suited for a sprightly lunch as for a leisurely weekend breakfast. Make it in a 9-inch (23 cm) frying pan if you don't have the mini versions, and divide into quarters to serve. You can fold three lightly beaten eggs into the sweet potato mixture, though those cakes will be frittata-esque in style, or balance a poached egg on top (with the avocado, of course, and some hot sauce).

1 Using a colander held under a cool tap, rinse the grated sweet potatoes until the water runs mostly clear. Squeeze the rinsed gratings in a clean kitchen towel to remove excess water, then transfer them into a large mixing bowl.

2 Add the onion, garlic, ginger, rice flour, cornstarch, the chopped chile, salt and pepper to taste, about 1 tablespoon of the cilantro and 2 tablespoons of the oil, and mix everything well.

3 Divide the remaining oil between 1½ × 6-inch (4 × 15 cm) cast-iron or heavy-bottomed frying pans—or a 9-inch (23 cm) pan to make a large cake—and place over high heat. Add one quarter of the potato mixture to each pan, or all of it to the large pan (it should sizzle loudly) and flatten firmly with a spatula. Reduce the heat to medium.

4 Cook each cake for 3 to 5 minutes (perhaps slightly longer for the larger version), then run a palette knife or spatula around the edge, transfer each cake out on to a flat plate, then slide back into its pan the other way up. (Don't attempt to flip these unless you're a black belt.) Return to the heat for about 3 minutes more until the underside is nicely browned.

5 Scoop the avocados out of their skins with a spoon and mash roughly with a little lime juice, the remaining cilantro, sliced chile and seasoning to taste. Serve each hot sweet potato cake with the avocado mixture spooned on top and lime quarters to squeeze over.

Overnight Smoky Baked Beans

Serves 6 to 8

- 1½ teaspoons cumin seeds
- 1 teaspoon coriander seeds
- 1 teaspoon hot smoked paprika
- 2½ cups (500 g) dried black beans
- 1½ tablespoons molasses
- 1 or 2 chipotle chiles in adobo, crushed, or 1 to 2 tablespoons chipotle chile paste
- 1 tablespoon oregano leaves or 1 teaspoon dried oregano
- 1 onion, chopped
- 2 garlic cloves, chopped
- 1 lime
- 1½ pounds (750 g) flavorful tomatoes, roughly chopped
- ½ teaspoon sea salt
- Freshly ground black pepper
- Greek or coconut yogurt or crumbled Wensleydale or feta, sliced avocado, cilantro sprigs and toasted bread or flatbreads, optional, to serve

Cooking beans overnight in a gentle oven negates the need for prior soaking and simmering and locks in every ounce of flavor. It really is as simple as mixing the ingredients the night before and leaving them to cook. Adding just-boiled water helps the beans keep their shape, and I have found that adding salt at the beginning of cooking doesn't make the skins tough (as was taught to us for years).

As with most cooked beans, this dish improves over the course of a few days and is just as suited to lunch or supper in place of a standard vegetarian chili. With time, the gentle heat from the chipotle peppers will increase and round out. Add as many peppers or as much chipotle paste as you like, but it might be best to err on the side of caution if small or timid people will be sharing your breakfast.

1 Preheat the oven to 300°F (140°C). Place a small frying pan over medium heat and add the cumin and coriander seeds and the smoked paprika. Toast, stirring often, for about 1 minute, until fragrant and a little darker in color. Crush the spices with a mortar and pestle or with the base of a sturdy jar.

2 Bring 5 cups (1.2 L) of water to a boil in a saucepan. Put the black beans in a large, sturdy Dutch oven and add the crushed spices. Stir in the molasses, chipotle chiles, oregano, onion, garlic, the juice of half the lime and all the chopped tomatoes. Add the salt and season generously with black pepper. Pour in the boiling water from the saucepan and cover with a well-fitting lid or a double layer of well-sealed foil. Slide straight into the oven and bake for 10 hours, stirring once or twice if possible. The liquid will evaporate, leaving a thick sauce behind, and the beans will be soft but not mushy. Rest for 10 minutes before serving, to allow the sauce to settle.

3 Stir well and divide the beans between warmed bowls. Top with spoonfuls of yogurt or crumbled cheese, sliced avocado and cilantro sprigs. Cut the remaining lime half into wedges and tuck beside each bowl for squeezing over. Serve with toasted bread or flatbreads, if you like. Alternatively, serve the beans on thick, buttered toast.

The Fluffiest Eggs on Toast

Serves 2

- 8 ounces (250 g) baby plum tomatoes
- 2 tablespoons olive oil
- Sea salt and freshly ground black pepper
- Large handful of basil leaves
- 1 tablespoon unsalted butter, plus more for the bread (optional)
- 6 eggs
- 2 tablespoons heavy cream
- 1 ripe avocado, halved
- 2 slices of rye bread
- 2 heaping tablespoons Charred Chile Salsa (page 34)

This really couldn't be simpler, but a little care and attention makes a good thing great. Cooking eggs low and slow with a touch of cream, and stirring only occasionally as they begin to set, yields a rich and fluffy scramble of large, irregular curds. Eat these just as they are or, as here, with basil-rich roasted tomatoes, avocado and a spike of Charred Chile Salsa.

1 Preheat the oven to 400°F (200°C). Toss the tomatoes with the olive oil and spread out in a small roasting pan. Season with salt and pepper and roast for 20 minutes, until the skins burst.

2 Meanwhile, finely shred 3 of the basil leaves. Melt the butter in a large frying pan set over very low heat. Crack the eggs into a mixing bowl and whisk very well with the shredded basil, cream, a pinch of salt and plenty of black pepper. Pour into the pan and leave to cook. The eggs will take 15 minutes to cook if the heat is low enough. Stir them very gently with a spatula now and then as the large and irregular curds set on the base of the pan. Take the eggs off the heat before they are cooked to your liking, as they will continue to cook for a minute or so.

3 Stir the remaining basil leaves into the roasting pan of warm tomatoes. Pit, peel and slice the avocado.

4 Toast the rye bread slices (and butter them if you like). Divide between 2 serving plates and top with the eggs, avocado and roasted tomatoes. Place a spoonful of salsa alongside.

Greek Coddled Eggs

Serves 2 to 4

- A little butter or olive oil, for the cups and foil
- 4 very fresh eggs
- ½ cup (120 g) full-fat Greek yogurt
- Small bunch of dill, chopped
- 3 scallions, trimmed and finely sliced
- ⅔ cup (100 g) crumbled feta
- Freshly ground black pepper
- Bread and butter, to serve

This is in no way authentic; the name is merely a nod to the ingredients (dill, feta, yogurt) used. If you want, replace the yogurt with light or heavy cream or crème fraîche, but please don't attempt any low-fat dairy swaps, as they will misbehave in the oven. *Low-fat* frequently also means artificially thickened and acidic; neither trait will be welcome here.

1 Preheat the oven to 350°F (180°C) and boil a kettle. Lightly grease 4 ovenproof cups, ramekins or shallow jars with butter.

2 Separate the eggs, putting the whites in a mixing bowl and very carefully putting the yolks on a plate, trying not to break them (if your eggs are fresh enough, the yolks should be pretty robust).

3 Beat the Greek yogurt, all but 1 tablespoon of the chopped dill, 2 of the sliced scallions, all but 1 tablespoon of the crumbled feta and plenty of black pepper into the egg whites. Don't worry if it looks slightly grainy. Divide this mixture between the cups, then gently drop a yolk into the middle of each. Season lightly with pepper again and cover each with a square of buttered foil. Put them into a small roasting pan.

4 Pour enough boiling water into the pan to reach halfway up the sides of the cups. Bake for 12 minutes, allowing a minute either way depending on whether your eggs are on the large or small side.

5 When there are 5 minutes before the egg timer goes off, put the bread into the oven to warm through, or slice it and make toast.

6 Take the foil lids off each egg and scatter with the remaining dill, scallion and feta. Serve with the warm bread or toast, buttered, for dipping.

Eggplant Shakshuka with Green Tahini

Serves 4 generously

For the herb-tahini sauce
- Handful of ice cubes
- 1 garlic clove, peeled
- 12 mint leaves
- Large bunch of flat-leaf parsley
- ¼ cup plus 1 tablespoon (75 g) light tahini, stirred
- Juice of 1 lemon
- Sea salt and freshly ground black pepper

For the shakshuka
- 1 teaspoon cumin seeds
- 2 tablespoons olive oil
- 1 onion, halved and finely sliced
- 1 red pepper, deseeded and finely sliced
- 1 smallish eggplant, finely chopped
- 3 plump garlic cloves, finely sliced
- 1 teaspoon sweet smoked paprika
- Pinch of cayenne pepper
- Two 14.5-ounce (400 g) cans plum tomatoes in juice
- 1 cup (150 g) crumbled feta, optional
- 6 very fresh eggs
- Crusty bread, to serve

To take this rather beautiful pan of simmering eggs from breakfast to brunch is a green tahini sauce, singing with fresh herbs and lemon. If the idea of tahini in the morning is too much, just skip it, though I promise the effect is subtle and resonant rather than bitter. Pockets of salty feta melting into the simmering panful are not authentic, but highly recommended unless you need this to be dairy-free.

1 Make the sauce first. It can be made up to 5 days ahead, covered and chilled until needed (stir well before using). Fill a large bowl with cold water and the ice. Bring a large saucepan of water to a boil and add the garlic clove. Cook for 45 seconds, then remove to the ice water with a slotted spoon. Reserve 6 mint leaves and a small handful of parsley leaves. Throw the other 6 mint leaves into the simmering water with the other parsley leaves and stalks. Cook for 15 to 20 seconds, then drain. Transfer to the ice water with the garlic, stir and let sit for a few seconds. Drain, then blend the garlic and herbs with the tahini, lemon juice and ⅔ cup (150 ml) of water until smooth. Season to taste and thin the sauce with more water, if you like.

2 Now on to the shakshuka: Toast the cumin seeds in a dry frying pan over medium heat, then crush with a mortar and pestle or with the base of a sturdy jar. Preheat the oven to 375°F (190°C), if you will be making the recipe right through. (If you are making the sauce ahead, don't preheat the oven until you're ready to eat.) Spoon the oil into a large, ovenproof frying pan (about 10 inches/25 cm in diameter) and set over medium-low heat. Add the onion, pepper and eggplant. Cook, stirring often, for 20 minutes, until very soft and sweet but only lightly browned. Add the garlic and cook for a further minute. Stir in the cumin, paprika and cayenne, cook for a few seconds, then add the tomatoes and their juice. Season well, being mindful of the salty feta if you're adding it. Increase the heat a notch and simmer for 10 minutes, breaking the tomatoes down with a spoon, until thickened.

3 Scatter with the crumbled feta, if using. Use the back of a spoon to create 6 wells in the sauce. Crack an egg into each and slide the pan into the oven. Bake until the eggs are just set (8 to 10 minutes), then put on the table, wrapping the hot handle in a cloth. I tend to (generously) drizzle the herb-tahini on with a spoon, but you can serve it alongside, if you prefer. Shower with the reserved herbs and eat with bread, or just as it is.

Jian Bing

Makes 4 large crepes

- ½ cup (80 g) spelt, white, or whole wheat flour
- 3 tablespoons (30 g) rye flour
- 1 tablespoon semolina flour
- 1 tablespoon cornstarch
- A little flavorless oil, for the pan
- 4 eggs
- 4 scallions, trimmed and finely sliced
- Sea salt and freshly ground white pepper
- Sriracha sauce, to taste

Jian Bing—or Beijing-style crepes to you and me—are simple and delicate pancakes, topped here with eggs, scrambled onto each crepe as it cooks. I've mixed rye and semolina flours with spelt to make a flavorful base. Crepes and pancakes make a fairly quick breakfast, if you make the batter the night before and keep it in the fridge overnight. Whisk in a splash of water if it has become too thick.

1 Combine the flours and cornstarch in a large mixing bowl. Make a well in the center and gradually whisk in 1 cup plus a few tablespoons if necessary (250 to 260 ml) of water to make a smooth, quite thin batter. Set aside for at least 30 minutes for the flours to swell. Beat well before making the crepes.

2 To make the crepes, have ready a very large crepe pan or frying pan, preferably as large as 12 inches (30 cm). If it is sturdy and nonstick, it will be a great help when releasing the crepes. Lightly wipe the pan with paper towels dipped in oil. While the pan is cold, add a small ladle of batter and swirl the pan slowly to coat the surface evenly and thinly.

3 Now put the pan over medium-high heat and cook for 1 minute, until the batter just sets. Crack an egg onto the crepe and immediately use a chopstick to gently mix the egg, scrambling it across the surface. Scatter with about 1 tablespoon of the sliced scallion and season to taste with salt and ground white pepper. Cook for 2 to 3 minutes, until the base of the crepe is browned and the egg layer on top is set. Flip the crepe, turn the heat off and leave to cook in the residual heat for 1 minute.

4 Flip the crepe back over, drizzle the egg with Sriracha sauce, fold in the sides and eat hot.

5 Repeat with the remaining batter and eggs—leaving a minute or so in between making each to allow the pan to cool slightly—to make 4 crepes.

chapter two

grazing

T HESE RECIPES ARE RELAXED ENOUGH to win anyone's affection. They cover the whole gamut from simple antipasti to side dishes to snack food to drinks party numbers; indeed many straddle those groups with ease. (Too many hours spent assembling thousands of identical canapés have possibly tainted my views on spiffy party food; you won't find that here.) The secret to successful "small food," I think, is that the flavors should be bright and intense enough to be satisfying in modest portions.

And there lies the winning formula to any miniature dish: Ramp every mouthful up a notch, adding a touch more spice or seasoning than you otherwise might, while keeping an eye on the balance of textures and temperatures. It could be as uncomplicated as something on toast, but taking your time to burnish pine nuts thoroughly, before crushing them into an unusual "butter" and topping with sweet-sour onions, ripe avocado and extra pine nuts for crunch (see page 58), makes an everyday idea great.

Step forward street food, the epitome of laid-back grazing food with lots of character. I won't lie: Some of the street-ish recipes here are projects. Making yeasted dough for Taiwanese-inspired steamed buns, forming Malaysian popiah wrappers, or even filling pot sticker dumplings takes time, but all are fun to do and to eat. I have tried my best not to overcomplicate or add expense with rare pantry items, destined for the back of the pantry after one use, instead sticking to widely available ingredients in the majority of cases. Where more esoteric foodstuffs are called for, it's because it is sometimes worth seeking out things you wouldn't normally buy to inject energy into your cooking. Soft corn tortillas and store-bought dumpling wrappers, for instance, both used in this chapter, aren't hard to find these days and are wise buys. Stock your freezer if you see them and defrost when needed. It is far easier now than it has ever been to track down such authentic and interesting items, with well-stocked supermarkets, specialty food shops and online suppliers.

Away from street food, the Mediterranean always delivers on relaxed starters and antipasti. As ever, they will shine if you are mindful of good ingredients. When tomatoes are plentiful, who could resist pairing them with mozzarella or burrata just as they are? But at the tail end of the season, when autumn is in full swing, large, "meaty" varieties are transformed by a couple of slow hours in the oven, bathed in oil and herbs (see page 67). With very little effort, you can produce a starter of exceptional flavor, and you only need good bread or a seasonal leaf to make it more substantial. Pile the fondue tomatoes, along with torn mozzarella, onto toasted bread to make a good-tempered platter for a party. Or show off with the easiest of homemade cheeses, requiring no special equipment, and be put off buying supermarket containers of ricotta forever. The flavor of a freshly made ricotta is exceptional, and pairs so well with the first new-season peas, or other sweet vegetables (see page 69).

One has to make certain assumptions when developing recipes, choosing a path between basic and expert that will, hopefully, be relevant to the majority of readers. With that in mind, I have supposed that the simplest of vegetable sides—such as steamed and dressed greens and roasted potatoes—do not need to be covered on these pages. Instead, I have written accompaniments with enough character to stand alone as humble kitchen suppers. Don't be afraid to vary them to suit your taste.

The Coconut-Chile Greens (page 52), for example, can be based on any variety of leaves and shoots beyond chard; try kale, cooking (not baby) spinach, spring greens, even broccoli. Make the recipe as written as an accompaniment to vegetable fritters or baked sweet potatoes or, to focus on it as a light main, scent basmati rice with a couple of cracked green cardamom pods as it steams and then finish the stir-fried greens with a generous dash of coconut cream, turning them into a curry of sorts to eat with the fragrant rice.

Creating a side dish with personality can be as straightforward as cooking or presenting a vegetable in a less conventional way. When brassicas are roasted at high temperatures they turn sweet and tender within and toasted—caramelized—on the outside, as the more delicate leaves or buds catch and scorch. Sweetheart (pointed or hispi) cabbages, for example, don't need much more than fierce heat and a tumble of oil to bring them to life, but you can vary the accent flavors, adding the buzz of Szechuan pepper and dried chile flakes, or smoky chipotle and lime juice, instead of the mustard and lemon I have suggested (see page 66).

Likewise, cooking radishes on the stove burner until burnished and sweet is an unexpected way to treat them, but as well-suited to side dish status when paired with a frittata or a rich, baked cheese as it is to lunch with decent bread and a handful of watercress.

These joyful grazing recipes are intended to be gutsy and a break from the norm. Have fun making them and serve them in whatever guise you wish; you'll find they are bold enough to hold their own.

Bhel Puri

Serves 4

- 8 medium new potatoes
- Sea salt and freshly ground black pepper
- ½ cup (100 g) plain yogurt
- 2 tablespoons mango chutney, plus more to serve
- Handful of cilantro leaves, roughly chopped
- 2 tablespoons tamarind paste
- 2 teaspoons palm sugar
- ½ teaspoon cumin seeds, toasted and crushed
- 1 or 2 green chiles, finely chopped
- 1 small pomegranate, seeds only
- ½ cucumber, peeled and roughly chopped
- Large handful of cherry tomatoes, roughly chopped
- 5 Medjool dates, pitted and chopped
- 2 shallots, very finely chopped
- 1 cup (25 g) puffed brown rice
- 6 cooked pappadams (a type of Indian bread), 2 roughly crushed, the rest to serve
- 2 limes, halved

Thought to have originated as a Mumbai street snack, this is such a riot of flavors and texture. With so many versions in circulation, I don't feel I need to apologize for this recipe being heavier on the fresh additions than most. Change it up at will, but bear in mind that it hinges on the contrast of sweet, sour, crunch and heat. Whatever the incarnation, a chilled beer on the side would be most welcome.

1 Put the potatoes in a small saucepan and cover with cool water. Add a large pinch of salt and bring to a boil. Reduce the heat and simmer gently for 18 to 20 minutes, until tender to the point of a knife. Drain and set aside to cool slightly, then peel and finely chop.

2 Combine the yogurt and mango chutney in a small bowl. Finely chop 1 tablespoon of the cilantro, add that, then season with a little salt.

3 Separately, in another small bowl, mix the tamarind paste with the sugar to take the edge off and splash in a little water to loosen.

4 Put the potatoes and all the remaining ingredients—except the yogurt and tamarind mixtures, puffed rice, pappadams and limes—in a large bowl, seasoning with salt and pepper and mixing together gently. Now fold in the puffed rice and crushed pappadams and divide the bhel puri between 4 serving bowls, cups or plates.

5 Add spoonfuls of both the yogurt mixture and the tamarind mixture to each portion, stirring through gently if wished.

6 Eat while the puffed rice and pappadams are still crunchy, using the rest of the pappadams for scooping up the bhel puri. Offer lime halves and more mango chutney alongside, so everyone can sharpen or sweeten their plate as they like.

Lemongrass Tofu Banh Mi

Serves 4

- 14 ounces (400 g) smoked tofu, sliced
- 2 red chiles, finely chopped
- 3 garlic cloves, finely chopped
- 1-inch (2.5 cm) piece fresh ginger root, peeled and finely chopped
- 2 lemongrass stalks, trimmed and finely sliced
- 2 tablespoons Vegetarian "Fish" Sauce (page 300) or light soy sauce, plus more for the baguettes
- 1 tablespoon palm sugar
- Sea salt
- ¼ teaspoon freshly ground white pepper
- 1 tablespoon peanut oil or other flavorless oil
- 2 small ficelles (thin French bread) or small, thin baguettes
- 3 tablespoons mayonnaise
- ½ small cucumber, sliced on the diagonal
- Handful of sprigs of cilantro
- 1 batch Quick Vietnamese Pickles (page 304)

Banh mi: a sandwich to beat all sandwiches. The airy, crisp-shelled baguettes that are used in Vietnam are often made with rice flour, but a very fresh wheat-flour loaf will do nicely here. (Use a baguette that's about 12 inches/30 cm long, to get the sandwiches the right size.) It's worth hollowing out some of the soft middle to make more room for the fillings. Use vegan mayonnaise if you want to make this a vegan recipe.

1 Dry the sliced tofu well with paper towels. Mix it in a bowl with the chiles, garlic, ginger, lemongrass, "fish" sauce and sugar. Set aside for 30 minutes, if you have the time, seasoning lightly with salt and the white pepper.

2 Place a large wok or frying pan over medium-high heat. Add the oil, followed by the tofu mixture. Sear the slices for 2 to 3 minutes on each side, until glazed and caramelized. Remove from the heat.

3 Preheat a broiler to low and warm the baguettes through, turning often, until crisp-edged and just-warm inside.

4 Split open the warmed baguettes, then cut each in half to make 4 split pieces. Pick out some of the inside of the bread, if you like, to make a bigger space for the filling. Brush the insides with a little more "fish" sauce and spread with mayonnaise and slices of cucumber. Now stuff in some tofu, a few sprigs of cilantro and a generous helping of drained pickles. Drizzle with any juices from the tofu pan and serve hot.

Coconut-Chile Greens

Serves 4

- Large bunch of rainbow chard
- Sea salt and freshly ground black pepper
- 3 tablespoons coconut butter
- 1½ teaspoons black mustard seeds
- 1 teaspoon cumin seeds
- 2 garlic cloves, finely chopped
- 1 red chile, finely chopped
- 1-inch (2.5 cm) piece fresh ginger root, peeled and finely grated
- Fat pinch of ground turmeric
- 1 cup (90 g) coarsely grated fresh coconut
- Juice of ½ lime, or to taste

Sturdy greens, including their stalks in the case of the chard family, can stand up to some serious spice. Should you have access to them, a handful of fresh curry leaves, thrown in with the mustard seeds, will add fragrance here. Add steamed rice of your choice, a fried egg or tofu, roasted roots such as carrots or parsnips and a handful of toasted nuts or seeds, to turn this into a comforting rice bowl.

1 Rinse the chard and drain it well. Cut the stems from the leaves. Bring a saucepan of water to a rapid boil, add a little salt and blanch the stalks for a minute or so, depending on their thickness. Drain the stalks, refresh under cool water, then cut into ¾-inch (2 cm) lengths. Roughly shred the chard leaves, too, but keep them separate.

2 In a wok or deep frying pan—one that has a lid and is large enough to hold the chard—melt the coconut butter over medium-high heat. Add the mustard and cumin seeds and heat through until they begin to sizzle. Add the garlic, chile, ginger and turmeric to the pan and cook, stirring, for a minute or so. Increase the heat and throw in the coconut, chard stalks and lime juice, with a decent pinch of salt.

3 Cover with a lid, reduce the heat and leave to simmer for 3 minutes, or until the stalks are completely tender. Stir in the leaves and continue to cook until they, too, are tender. Check the seasoning and add more lime juice, salt or pepper, if you like.

Spring Lentils in Radicchio Cups

Serves 4 / Makes 20

- 1 cup (200 g) small green French lentils
- ¼ cup (60 ml) plus 2 tablespoons olive oil
- 3 shallots, very finely chopped
- Sea salt and freshly ground black pepper
- ½ garlic clove, crushed
- 3 tablespoons red wine vinegar, or to taste
- 1 teaspoon Dijon mustard
- 1 teaspoon grated horseradish
- 1 teaspoon mild honey
- 2 tablespoons finely chopped chives
- 2 tablespoons finely chopped tarragon leaves
- ¾ cup (100 g) chopped radishes
- Handful of young (slim) sprigs of watercress, any coarse stalks removed
- ⅔ cup (75 g) walnut pieces, toasted
- 2 heads red radicchio, leaves separated

This salad doesn't have to be served in radicchio leaves, but do shred the heads finely and stir them through the lentils if you aren't using them as serving vessels: That contrast of crisp, bitter leaf with sweet shallot dressing, fiery radish and nutty lentil is what makes this simple recipe a winning one. A little horseradish gives extra poke, but be more generous with the mustard if you don't have any on hand.

1 Cover the lentils with plenty of water in a saucepan, bring to a boil and simmer for 20 to 25 minutes, until tender but still holding their shape.

2 Meanwhile, put 2 tablespoons of the oil in a saucepan. Place over low heat and add the shallots with a fat pinch of salt. Cook very gently for 10 minutes, stirring often, until they begin to soften, but not to color. Remove from the heat and stir in the garlic, vinegar, mustard, horseradish and honey. Gradually whisk in the remaining oil to make a thick dressing. Stir in the chives and tarragon and check the seasoning, adding more salt, pepper or vinegar, as needed.

3 Drain the cooked lentils well, transfer into a large bowl and combine with the radishes, watercress, walnuts and enough dressing to coat. Season to taste. (Any extra dressing will keep well in the fridge for a week or so; loosen it with a little boiling water when needed.)

4 Fill each radicchio leaf with a spoon of warm lentil salad and serve soon.

Squash and Sesame Fritters

Makes about 16

For the fritters

- One 3-pound (900 g) piece of dense winter squash, plus 2 tablespoons seeds if needed
- 2 tablespoons olive oil, plus more to cook
- ½ cup (125 ml) vegetable stock
- ½ cup (100 g) whole-grain couscous
- 1 tablespoon unbleached all-purpose flour or spelt flour
- 1 egg, lightly beaten
- Small handful of basil leaves, shredded
- Finely grated zest of 1 unwaxed lemon, plus lemon wedges to serve, optional
- 3 tablespoons sesame seeds, toasted
- Peppery salad leaves, to serve

For the sesame-yogurt sauce

- ¼ cup (60 g) plain yogurt
- Juice of 1 lemon
- 2 tablespoons light tahini
- 1 garlic clove, crushed
- Sea salt and freshly ground black pepper

The winter squash you choose here is the key to success. Best bet: the grey-blue Crown Prince for its dense, sweet and firm flesh. Butternut squash will do, but the batter may need a touch more flour. Hold your nerve though—too much will make a gluey fritter; better instead to leave the fritters well alone when frying and to use enough oil. A mild sesame and yogurt sauce balances the squash's sweetness.

❶ Preheat the oven to 400°F (200°C). If the squash seeds are plump and shiny, scoop them out and set aside (if they are flat and wizened, use store-bought pumpkin seeds instead). Slice the flesh into slim wedges, skin and all, and toss with the 2 tablespoons oil in a roasting pan. Roast for 35 minutes, until soft and browned. Reduce the oven temperature to a warming setting.

❷ Meanwhile, bring the stock to a boil in a small pan. Put the couscous in a bowl and pour the hot stock over to cover. Cover with a plate, set aside for 5 minutes, then fluff up with a fork and leave to cool.

❸ To make the sesame-yogurt sauce, combine all the ingredients in a small bowl with ⅓ cup (90 ml) of hot water, seasoning to taste.

❹ If they were worth having, rinse the reserved squash seeds, removing any orange fibers clinging to them. Boil a kettle and pour enough water over the seeds to cover. Let steep for 15 minutes, then drain. Pare the now-soft skin from the squash with a small knife and put the flesh in a mixing bowl. Mash it lightly. Add the cooked couscous, flour, egg, basil, lemon zest and half the toasted sesame seeds. Mix together well.

❺ Set a large frying pan over medium heat. Add enough olive oil to form a thin film across the surface. Add the drained (or store-bought) seeds and cook for a few minutes, stirring, until golden. Remove to a plate.

❻ Make sure there is still a covering of oil in the pan and heap in spoonfuls of batter to make patties, being sure not to crowd the pan. Cook for 2 to 3 minutes on each side until golden and crisp-edged, reducing the heat a little if they color too fast. Remove to a plate and keep warm in the oven. Repeat to cook all the fritters; you should have about 16, depending on size.

❼ Serve the hot fritters with the fried seeds, the remaining sesame seeds and a handful of peppery salad leaves, offering the sauce alongside and lemon wedges, if you like.

Pot Stickers with Black Vinegar and Chile

Makes 30

Dumpling-making, as with any fussy kitchen task, takes patience and probably shouldn't be attempted during fraught moments. If you are reasonably dexterous, however, an army of plump beauties will be just reward for time spent pleating wrappers together.

You can also use a soy-based salad dressing (page 221), minus the peanut oil, as a dipping sauce here, if you prefer.

For the dipping sauce

- ¼ cup (60 ml) light soy sauce
- 3 tablespoons black vinegar
- 1 tablespoon toasted sesame oil
- 1 teaspoon unrefined sugar
- 1 green chile, finely chopped

For the pot stickers

- 3 tablespoons sunflower oil
- 2 garlic cloves, crushed
- 1½-inch (4 cm) piece fresh ginger root, peeled and finely chopped
- 2 cups (150 g) finely chopped shiitake mushrooms
- 3 scallions, trimmed and finely sliced
- 2 carrots, finely grated
- 7 ounces (200 g) firm smoked tofu, drained and crumbled
- 10 cups (225 g) blanched, dried and chopped spinach (see page 70)
- Small bunch of cilantro, finely chopped
- 1 tablespoon light soy sauce
- 1 teaspoon toasted sesame oil
- ½ teaspoon freshly ground white pepper
- Sea salt
- 30 round dumpling wrappers

1 Start with the dipping sauce. Combine all the ingredients and set aside.

2 Put 1 tablespoon of the sunflower oil, the garlic and ginger in a wok and set over medium heat. Cook, stirring, for a minute, until the mixture sizzles, then add the mushrooms, scallions and carrots. Stir-fry for 5 minutes or so, until the mixture softens and any liquid evaporates. Remove from the heat and stir in the tofu, spinach and cilantro, followed by the soy sauce, sesame oil, white pepper and a generous pinch of salt. Allow to cool.

3 Place 1 firmly packed heaping teaspoon of this filling in the middle of a wrapper and lightly brush the border with water. (I use a dampened finger rather than fussing with a pastry brush.) Fold into a half-moon shape, making about 5 pleats to seal. This is all a matter of practice. If you find pleating too fussy, simply press the edges together to make a simple half-moon. If you're feeling brave, to make each pleat, fold the wrapper slightly between your thumb and forefinger, pushing your other thumb in to flatten and secure the pleat. I find the best way is to start in the middle with a single pleat, then work down each side in turn with 2 to 3 pleats. Press the edges firmly to seal, but take care not to crush the pastry or you'll ruin the pleating effect. You should have a curved dumpling.

4 Line a tray with nonstick parchment paper. Add the dumpling, upright, so the seam is on top. Cover with a kitchen towel while you make the rest.

5 Pour 1 tablespoon of the remaining oil into a large, nonstick frying pan and set over medium heat. Add half the dumplings, base-down. Fry undisturbed for about 2 minutes, until golden underneath. Pour ¾ cup (200 ml) water into the pan, bring to a boil, then reduce the heat slightly. Cover with a lid or a large tray and simmer for 7 to 8 minutes, until no liquid remains. Listen for a change in sound: When the liquid has gone, the pan will hiss. Serve immediately with half the dipping sauce. Repeat to cook the remaining dumplings.

Rye Toasts with Pine Nut Butter and Avocado

Serves 2 to 3

- 2½ tablespoons mild-flavored oil, such as canola or olive
- 1 red onion, sliced
- Sea salt and freshly ground black pepper
- 1 teaspoon finely chopped rosemary leaves
- 2½ tablespoons sherry vinegar, or to taste
- ½ cup (75 g) pine nuts
- ½ garlic clove, crushed
- 1 ripe avocado, halved
- 3 or 4 slices of rye bread

An indulgent snack for missed-breakfast days, or an energy-rich pick-me-up. Pine nuts are expensive enough to make any cook wince, so I don't advocate making jars of "butter." In small amounts, though, it makes a fabulous spread or pasta sauce. Watch them like a hawk when toasting (writes the queen of burning nuts), but take your time: You want an even, deep golden color for the best flavor.

1 Put 2 tablespoons of the oil and the onion in a saucepan with a pinch of salt and set over medium-low heat. Fry gently for 15 minutes, stirring often, until soft and beginning to brown. Increase the heat and add the rosemary and a scant 2 tablespoons of the sherry vinegar, cooking and stirring until the vinegar has evaporated and the onions are slightly sticky. Set aside.

2 Put the pine nuts in a frying pan with a meager splash of oil (about the remaining ½ tablespoon) and cook over medium-low heat, shaking the pan often, until the nuts are truly golden all over. Take this too far and you'll introduce bitter notes, but don't let that break your nerve: Undertoasting will make for an insipid butter and, with so few ingredients, there is nowhere to hide. Go for broke. Remove 1 tablespoon of the nuts, draining as you do so, and set aside.

3 With a mortar and pestle, crush the remaining toasted nuts, with their oil and the garlic, until they release their oils and turn from mealy to buttery. Add the remaining ½ tablespoon sherry vinegar, or to taste—just to cut the richness—and season with salt and pepper. If you are making this in advance, it can now be covered and chilled for a few days.

4 Pit the avocado and scoop out the flesh. Chop it roughly with a spoon.

5 Toast the bread slices on both sides under a hot broiler or in a smoking-hot griddle pan. Spread pine nut butter over each slice, topping with the avocado and fried onions. Season well, cut each in half and scatter with the reserved, golden pine nuts to finish.

Tiny Baked Potatoes with Spiced Chickpeas

Serves 6 to 8 at a party as nibbles

- 3¼ pounds (1.5 kg) new potatoes
- ¼ cup (60 ml) olive oil
- Sea salt and freshly ground black pepper
- One 15-ounce (400 g) can chickpeas, rinsed and thoroughly drained
- 1 teaspoon cumin seeds
- 1½ teaspoons nigella seeds
- ½ teaspoon hot smoked paprika
- Finely grated zest and a squeeze of juice from 1 unwaxed lemon
- 1 teaspoon honey
- Bunch of scallions, trimmed
- ⅔ cup (150 g) sour cream
- 2 to 3 tablespoons mango chutney

f you're ever in need of a vegetarian canapé—or at least a plate of something for a party if *canapé* sounds passé—hot baked potatoes, topped with a scallion sour cream and wonderfully crisp, spiced chickpeas should fit the bill. Season these more than you would normally think wise, bearing in mind that they are only small mouthfuls and need to carry a bit of a kick.

1 Preheat the oven to 400°F (200°C).

2 Prick each potato with the tip of a knife, toss with half the oil and spread out on a large baking sheet. Season well with salt and bake for 45 minutes, shaking the pan to redistribute halfway through the cooking time.

3 Meanwhile, transfer the chickpeas into a bowl lined with paper towels and pat dry to get as much moisture off them as possible. Whip out the paper towels and toss with the remaining oil, cumin seeds, 1 teaspoon of the nigella seeds and the paprika. Season well and spread out in a roasting pan.

4 Roast for 10 to 15 minutes, depending on the size of the chickpeas, until just beginning to brown. Stir through the lemon zest and honey and return to the oven for a further 5 to 10 minutes, until well browned and crisp.

5 Finely chop half the scallions and stir into the sour cream with a little lemon juice and seasoning to taste. Finely slice the remaining scallions on the diagonal and set aside.

6 Let the potatoes cool for 10 minutes before handling, so that they aren't piping hot. Make a small cut in the top of each and squeeze the sides gently to open.

7 Add 1 heaping teaspoon of the scallion sour cream to each potato, with a little mango chutney. Spoon the chickpeas over top. Scatter with the sliced scallions and remaining nigella seeds, plus a little more black pepper.

Squash Bao

Makes 8

For the bao
- 3¼ cups (450 g) bread flour, plus more if needed
- ¼ cup (50 g) unrefined superfine sugar
- 2¼ teaspoons (7 g) instant yeast

For the filling
- 1½ pounds (700 g) winter squash, peeled, deseeded and cut into batons
- 3 tablespoons toasted sesame oil
- 2 tablespoons dark soy sauce
- 1 tablespoon peeled and finely grated fresh ginger root
- 1 tablespoon honey
- 1 teaspoon five-spice powder
- ½ teaspoon chile flakes
- ½ large cucumber
- 2 tablespoons mirin
- 1 tablespoon rice wine vinegar
- 1 teaspoon unrefined superfine sugar
- Pinch of freshly ground white pepper
- 3 scallions, finely sliced
- Handful of sprigs of cilantro
- ¾ cup (100 g) salted roasted cashews, crushed

This version of the light steamed buns, commonly—and erroneously—known as just *bao* and often made with rice flour in the mix, can never be truly authentic due to the lack of meat, so I've thrown caution to the wind with an umami-rich stuffing of roasted squash, pickled cucumber and salty cashews. As with the Popiah with Shredded Vegetables (page 73), it's refined flour all the way here.

❶ Mix the flour, sugar, yeast and 1 cup (225 ml) of water in a stand mixer fitted with a dough hook, or use a large bowl and wooden spoon. Knead for 8 to 10 minutes, until smooth and elastic. The dough will be quite stiff, but flours can differ and the weather might be particularly wet or dry, so add up to 1 tablespoon more flour or water, as needed. Cover with a damp kitchen towel and leave to proof for about 1½ hours, or until doubled in size. Or chill the dough, letting it rise overnight, and return to room temperature before shaping.

❷ Preheat the oven to 425°F (220°C). Toss the squash in a roasting pan with 2 tablespoons of the sesame oil, the soy sauce, ginger, honey, five-spice and half the chile flakes. Roast for 30 minutes, flipping halfway, until glazed and soft.

❸ Shred or slice the cucumber into a bowl. Put the remaining chile flakes in a small saucepan with the mirin, rice vinegar and sugar. Bring to a boil, then reduce the heat and simmer briskly until the liquid is reduced to about 1 tablespoon. Pour over the cucumber, adding the white pepper and remaining sesame oil. Toss to coat and set aside for 10 minutes before eating, or chill for up to 5 days.

❹ Cut out sixteen 4 × 6-inch (10 × 16 cm) squares of nonstick parchment or wax paper. Punch down the dough and divide into 8 even rounds. Roll each out on a large piece of nonstick paper to form ovals, about 5 inches (12 cm) long and 3½ inches (9 cm) wide. Stick a cutout square of paper on top and fold the ovals in half over them. Sit each on a second square of cutout paper. Cover loosely with plastic wrap and leave in a warm place for 30 minutes, until risen.

❺ Set a large steamer, preferably with 2 tiers, over medium heat and get the water boiling. Arrange the buns in the steamer baskets, spaced at least 1 inch (3 cm) apart, and steam—not too fiercely—for 10 to 12 minutes until puffed, shiny and cooked through. Split the buns open, removing the papers, and fill with roasted squash, drained cucumber, sliced scallions, cilantro sprigs and lots of crushed cashews for texture.

Aloo Methi

Serves 4

- 1¼ teaspoons coriander seeds
- 1¼ teaspoons cumin seeds
- 3 pounds (900 g) large, waxy potatoes
- Sea salt and freshly ground black pepper
- 1 large (beefsteak) tomato, halved
- 3 tablespoons ghee or mild-flavored oil
- 1¼ teaspoons garam masala
- 1 teaspoon ground turmeric
- Large pinch of hot chili powder
- 1 large onion, chopped
- 1-inch (2.5 cm) piece fresh ginger root, peeled and finely grated
- 2 plump garlic cloves, crushed
- Leaves from 2 bunches of fenugreek, chopped
- Squeeze of lemon juice, if needed

Fresh fenugreek has a slightly bitter, aromatic flavor, with soft green leaves resembling clover. If you can't find it (try Indian and Middle Eastern grocers and the ethnic sections of larger supermarkets), add a scant teaspoon of fenugreek seeds with the other spices instead and stir in finely chopped spinach near the end of cooking; the flavor won't be the same, but the color and chlorophyll hit will be comparable.

1 Start by toasting the spices: Put the coriander and cumin seeds in a dry frying pan and place over medium-low heat, stirring occasionally until their fragrance is heightened and they turn a shade darker. This should take 1 to 2 minutes. Transfer into a mortar and crush with the pestle.

2 Peel the potatoes and cut into 1-inch (3 cm) pieces. Put into a saucepan, cover with water, add a generous pinch of salt, then place over medium heat. Bring to a boil. Reduce the heat a little and simmer for 10 to 12 minutes, until just tender but holding their shape. Drain and set aside. (This can be done a couple of hours ahead or the day before; chill the potatoes until needed.)

3 Coarsely grate the halved tomato, cut side first, leaving only the empty skin behind (discard this). Sweep the grated flesh into a bowl.

4 Put half the ghee in a deep frying pan or wok and set over medium-high heat. Add the potatoes and cook, stirring occasionally, until browned on all sides. Add the ground coriander and cumin along with the garam masala, turmeric and chili powder. Cook for a minute, then stir in the tomato and bring to a boil. Scoop out of the pan and into a bowl.

5 Return the empty pan to the heat, reducing the heat a notch. Add the onion with the remaining ghee and fry gently for 10 minutes, stirring often, until very soft and turning brown. Stir in the ginger and garlic and cook through for a minute. Stir in the fenugreek leaves and cook, stirring, for a couple of minutes, until wilted.

6 Return the spiced potato mixture to the pan and heat through. Taste and adjust the seasoning, adding a dash of lemon juice to brighten the dish, if you feel that's a good idea.

Corn Tortillas with Avocado and Charred Scallions

Makes 8

For the tomatillo salsa
- 6 small tomatillos, husked and halved
- 1 green chile, halved and deseeded
- 1 plump garlic clove, peeled
- 2 to 4 tablespoons lime juice, plus lime halves to serve
- Large handful of sprigs of cilantro
- ½ sweet white onion, finely chopped
- Sea salt

For the tortillas
- 2 ripe avocados, halved, pitted and sliced
- 1 tablespoon lime juice
- Bunch of scallions, trimmed
- 1 tablespoon olive oil
- 8 small, soft, corn tortillas
- ⅔ cup (100 g) crumbled Wensleydale or feta
- Hot chile sauce, to serve

've stayed away from true Mexican queso fresco, as I haven't been able to find any made without animal rennet. Cue vegetarian-friendly Wensleydale or feta. If you can't get fresh tomatillos, or they aren't in season, use a can, drained and blended with a sautéed garlic clove and a deseeded green chile. Or make the salsa with vine tomatoes instead. Not the same, but also delicious in its way.

1 For the salsa, preheat the broiler to medium. Arrange the tomatillos, cut sides down, halved chile and garlic clove in a small roasting pan and broil for 4 to 5 minutes. Remove the garlic and set aside. Turn the tomatillos and chile over and return to the broiler for a further 5 minutes, until softened and charred in places. Blend in a mini food processor with 2 tablespoons of the lime juice and half the cilantro to make a lumpy purée. Add a splash of water, if needed (this is a sharp and watery salsa). Rinse the onion in a sieve held under cool, running water, drain well and stir into the salsa. Season with salt to taste and add the rest of the lime juice, if you like.

2 Halve, pit and slice the avocados, tossing them with the lime juice to keep them from browning.

3 Set a griddle pan over high heat until smoking hot. Toss the whole scallions with the olive oil. Cook in the griddle pan, running the scallions crossways. Cook for 2 to 3 minutes, then turn with tongs and cook for a further 2 to 3 minutes, until charred with lines all over and slightly softened. Remove and cut each scallion in half through its middle.

4 Keep the pan on the high heat and add a tortilla, cooking it for about 20 seconds on each side, until charred, but still soft. Repeat to heat all the tortillas; as you heat them, pile up and wrap loosely in a sheet of foil covered with a kitchen towel.

5 When all the tortillas are warm, top each with a pile of scallions, tomatillo salsa, sliced avocado, the remaining sprigs of cilantro and the crumbled Wensleydale. Shake hot sauce over the top and eat.

Charred Sweetheart Cabbage

Serves 4 as a side dish,
or 2 as a main course

- 2 sweetheart (hispi or pointed) cabbages
- Juice of 1 lemon
- 3 tablespoons olive oil
- 1 teaspoon whole-grain mustard
- Sea salt and freshly ground black pepper

Unsurprisingly, given they are in the same family, cabbage roasts as well as cauliflower or broccoli, taking on the same sweet notes, tempered with charred edges. As an easy accompaniment, it is hard to beat. Play with the flavors as you wish; I have had success swapping the mustard and lemon out for lime, chile and sesame, serving that version with soy sauce and egg-fried rice as a frugal supper.

1 Preheat the oven to 425°F (220°C).

2 Trim the cabbage bases, keeping them as intact as possible, and cut each head into delicate quarters from tip to base. Combine the lemon juice, olive oil and mustard in a small bowl and spoon or brush generously over the cabbage wedges on a large baking sheet. Turn the wedges to coat, then season with salt and pepper, making sure they are spaced out well. If they are too close together, they will steam; you want them to color.

3 Roast for 15 minutes, then turn the slices over with tongs and roast for a further 15 minutes, until charred in places, tender and well browned. Serve as a side dish or as a light main event with a steamed grain.

Fondue Tomatoes with Mozzarella

Serves 4

- 12 large, ripe tomatoes
- ¼ cup plus 2 tablespoons (90 ml) olive oil
- 2 garlic cloves, unpeeled
- A few sprigs of oregano
- A few sprigs of thyme
- 4 slices of sturdy bread, ideally a sourdough
- 2 mozzarella balls, drained
- Good balsamic vinegar, to taste

A beautifully simple, aromatic way with tomatoes. For the best flavor, choose the ripest you can find, ideally something with a low water content, such as oxheart or a large plum type. It's very hard to find vegetarian buffalo mozzarella, so stick to cow's milk, or a richer burrata made with vegetarian rennet. Serve on a base of good bread, toasted or not. Alternatively, keep the tomatoes chilled and use within a week, returning them to room temperature or even warming through when needed. They can be mashed with a fork to make a rich pasta sauce, in which case it's a good idea to double the recipe to make a generous amount.

1 Preheat the oven to 300°F (150°C).

2 Halve the tomatoes through their middles. Pour the olive oil into a large baking dish or roasting pan; it should be large enough to fit the tomatoes in a single layer with room to spare (if they fit too snugly they will steam). Bruise the garlic cloves by giving them a firm smash with the base of a glass and add to the oil with the herb sprigs.

3 Arrange the tomatoes in the oil, cut sides down, and roast for 2 hours. By this time, the tomatoes should be soft, sweet and concentrated in flavor. You can remove the skins if you wish—they will slide off easily—or leave them as is. Remove the skins from the garlic and mash the cloves into the oil, removing any hard herb stalks as you go.

4 Lightly toast the bread slices under a hot broiler.

5 Divide the warm tomatoes between the toasts with the mozzarella, torn into pieces, the herb-flavored oil from the dish and a little balsamic vinegar. It shouldn't need much.

The First Peas with Fresh Ricotta

Serves 4 to 6

- 2 quarts (2 L) whole, fresh cow's milk
- ⅔ cup (150 ml) heavy cream
- ¼ to ½ teaspoon sea salt, plus more to serve
- 3 to 4 tablespoons lemon juice, plus more to serve
- 4½ pounds (2 kg) fresh peas in the pod
- Freshly ground black pepper
- Extra virgin olive oil

A recipe to celebrate early summer's dairy and peas. Fresh cheese really is simple to make, but you can of course use a very fresh, store-bought ricotta instead. Unfortunately, the stuff in supermarket containers won't cut it here. If your peas are homegrown or very fresh, don't bother to cook them. For more mature peas, adding a few pea pods to the cooking water is a good trick to intensify their sweetness.

1 Pour the milk, cream and salt into a large saucepan and set over medium heat. Bring the milk to steaming point: just below a boil at around 200°F (93°C), if you have a thermometer. Stir occasionally, scraping the bottom of the saucepan to make sure the milk doesn't scorch as it heats through. When ready, the surface of the milk will look steamy and slightly foamy.

2 Reduce the heat a notch, add 3 tablespoons of the lemon juice and stir gently. The milk should begin to curdle. Remove from the heat, cover the pan and let stand for 10 minutes. The curds should have completely separated and the whey should look yellow and watery. If the magic hasn't happened, try adding another 1 tablespoon of lemon juice.

3 Set a strainer or colander over a mixing bowl and line it with muslin, a nut milk bag, or other straining cloth. Carefully scoop or pour the curds into the strainer, letting the whey collect in the bowl beneath. Leave in a cool place for 1 hour.

4 The ricotta—you should have about 1⅔ cups (400 g)—is now ready to eat, or can be covered and chilled for 2 days.

5 Pod the peas, preferably with an extra pair of hands to help. Taste and decide if they are sweet and young enough to eat raw. If they are good as is, transfer to a bowl; if they need blanching, reserve a small handful of the pods and bring a large saucepan of water up to a rolling boil. Add the reserved pods and a fat pinch of salt and transfer in the peas. Boil for about 4 minutes, then drain and transfer to a bowl, removing the pods.

6 Either way, dress the raw or cooked peas with salt, pepper, extra virgin olive oil and lemon juice to taste. Eat with spoonfuls of fresh ricotta.

Squash, Bulgur and Spinach Kibbeh

Serves 4, with accompaniments

- 3¼ pounds (1.5 kg) kabocha squash (about 6 inches/15 cm in diameter)
- 4 fresh bay leaves
- 3 tablespoons olive oil
- Sea salt and freshly ground black pepper
- 1 teaspoon coriander seeds
- 1 teaspoon cumin seeds
- 10 cups (300 g) large-leafed cooking spinach
- 1½ cups (200 g) bulgur wheat
- 2 tablespoons unbleached all-purpose flour or spelt flour
- 1 scant teaspoon ground allspice
- ⅔ cup (100 g) pine nuts
- 1 batch Warm Tahini Dressing (page 298)
- Pickled Sour Cherries (page 299), warm flatbreads and salad leaves, to serve

These crisp-shelled baked kibbeh go well with Warm Tahini Dressing and Pickled Sour Cherries, warmed flatbreads and a large salad. I suggest making the kibbeh slightly heftier than is traditional; forming delicate, thin-shelled torpedoes is a job for experts and requires a fine—and hard to source—type of bulgur in the shell. Use a firm, dry squash; this won't work with wet butternut squash.

1 Preheat the oven to 375°F (190°C).

2 To make the kibbeh shell, start by slicing the squash into wedges around the stalk. Use a sturdy knife and a well-balanced chopping board to avoid accidents. Scoop out the seeds and fibers with a soup spoon. Weigh out about 1½ pounds (700 g) of squash and peel those wedges with a vegetable peeler. Cut the orange flesh into 1-inch (3 cm) cubes. You will need 1¼ pounds (600 g) prepared, raw weight, so cut off an extra bit to peel and cube if needed. Cut the remaining squash into 8 small wedges (there is no need to peel these, though you are welcome to do so if you wish). Put the cubed squash in a small roasting pan and the wedges and bay leaves in another. Divide the olive oil between the pans, season with salt and pepper and toss to coat. Roast both pans for about 35 minutes, until soft and caramelized. (If you are making the kibbeh mixture in advance, to bake and finish in a day or so, do not bake the pan of squash wedges now. Instead, cover with plastic wrap and chill until you are ready to bake the finished kibbeh.)

3 Meanwhile, toast the coriander and cumin seeds in a dry frying pan set over medium heat. Shake and stir until they are fragrant and slightly darker. Crush to a rough powder with a mortar and pestle and set aside.

4 Remove the coarse stalks from the spinach leaves, then rinse the leaves to remove any grit and dirt. Bring a saucepan of water to a boil, add the leaves and blanch for 30 seconds or so, until just wilted. Drain in a colander. Wring out in a kitchen towel and chop half the leaves finely and half roughly. Set the roughly chopped half aside.

recipe continues . . .

5 Soak the bulgur in enough cool water to cover generously, setting it aside for 10 minutes. Drain well and, using your hands, squeeze out as much water as you can. Transfer to another kitchen towel and twist to extract even more moisture. Transfer into a large bowl and add the roasted squash cubes. Crush the bulgur and squash mixture with a potato masher, making sure no large lumps remain. Add the finely chopped portion of spinach, the flour, crushed coriander and cumin, half the ground allspice and a seasoning of salt and pepper. Knead until the mixture is thoroughly blended. Place the bowl in the refrigerator for 30 minutes, if you have time, to make the paste easier to work with.

6 To make the filling, toast the pine nuts in a dry frying pan over medium heat, shaking often, until golden. Add to the reserved roughly chopped spinach with the remaining allspice and season well.

7 To form the kibbeh, divide the squash mixture into about 20 large walnut-sized pieces and roll each into a ball. Take a ball, stick a finger into the center to form a hollow, stuff 1 scant teaspoon of the spinach mixture in and mold the squash back around it to enclose, forming the kibbeh into a torpedo shape. Repeat to use all the squash balls and filling. At this stage, the shaped kibbeh may be spaced out on 2 baking sheets lined with nonstick parchment paper, covered and chilled for up to 48 hours. Leave out at room temperature for 30 minutes before proceeding.

8 Preheat the oven to 375°F (190°C). If you did not roast them earlier, put the prepared tray of squash wedges into the oven and cook for 10 minutes, then slide the kibbeh trays in and set a timer for 20 minutes. When cooked, they should be golden brown and crisp, so turn each one over and give them an extra 5 minutes, if need be. The squash wedges should be soft and browned. (If your squash is already roasted, just return it to the oven for a few minutes to warm through.)

9 Serve the hot kibbeh with spoonfuls of warm tahini dressing and the hot roasted squash wedges (include the bay leaves for decoration, if you like). Pickled cherries, warm flatbreads and a green salad make perfect accompaniments and turn this into a feast.

Popiah with Shredded Vegetables

Serves 4

For the dough
- 1 teaspoon fine salt
- 4¼ cups (500 g) unbleached all-purpose flour

For the filling
- 1 tablespoon peanut oil
- 2 garlic cloves, crushed
- 2 large carrots, shredded or coarsely grated
- 7 ounces (200 g) pole or runner beans, sliced finely on the diagonal
- 6 ounces (160 g) store-bought marinated tofu cubes (ideally those in tamari)
- 2 tablespoons light soy sauce
- ⅓ cup plus 2 tablespoons (105 g) hoisin sauce
- 3 to 4 tablespoons Sriracha sauce, or Sambal Oelek (page 304)
- 20 soft lettuce leaves
- ¾ cup (100 g) cashews, toasted (see page 149) and crushed
- 1 cup (100 g) bean sprouts

fell for a more involved and authentic incarnation of these fresh spring rolls in Malaysia and have made them at home ever since. Gluten is the master of the ingenious wrappers; developing the gluten in wheat flour forms a stretchy dough that can be dabbed across a frying pan in a paper-thin layer. If gluten is not your friend, try making them with Vietnamese rice paper wrappers instead.

1 Start the dough the day before: Dissolve the salt in 2 cups (450 ml) of cool water. Put the flour in a bowl and add the salted water as you mix with a wooden spoon into a very wet dough (use your hand if it feels easier). Now for the strange bit: Pour cold water into the bowl to cover the dough. Transfer to the fridge and chill overnight, or for at least 6 hours. Tip the bowl to drain the water off. It is best to knead this using a stand mixer fitted with a dough hook, as it takes about 15 minutes for the dough to collect around the hook and be smooth and very elastic. You can achieve this by hand, by stretching the dough up and slapping it back down, but it is hard work.

2 For the filling, put the oil and garlic in a cold frying pan or wok and set over medium heat. Sizzle gently for 1 minute. Before the garlic colors, add the carrots and beans. Stir-fry for 3 minutes, until softer. Stir in the tofu and soy sauce and cook over high heat for a further 2 minutes. Set aside.

3 Place a frying pan over medium heat. Pick some or all of the dough up and, being careful not to let your hand touch the pan, wipe the dough briefly over the pan to coat. Let the dough fall back into the bowl and cook your thin crepe until the edges start to lift. Use a spatula to lift an edge up enough to peel the still-soft crepe out of the pan. Cover loosely with plastic wrap and repeat to cook the remaining crepes, layering them between squares of parchment paper. This makes more than needed, but use the extra to practice with (or freeze excess crepes for another time).

4 Spread 1 scant teaspoon of hoisin sauce over the center of the uncooked side of a wrapper. Top with a little Sriracha to taste, and a lettuce leaf. Spoon 1 heaping tablespoon of the filling over the leaf in the part of the crepe nearest to you, leaving any excess liquid in the pan. Top with crushed cashews and a few bean sprouts. Fold in the left and right sides to cover the ends of the filling, then roll away from you to make a roll. Repeat to fill all the wrappers and eat as soon as possible.

Baked Polenta and Sweet Potato with Halloumi Salsa

Serves 4 as a main course, or 6 as a side dish

For the polenta
- 2 to 4 tablespoons unsalted butter or olive oil, plus more for the dish
- 3⅓ cups (800 ml) milk
- 1⅔ cups (300 g) coarse cornmeal or polenta
- Sea salt and freshly ground black pepper
- 3 medium sweet potatoes, peeled and finely chopped
- 9 ounces (250 g) halloumi, coarsely grated

For the salsa
- 1 large lemon
- 1⅓ cups (200 g) chopped cherry tomatoes
- Handful of green olives, halved and pitted
- Handful of flat-leaf parsley leaves
- Extra virgin olive oil, to taste

Simmering polenta is a minefield for bare-armed cooks; roasting it in the oven yields tender, creamy results with little hands-on time and no third-degree burns. Serve as an accompaniment to roasted vegetables, or as a main course with peppery salad leaves. Make only the polenta component if you are after a comforting, soft and simple accompaniment.

Here, a polenta-sweet potato mash bakes until brown on top and fluffy within. Just before serving, a feisty salsa is spooned over to wake everything up.

❶ Preheat the oven to 350°F (180°C). Grease a large, ovenproof dish with butter. Mix the milk, cornmeal, ½ teaspoon of salt and 2 tablespoons of the butter in the dish with 3¾ cups (900 ml) of water. Bake, uncovered, for 40 minutes (don't worry if it looks terrible as it cooks; it will come together).

❷ Meanwhile, toss the sweet potatoes with 2 tablespoons of the olive oil in a roasting pan, season, spread out and slide into the oven below the polenta. Cook for 40 to 45 minutes, until tender and colored at the edges.

❸ Stir the cooked polenta and bake for a further 10 minutes. Remove from the oven, stir in 1½ cups (150 g) of the halloumi and let the polenta rest for a minute. Add the roasted sweet potatoes. Mash as much as you would like the sweet potatoes to be broken down (keep it rustic by barely crushing them, or mash thoroughly). Taste and adjust the seasoning if needed.

❹ Keep in the dish, or divide between 4 small ovenproof dishes to make individual servings. Dot with the remaining 2 tablespoons butter and return to the oven for 15 minutes, until piping hot and beginning to brown.

❺ Meanwhile, make the salsa. Pare the skin and pith from the lemon, cutting the flesh out in segments and leaving the membranes behind. Chop roughly and toss with the tomatoes, remaining grated halloumi, the olives, parsley and extra virgin olive oil. Spoon over the baked polenta and serve.

Butter-Glazed Radishes with Capers and Walnuts

Serves 4 as a light lunch, starter or side dish

- 2 tablespoons salted butter
- 1 tablespoon olive oil
- 1 tablespoon capers, rinsed and dried
- 20 to 25 radishes, halved or quartered if large
- 2 shallots, very finely chopped
- 1 garlic clove, finely chopped
- ⅓ cup (50 g) walnut halves, toasted and roughly crushed
- Leaves from 2 sprigs of oregano
- 2 tablespoons sherry vinegar
- Sea salt and freshly ground black pepper
- Walnut bread, to serve, optional

f you tire of crisp, raw radishes by the end of the summer, try roasting them or, as in the recipe below, caramelizing them in a frying pan. Lightly cooked as a vegetable, glazed with buttery vinegar, tempered with the saline hit of fried capers and bolstered by a handful of toasted walnuts for autumn, whole radishes take on a sweet, mild flavor.

❶ Melt the butter and olive oil in a large, heavy-based frying pan set over medium heat. Add the capers and fry until they start to sizzle. Add the radishes and shallots and cook, stirring occasionally, for 8 minutes, until they are translucent and browned at the edges. Stir in the garlic, walnuts and oregano and cook for 2 to 3 minutes more.

❷ Now increase the heat and pour in the vinegar. Bubble this down, tossing the mixture together, until the radishes are shiny and glazed. Season generously and serve with the walnut bread as a light lunch or starter, or on its own as a side dish. It works very well next to cheese on toast, a whole baked cheese, or even an herby omelet or frittata.

quick

"QUICK" IS A VAGUE LABEL in our hurried times, and my idea of speedy cooking may not match yours. So, for the sake of clarity, in this chapter I term thirty minutes or so spent making a home-cooked recipe from scratch as "quick"; any less is really pushing it unless you're simply throwing a salad together or happen to have a nifty sous chef on hand. Speed doesn't have to mean compromise or stingy portions—there are substantial and satisfying recipes here—but producing supper on the double will require a little forethought and a handful of good tools.

The difference between most home cooks versus the professionals? Keeping a good chef's knife sharp. (Arguably, properly seasoning food, too, but that is a separate gripe.) If your knife is sharpened and your hand practiced, you really will need little more in the way of equipment.

In the interests of chopping or blending modest quantities in seconds, a mini food processor will prove even more useful than its larger equivalent, as well as cheaper. I blend many a pesto or curry base in mine . . . failing that, use a mortar and pestle. . . . Otherwise, simply rely on your decent chef's knife which, naturally, has a deep enough blade to turn on its side for crushing and bruising ingredients. Keep chopping and you will get faster at it, I promise.

A box grater, a speed peeler and a shredder version of the same will all work double-time for you; they are cheap and make short work of crisp vegetables. Hand blenders take up little space but will save you the bother of blending soup in batches; you can simply blend a quick soup in the pot with very little waste or cleaning up.

Incidentally, if you ever have five extra minutes when crushing garlic, chopping chile or grating ginger, fill the indentations of an ice cube tray with any excess. Freeze, then transfer into freezer bags and keep on hand to buy time on another, busier day.

The vast majority of quick recipes are born on a hot stove top, rather than in the oven. Hardly surprising, when Asian and East Asian countries with their strong tradition of quick-fire cooking and street food provide so much inspiration. Getting everything prepped and lined up before you start to cook is so important for speed and never more vital than when stir-frying. You will have the heat up as high as it will go so it's essential to stand by, stirring when needed to prevent ingredients catching. Reducing the heat to give you time to chop the next ingredient will lead to a waterlogged wokful. Either way, dawdling over a stir-fry won't end well.

A wok is extremely useful then, but you will also need a form of sturdy frying pan or griddle to bring up to smoking-hot temperatures. A generous-sized version, suited to cooking large batches at once, will be a sound investment. Ditto at least one large, robust roasting pan that won't crowd its contents and is built to withstand fiery roasts such as those in this chapter—and even the odd spell directly on the cooktop—without buckling.

This is a book to celebrate vegetables and that applies to this Quick chapter as much as to any of the others. Choose varieties wisely, or simply slice them thinly to get them cooked in double-quick time. Green vegetables, salads and shoots, brassicas, peppers, corn, tomatoes, or any other vegetables suited to eating raw are ideal for hasty cooking methods; they will need little more than a flash in the pan and a confident hand with the spices and aromatics. Root vegetables and tough tubers, more commonly suited to slower cooking, shouldn't be ruled out though. They can be adapted to suit a quicker cooking style but will only be your friends if you cut them up small or slice them very thinly to expose as much surface area as possible.

It will serve you well to memorize a few simple recipes that can be adapted to suit mood and season. My swift and bold staples include egg-fried rice (get into the habit of cooking extra rice and chill what you don't need, ready to revive the following day); the simplest rice paper rolls with a satay-style nut butter dip; quick tofu or lentil patties with salad and interesting homemade pestos (throw in some kale or watercress or chile and vary the nuts or seeds) to be stirred through anything from pasta and roasted tomatoes to cooked grains and sautéed vegetables.

Eggs are an obvious godsend for the hurried, and hungry, cook. I suppose it's a rare kitchen supper–style recipe that *wouldn't* welcome an extra fried or poached egg on top. From this chapter, I'd recommend adding an egg to the Twice-Cooked Leeks with Goat Curd, Horta on Toast with Sweet Pepper and Chile Jam or even the Vegetarian Pad Thai (pages 85, 90 and 102), if you are ravenous. But, because of those Asian and East Asian influences, there is a lot of egg-free and dairy-free fodder in this chapter, too. Try the Crisp Tofu Stir-Fry with Black Beans (page 94); it is vegan and proud.

Once that initial assembling, prepping and chopping time is out of the way, this chapter is vegetarian cooking as theater. Enjoy showing off with some fast but simple techniques and flashy flavors.

Thai Green Sweet Corn Soup

Serves 4

- ¾ cup (100 g) roughly chopped cashews
- 2 shallots, roughly chopped
- 1 fat garlic clove, smashed
- 1-inch (2.5 cm) piece fresh ginger root, peeled and roughly chopped
- 2 fresh or frozen makrut lime leaves
- 2 lemongrass stalks, outer layers removed, inner roughly chopped
- 1 green chile, deseeded if you prefer, roughly chopped
- Small bunch of cilantro, stalks and leaves separated
- 2 tablespoons peanut oil
- 2 large ears sweet corn, kernels sliced off and corncobs discarded
- One 13.5-ounce (400 ml) can coconut milk
- 1⅔ cups (400 ml) vegetable stock (fill the emptied coconut milk can to measure out)
- 1 or 2 squeezes of lime juice, or to taste
- Small handful of baby Thai basil or cilantro leaves, to serve

Considering its lively base, loosely borrowed from a Thai green curry paste, this is a surprisingly soothing (vegan) soup thanks to the richness lent by sweet corn, coconut and cashews. If you need to cut corners here, use a couple of spoons of a good-quality store-bought Thai green curry paste and 1½ cups (250 g) frozen corn kernels in place of the fresh varieties in the recipe.

1 Cover the cashews with water and set aside to soften for 15 minutes.

2 Blend the shallots, garlic, ginger, makrut lime leaves, lemongrass, green chile and cilantro stalks together in the small bowl of a food processor. Scrape the processor bowl down a couple of times between pulses, until the mixture is very finely chopped.

3 Put the peanut oil in a large saucepan set over medium-low heat. Add the blended mixture and fry gently for 10 minutes, stirring often, until soft and fragrant, but not highly colored.

4 Drain the cashews and add to the pan, cooking for a couple of minutes. Transfer in the corn and cook for 5 minutes more, stirring often. Now pour in the coconut milk and vegetable stock. Bring to a boil, then reduce the heat and simmer gently for 15 to 20 minutes. Stir in the cilantro leaves.

5 Blend in the pan until most of the soup is smooth, using a hand blender, or keep half a cupful back and blend the rest in 2 batches in a freestanding blender. Either way, keeping a small amount of soup unblended adds welcome texture.

6 Taste and adjust the seasoning as needed: A squeeze of lime juice should perk the flavors up, so add a little, then taste and see if you want any more. Divide between warmed bowls and scatter with baby Thai basil or cilantro leaves, for extra fragrance.

Blackened Baby Eggplant with Summer Herbs

Serves 4

- 1 fresh bay leaf
- 1 cup (200 g) brown rice, rinsed
- Sea salt and freshly ground black pepper
- 8 to 12 baby eggplants, depending on size
- Olive oil
- 1 large shallot, finely chopped
- 10.5 ounces (300 g) baby plum tomatoes
- 3 tablespoons red wine vinegar, or to taste
- Extra virgin olive oil, to taste
- Handful of chervil or mint leaves
- ¼ cup (60 g) plain yogurt
- 1 tablespoon light tahini
- Small handful of flat-leaf parsley leaves
- Handful of watercress, coarse stalks removed
- ½ teaspoon hot smoked paprika

A delicate supper for warm evenings. I suggest using the widely available baby eggplant, but slices of larger, regular eggplant will work perfectly, too. Brush them with olive oil and cook in a smoking-hot griddle or frying pan until tender and well marked on both sides. The more dramatic-looking wild rice is particularly good here in place of the brown, though it will take longer to cook.

1 Scrunch the bay leaf in your hand to bruise it, then throw it into a medium saucepan with the rice and enough water to cover by a good 1½ inches (4 cm). Add a fat pinch of salt and bring to a boil. Cover, reduce the heat and simmer for 25 minutes, or until the grains are just tender, but not mushy. Drain and remove the bay leaf. Cover and keep warm.

2 Preheat the broiler to medium. Pierce a few holes in each eggplant with the tip of a knife. Coat with the regular olive oil and arrange on a rack set in a roasting pan. Broil for 12 minutes, turning the eggplants with tongs every 3 minutes, until blackened on the outside and soft within. Alternatively, cook the eggplants in a smoking-hot griddle pan for about the same amount of time, turning until evenly blackened.

3 Put a splash more regular olive oil and the shallot in a large frying pan. Cook over medium heat for 5 minutes, stirring often, until softened but not colored. Add the tomatoes, increase the heat and cook, stirring now and then, for 5 minutes, until they begin to burst. Use the back of a spoon to crush about half the tomatoes roughly. Remove the pan from the heat and stir in 1 to 2 tablespoons of the vinegar and a good splash of extra virgin olive oil. Finely chop a couple of tablespoons' worth of the chervil or mint leaves and stir them in, too, seasoning the dressing well.

4 Combine the yogurt, tahini and remaining vinegar, to taste, with 2 to 3 tablespoons of water to make a dressing with the consistency of light cream. Finely chop the parsley and stir this in, too.

5 Divide the rice between warmed plates, topping with 2 or 3 eggplants and the warm tomato dressing. Tuck a little watercress in beside the rice. Finish with spoonfuls of the yogurt-herb mixture, a little more extra virgin olive oil, pinches of paprika and the remaining chervil or mint leaves.

Twice-Cooked Leeks with Goat Curd

Serves 4 as a starter or side dish

- ½ cup (75 g) shelled hazelnuts
- 6 medium leeks, trimmed
- Sea salt and freshly ground black pepper
- 3 fresh bay leaves, scrunched up
- ¼ cup (60 ml) cold-pressed canola oil, plus more to coat
- 1 tablespoon chopped tarragon leaves
- 1 teaspoon whole-grain mustard
- 1 teaspoon finely grated zest and the juice of 1 unwaxed lemon
- ⅔ cup (100 g) goat curd, or soft goat cheese

Giving leeks a quick blanch before charring them in a griddle pan renders them tender inside with a smoky, caramelized outer in no time. Perfect eaten, as here, with a simple dressing and a mousse-like goat curd. To take the dish from starter or side dish to main course, serve the leeks on a bed of very soft polenta (page 75), in which case you might want to swap the oil in the dressing for melted butter, whisking the dressing together in the warm pan in which you melted the butter.

1 Preheat the oven to 375°F (190°C).

2 Spread the hazelnuts out on a tray and roast for 5 to 6 minutes, shaking the tray once as they cook to a golden brown. Let cool slightly, then roughly chop and set aside.

3 Halve the leeks from top to bottom, washing them well to remove any grit stuck between the leaves.

4 Bring a large saucepan or stockpot of water up to a rolling boil. Throw a generous pinch of salt and the bay leaves into the water, followed by the leeks. Boil for 4 to 5 minutes, until tender, then transfer into a colander and drain thoroughly. Coat lightly with oil.

5 To make the dressing, whisk together the ¼ cup (60 ml) of canola oil, the tarragon, mustard and lemon zest and juice, seasoning to taste.

6 Put a griddle pan over high heat until smoking hot. Lay half the leeks out in the pan and weigh down with the base of the saucepan you used to blanch them. Cook for 1 to 2 minutes, until well marked with griddle lines, then turn and repeat on the other side. Remove to a plate and cook the remaining leeks in the same way.

7 Season the griddled leeks well and divide between warmed serving plates. Spoon the dressing over and top with spoonfuls of goat curd and a scattering of the toasted hazelnuts.

Son-in-Law Eggs with Green Mango

Serves 4 generously

- ⅓ cup (50 g) unsalted peanuts
- 4 duck eggs, not newly laid, at room temperature
- Peanut oil
- 1 dried chile
- Handful of little red Thai shallots, finely sliced
- 2 garlic cloves, finely sliced
- 1- to 1½-inch (2.5 to 4 cm) piece fresh ginger root, peeled and sliced into fine matchsticks
- ½ cup (100 ml; ½ batch) Sweet-Sour Tamarind Sauce (page 308)
- Handful of Thai basil leaves
- 2 little green mangos, peeled and sliced around the pit
- 2 baby cucumbers, sliced
- 1 lime, ½ juiced, ½ cut into slim wedges
- Sea salt
- A few sprigs of cilantro, optional

Various theories float around to explain the name. . . . The more risqué may put you off your supper; the most popular (and placid) version has this pegged as a dish with which to impress prospective in-laws. It is a perfect summation of why it is a travesty to exclude vegetarians from Southeast Asian recipes traditionally seasoned with fish sauce. Granny Smith apples make an easy substitute for green mangos.

1 Preheat the oven to 375°F (190°C). Spread the peanuts out in a baking pan and roast for 5 to 6 minutes, until golden. (Set a timer for 4 minutes and check every minute from then on.) You can do this in a dry pan on the stove, but I find roasting nuts lends a deeper flavor. Either way, let cool before chopping quite finely, or crushing with a mortar and pestle.

2 Bring a pan of water—enough to cover the eggs—to a boil, then reduce the heat to a gentle simmer. Gently lower the eggs into the water and cook for 7 minutes (or 30 seconds more or less if they are very large or particularly small). Drain, then peel under cool, running water and pat dry.

3 To make the sauce, add a good pour of peanut oil to a wok or frying pan—enough to cover the base generously—and set over medium heat. Throw in the dried chile and cook for about 10 seconds, until a shade darker. Remove to a plate lined with paper towels, leaving the oil behind. Now add all but 1 tablespoon of the sliced shallots to the wok and fry slowly for 5 to 7 minutes, stirring, until they have become a deep and rich golden color and appear shriveled. Remove to the paper towel with a slotted spoon. Add the garlic and half the ginger to the wok and cook slowly for 2 to 3 minutes, until pale golden and crisp. Add to the shallots, first draining them of excess oil. Lastly, add the eggs to the wok, cooking slowly until golden-brown on all sides and puffed in places. Drain on paper towels. Wipe the wok or pan out with paper towels, then return to a low heat. Add the tamarind sauce and warm through for a minute or so.

4 Toss the reserved, uncooked shallots and ginger with the Thai basil, green mangos, cucumbers, lime juice to taste and a pinch of salt. Halve the eggs and divide between individual plates with the sauce. Shower with the fried shallot mix and the salad, adding the peanuts. Add a cilantro sprig or 2 if you like, and tuck in a lime wedge, for squeezing over as you eat.

Smoky Thai-Style Tofu Cakes with Green Pod Salad

Serves 4

For the tofu cakes

- 1- to 1½-inch (2.5 to 4 cm) piece galangal or fresh ginger root, peeled and chopped
- 1 large garlic clove
- 1 red chile, deseeded
- 2 lemongrass stalks, trimmed and sliced
- Sea salt and freshly ground black pepper
- 4 tablespoons crunchy peanut butter
- 2 fresh or frozen makrut lime leaves, very finely sliced
- 1 medium carrot, finely grated
- 14 ounces (400 g) firm, smoked tofu, crumbled
- 2 eggs, lightly beaten
- 3 tablespoons peanut oil

For the salad

- ⅔ cup (100 g) edamame or soybeans, fresh or frozen
- Juice of 1 lime
- 1 to 2 tablespoons light soy sauce
- A little sugar or honey, optional
- 7 ounces (200 g) sugar snap peas, sliced on the diagonal

A light, aromatic lunch or supper. Tofu is surprisingly filling, but you might want to add steamed rice on the side to keep larger appetites happy. If you can't find frozen or fresh makrut lime leaves (incidentally, the fresh ones I used for this were grown not three miles from where I sit in East Sussex), finely grate the zest of the lime used in the dressing and stir that in instead. Plain, firm tofu works just as well as smoked.

1 With a sturdy mortar and pestle, pound together the galangal, garlic, chile and lemongrass with a generous pinch of salt to form a paste. You could also use a mini food processor here, stopping to scrape down the sides now and then. Dump into a mixing bowl (don't wash the mortar out!) and stir in 3 tablespoons of the peanut butter, the makrut lime leaves, grated carrot and tofu, working the mixture together with the back of a spoon. Taste and season accordingly with salt and pepper, then stir in the eggs.

2 Scoop slightly heaping soup spoonfuls of the mixture up, pressing them together firmly to make 12 patties about 2 inches (5 to 6 cm) in diameter and ⅜ inch (1 cm) thick. Space out on a plate.

3 To make the salad, steam the edamame for 4 minutes, then drain well. Stir together the remaining 1 tablespoon of peanut butter, the lime juice and soy sauce to taste in the mortar you used to make the patties or, failing that, a mixing bowl. You can add a little sugar or honey to balance, if you like, but I think astringent is good here. Toss the raw sliced sugar snap peas and the edamame through this dressing.

4 Put a large frying pan over medium heat, add half the oil and fry half the patties for 2 to 3 minutes on the first side, flipping over with a spatula when golden brown and cooking for 2 to 3 minutes more. Remove to a plate and keep warm. Repeat with the remaining oil and tofu cakes. Serve the green pod salad with the hot tofu cakes.

Rye Migas, Baked Feta and Hot Caper Salsa

Serves 4

- 6 slices (250 g) rye sourdough bread, stale if possible, crusts removed
- 1½ tablespoons capers
- 1 small unwaxed lemon
- 1 shallot, finely chopped
- 1 green chile, finely chopped
- Leaves from 4 sprigs of oregano, chopped
- Freshly ground black pepper
- 14 ounces (400 g) feta, drained
- Olive oil
- 1 fat garlic clove, chopped
- 6½ cups (200 g) sliced kale, ribs removed
- ½ teaspoon sweet smoked paprika

Bold flavors and textures for a late summer meal. It is so important to use a decent (stale) bread with a bit of body here. Anything flimsy will turn soggy once doused in water. Use a good sourdough, rye-based if you can find it, for a mild, sweet flavor. Swap green beans, halved through the middle, for the kale if you prefer a sweeter vegetable; add a splash of water as they cook and allow an extra minute or so in the pan.

1 Preheat the oven to 375°F (190°C).

2 Cut the crustless bread into rough cubes and transfer to a mixing bowl. Sprinkle with ¼ cup (60 ml) water, toss gently and set aside for 15 minutes.

3 Meanwhile, rinse and drain the capers to remove excess salt or brine. Slice half the lemon and juice the other half. Combine the lemon juice with the capers, shallot, chile and oregano. Season with lots of pepper.

4 Cut the feta into 4 even portions. Place each feta block in the center of a sheet of foil on a baking sheet. Top each with a lemon slice and one quarter of the caper salsa. Drizzle generously with olive oil. Scrunch up the foil to make 4 generously tented but tightly sealed parcels. Bake for 15 minutes, until the cheese has softened.

5 Firmly squeeze the water from the bread cubes and put them on a plate.

6 Pour enough oil into a frying pan to form a thin film over the base when swirled. Add the garlic, place over medium-high heat, warm through for a few seconds, then throw in the kale. Stir-fry briskly for a couple of minutes until softened. Season, transfer into a bowl and keep warm. Add the bread to the pan with a little more oil. Cook for 5 minutes, stirring almost constantly, until golden and crisp. Season well with pepper (remembering how salty the feta will be) and the paprika.

7 Divide the fried bread and kale between warmed plates with the baked feta and salsa.

Horta on Toast with Sweet Pepper and Chile Jam

Serves 4

- 2 plump garlic cloves, preferably mild, spring garlic
- 1 pound 10 ounces (750 g) mixed green leaves and shoots, such as large spinach leaves, kale, chard, sprue (very young) asparagus, mustard leaves, wild garlic, hop shoots, watercress . . .
- 3 tablespoons olive oil
- 1 mild red chile, finely sliced
- Sea salt and freshly ground black pepper
- 4 large slices of rye or sourdough bread
- Extra virgin olive oil, to serve
- ½ lemon
- Sweet Pepper and Chile Jam (page 295)

Horta (or *khorta*) is a Greek catch-all term for greens, usually braised or boiled with plenty of olive oil and lemon. Use any mixture of robust greens you like, wild or not; anything from the first asparagus, to chard or large spinach leaves, to peppery watercress will be superb. A softly poached or fried egg, or a crumble of feta, on top is an excellent addition . . . but ruins the recipe's current vegan credentials.

1. Finely slice 1 garlic clove and halve the other. Wash well and trim all the greens, removing any coarse stalks and slicing leaves.

2. Warm the regular olive oil in a large frying pan over medium heat. Add the sliced garlic and chile and cook for a minute. Throw in the greens and stir-fry for 3 to 4 minutes over medium-high heat, tossing the pan often, until the greens are wilted but still retain a bit of bite. Season well with salt and pepper.

3. Toast or broil the bread until slightly charred, then rub a side of each slice with the cut sides of the halved garlic clove.

4. Divide the greens between the toasted bread slices—piling them high—with a few drops of extra virgin olive oil, a squeeze of lemon juice and a good spoonful of pepper and chile jam.

Crisp Tofu Stir-Fry with Black Beans

Serves 2 to 3

- 14 ounces (400 g) firm tofu, drained
- 1 tablespoon fermented salted black beans (from Chinese groceries and online)
- 2 garlic cloves, finely chopped
- 1-inch (2.5 cm) piece fresh ginger root, peeled and finely chopped
- 2 tablespoons dark soy sauce
- 3½ tablespoons cornstarch
- 2 tablespoons Shaoxing rice wine
- 2 medium carrots, scrubbed
- 4 scallions, trimmed
- 1 tablespoon five-spice powder
- 1 teaspoon chile flakes
- ¼ cup (60 ml) peanut oil
- 7 ounces (200 g) gai lan (Chinese broccoli), or pak or bok choy, chopped into 2-inch (5 cm) lengths
- Sea salt

The trick to this recipe lies in its contrasting textures. Tofu is pressed to extract the water that stops it from forming a crisp coating once fried. When the tofu and vegetables are cooked, barely toss them together, to prevent sogginess. Stalky gai lan (Chinese broccoli) is excellent stir-fried, a bit like firm pak choy, but use any pak or bok choy, broccoli or sliced cabbage. You'll want steamed rice on the side.

1 Turn the oven to a very low warming setting.

2 Place the tofu on a plate lined with 2 layers of paper towels. Cover with another 2 layers of paper towels, then another plate, and press firmly. Weigh down with a couple of unopened cans. Set aside for 10 minutes.

3 Rinse and drain the salted black beans. In a small bowl, mash them with the garlic, ginger and soy sauce. Put ½ tablespoon of the cornstarch in another small bowl, then gradually add 3 tablespoons of water and the rice wine. Slice the carrots on a steep diagonal. Halve the scallions from top to bottom and cut into thumb-height lengths.

4 Combine the remaining 3 tablespoons cornstarch, the five-spice and chile flakes on a plate.

5 Pat the tofu dry with more paper towels and cut into ¾-inch (2 cm) cubes. Roll the cubes in the cornstarch mixture until well coated on all sides, dusting off the excess. Put 3 tablespoons of the oil in a large frying pan or wok. Turn on the heat under the pan to medium-high and fry the tofu cubes, turning carefully with tongs every minute or so, until crisp and golden on all sides; this will take about 5 minutes. Transfer to a plate lined with paper towels and keep warm in the oven. Wipe the pan out.

6 Put the remaining 1 tablespoon of oil in the pan and set over high heat until smoking. Keeping the heat very high and the ingredients moving throughout, throw in the carrots and stir-fry for 30 seconds or so. Add the gai lan and cook for another 30 seconds. Stir in the black bean mixture and the scallions and cook for 30 seconds, then stir and add the rice wine mixture. Stir-fry for a minute or so until thickened and glossy, then season with a little salt and divide between warmed plates with the crisp tofu.

HOW TO MAKE TOFU DELICIOUS

Let's be real: Tofu doesn't get the best reception outside its native East and Southeast Asia, where it is understood and justly celebrated. When treated correctly, this valuable, protein-dense weapon in the vegetarian or vegan cook's arsenal is rich in B vitamins. In its simplest form, it is made from only soy milk and the coagulant nigari (magnesium chloride). (As with any packaged food, if you worry about how it is made or what it contains, check the label and stay away from additives you don't want.)

The problem—in Western countries at least—isn't just that we're not sure what to do with it, but also that the tofu available to us in the recent past was rarely of the best quality. We can now buy good, firm tofu in supermarkets and smoked or marinated tofu in specialty shops. Those firm varieties are perfect in stir-fries, absorbing sauces like a sponge.

Go to any Chinatown and you'll find frozen, spongy tofu to simmer in broths; inari pouches to swell with sushi rice; fermented, salted jarfuls in sauce or not; dried sheets to use as dumpling wrappers, to name a few. (Don't bother with the musty blocks of silken tofu in shelf-stable packages.)

Let's assume, for simplicity's sake, we are dealing with blocks of firm tofu (whether smoked or flavored is up to you). These crumble beautifully, ready to scramble as you would eggs, or bind patties such as Smoky Thai-Style Tofu Cakes with Green Pod Salad (page 88). Whatever recipe you use, don't be shy. Add bold flavors, such as ginger, garlic, sesame oil, lime leaves, black beans, Szechuan pepper, wasabi or chile, and use natural sweeteners (honey, palm sugar and so on) to glaze. Less conventional, but no less successful, are typically Asian spices such as cumin and coriander, or complex curry blends, or—from even further afield—smoky chipotle. You simply can't be coy with tofu, or your dish will be bland.

Texture is one of tofu's most interesting characteristics. Again, I will look at the firm blocks, though I give a recipe for steaming silken tofu doused with a sweet-sharp-salty dressing in the Raw-ish chapter (page 257), celebrating its delicate wobble. Firm tofu is particularly useful to the cook; not only will it stand up to a tumble around a frying pan or flash under a broiler, it will hold a flavorful coating, adding a second texture when crisp outer gives way to soft inner. Cornstarch and potato flour prove to be excellent coatings, frying up crisp and golden. Increase the contrast (and live life on the edge) by triple-coating softer cubed tofu in salted, spiced flour, then beaten egg, then bread crumbs. Fry until crisp, then toss with a fiery relish, such as Sambal Oelek or Caramelized Peanut Sauce (pages 304 and 305). Offer lime wedges and soy sauce on the side. Delicious!

A Summer Salad

Serves 4 generously

For the dressing

- Finely grated zest and juice of 1 small unwaxed lemon
- 2 teaspoons whole-grain mustard
- ¼ cup (60 ml) extra virgin olive oil
- Sea salt and freshly ground black pepper

For the salad

- 1 pound (500 g) new potatoes
- Handful of mint leaves, shredded if large, plus 1 sprig of mint
- 12 quail eggs (see recipe introduction)
- 1½ cups (200 g) shelled peas, fresh or frozen
- 2 tablespoons mild olive oil
- 2 large handfuls of pea shoots

Familiar flavors run riot in this warm salad: tender pea shoots against hot peas and cool mint; a sharp, mustard-citrus dressing; new potatoes crisp from the pan; and soft-boiled quail eggs. Try to make sure the eggs you buy aren't too fresh, or you'll have a terrible time peeling them. (If they are older, air pockets develop inside, separating the membrane from the white and making them easier to peel.)

1 To make the dressing, shake the lemon zest and juice, mustard and extra virgin olive oil together with 1 tablespoon of water in a lidded jar and season with salt and pepper to taste. Set aside.

2 Put the potatoes in a saucepan with enough cool water to cover generously. Add a large pinch of salt and the mint sprig, bring to a boil, reduce the heat and simmer for about 15 minutes, depending on size, until almost tender to the point of a knife.

3 Have a bowl of ice water ready in the fridge. Bring a small pan of water to a rolling boil. Have a timer ready and set it as you drop the eggs in. Boil them for exactly 3 minutes, then transfer to the ice water bowl with a slotted spoon. Carefully peel, then cut in half. Separately steam the peas, or simmer them in salted, boiling water, for 2 to 3 minutes. Drain well.

4 Drain the potatoes thoroughly and slice into thick coins as soon as they are cool enough to handle (or wear rubber gloves and slice immediately). Put a frying pan over high heat and add the regular olive oil. Fry the potato slices on both sides, until they are crisp and golden.

5 Gently toss the warm potatoes and peas with the dressing, shredded mint, pea shoots and halved quail eggs and serve on a platter or in a serving bowl.

Stalk Soup

Serves 4 generously

- 1 pound 10 ounces (750 g; 2 smallish) stalky broccoli heads
- 1 large leek, washed and sliced
- 1 celery stalk, chopped
- 2 tablespoons olive oil
- Sea salt and freshly ground black pepper
- ⅓ cup (50 g) chopped almonds
- 3 tablespoons basmati rice
- 1 quart (1 L) vegetable stock
- Handful of sliced almonds
- Handful of watercress
- Squeeze of lemon juice

have kept simplicity and comfort at the forefront in this vegan soup, braced with almonds and rice to give a silky texture without added cream. If you want to vamp up the flavors, strong cheese is an option: 1½ cups (150 g) grated cheddar or crumbled blue cheese, stirred into the blended soup over gentle heat, pairs beautifully. Or keep it dairy-free and top with caramelized onions or spoonfuls of vegan pesto.

1 Roughly chop the broccoli heads, including the stalks. Set aside.

2 In a large saucepan or casserole set over medium-low heat, soften the leek and celery in the olive oil with a pinch of salt. They will take about 10 minutes to soften and become sweet. Add the broccoli, chopped almonds and rice, turning to coat in the oil for a minute or so. Pour in the stock, then bring to a boil, partially cover, then reduce the heat and simmer for 20 minutes.

3 Meanwhile, toast the sliced almonds in a small frying pan set over medium heat, tossing the pan often until the nuts are deeply golden. Set aside.

4 Stir the watercress into the cooked soup and simmer uncovered for a minute more, then remove from the heat and blend until very smooth, either in the pan using a hand blender, or in batches in a freestanding blender. Reheat the soup gently, then add the lemon juice and adjust the seasoning to taste. Serve scattered with the toasted sliced almonds.

Celery Root and Chestnut Soup with Oregano

Serves 3

- 1 large celery root, about 1½ pounds (700 g) total weight, peeled and cubed
- Squeeze of lemon juice, plus more if needed
- 2 celery stalks, finely chopped
- 1 onion, finely chopped
- 2 garlic cloves, chopped
- 1 teaspoon olive oil
- 3 tablespoons salted butter
- 2 cups (200 g) cooked, peeled chestnuts
- Leaves from 4 sprigs of oregano
- 1 quart (1 L) vegetable stock
- Small handful of green celery root or celery leaves, if you have them
- Sea salt and freshly ground black pepper
- 3 teaspoons crème fraiche, optional

With good bread and butter on the side, this autumnal, velveteen soup makes for a handsome kitchen supper on a cold night. It does, however, also feel fancy enough to masquerade as a starter, in which case you can stretch it to serve six in delicate portions. Do add the crème fraîche and the final, buttery chestnut flourish if this is destined for a dinner party or similar.

1 Drop the cubed celery root into a bowl of cold water with the squeeze of lemon juice. This will keep it from browning.

2 In a large saucepan, gently cook the celery, onion and garlic in the oil and half the butter for 10 minutes, until soft and translucent but not brown. Stir in 1½ cups (150 g) of the chestnuts, half the oregano and the drained celery root and cook for 5 minutes more. Pour in the stock. Bring to a boil, then reduce the heat and simmer for about 15 minutes.

3 Purée in a blender until completely smooth, either in the pan using a hand blender, or in batches in a freestanding blender. For a truly velvety soup, pass through a sieve as well. Return to the original saucepan.

4 Meanwhile, roughly crumble the reserved chestnuts. Melt the remaining butter in a frying pan set over medium heat until foaming. Add the chestnuts and remaining oregano and cook for a few minutes, stirring often, until turning golden. Stir in the green celery root or leaves, if you have any, and cook for a minute more, until the chestnuts are crisp.

5 Adjust the seasoning in the soup with salt and pepper; you may wish to add a spike of lemon juice to brighten the flavors. Reheat gently and divide between warmed bowls. Finish each serving with a spoonful of buttery, fried chestnuts and oregano and 1 teaspoon crème fraîche, if you like.

Tomato-Lentil Rasam with Spelt

Serves 4

- ½ cup (100 g) pearled spelt
- ½ cup (100 g) red lentils, rinsed
- ½- to 1-inch (1.3 to 2.5 cm) piece fresh turmeric, peeled and finely chopped, or ½ teaspoon ground turmeric
- 1 teaspoon black peppercorns
- 1 teaspoon cumin seeds
- 2 garlic cloves, peeled
- 1 tablespoon ghee or unsalted butter
- 3 shallots, finely sliced
- 1 teaspoon brown mustard seeds
- ½ teaspoon chile flakes
- Pinch of asafetida (hing), optional
- 3 medium tomatoes, chopped
- 1 tablespoon raw cane sugar
- 1 tablespoon tamarind purée (see page 308 for how to soak and strain tamarind pulp)
- Sea salt

n no way a traditional *rasam*, or even a traditional way to eat it. Rasam, a spiced, sour broth of sorts, is usually served in cups alongside a dal or similar, as a gentle, nutritious accompaniment. However, sometimes restorative suppers such as this are called for, and, with its spelt grains and burlier-than-average broth, this is also extremely cheap, assuming you have a good spice pantry to draw on.

1 Cover the spelt and lentils with 3½ cups (800 ml) of water in a small saucepan and bring to a boil. Cover, reduce the heat and simmer for 20 minutes, then add the turmeric and continue to simmer for 10 minutes more, until the lentils are very tender and the mixture is thick. Beat well with a wooden spoon to break the lentils down into a rough purée.

2 Meanwhile, crush the peppercorns and cumin seeds with a mortar and pestle, adding the garlic cloves once the spices are crushed and pounding them, too, to a purée.

3 Melt the ghee in a larger saucepan set over medium-high heat. Add the shallots, mustard seeds and chile flakes and cook, stirring often, for about 7 minutes, until the shallots begin to sizzle and the mustard seeds begin to pop. Stir in the spiced garlic mixture and asafetida, if using. Cook for a further minute. Add two thirds of the chopped tomatoes, the sugar and tamarind and cook for 2 minutes more.

4 Pour in 1⅔ cups (400 ml) of water, season with salt and bring to a boil. Stir in the lentil mixture and remaining chopped tomatoes, reduce the heat and simmer for 5 minutes, until piping hot.

Vegetarian Pad Thai

Serves 2

- 3.5 ounces (100 g) flat rice noodles
- ⅓ cup (40 g) unsalted peanuts
- ¼ cup (60 g) tamarind purée (see page 308 for how to soak and strain tamarind pulp)
- ¼ cup (60 ml) Vegetarian "Fish" Sauce (page 300), or light soy sauce
- 1 to 2 tablespoons palm sugar or brown sugar, to taste
- ½ teaspoon hot chili powder
- 3 tablespoons peanut oil
- 6 ounces (160 g) store-bought marinated tofu cubes (ideally those in tamari)
- 1 garlic clove, finely chopped
- 2 medium eggs
- 1 heaping tablespoon chopped, preserved radish, optional (from Thai groceries)
- 1 cup (100 g) bean sprouts
- 2 tablespoons chopped Chinese or garlic chives, scallion tops, or regular chives
- Lime wedges, to serve

You can make an excellent vegetarian pad Thai, and here it is. Of course, dried shrimp and fish sauce don't feature, but you can make my Vegetarian "Fish" Sauce, or just use light soy sauce. The recipe only serves two and with good reason: Overfilling a wok causes the contents to steam and simmer rather than fry, making any stir-fry soggy. Successful pad Thai is made in small quantities.

1 First, soak the rice noodles in plenty of lukewarm water for 20 minutes.

2 Meanwhile, preheat the oven to 375°F (190°C), spread the peanuts out on a baking sheet and roast for 6 to 7 minutes, shaking the tray halfway through, until golden. Cool, then crush or chop quite finely.

3 Put the tamarind purée, "fish" sauce and 1 tablespoon of the sugar in a small saucepan with 1 tablespoon of water. Heat gently for 5 minutes, then add the chili powder. Taste and stir in the remaining sugar, if you wish. There should be a good balance of salty, sour, sweet and hot.

4 Drain the noodles thoroughly. Have the tamarind sauce on hand, with all the remaining prepared ingredients and a small dish of water.

5 Set a wok over high heat and add 2 tablespoons of the peanut oil. Once smoking hot, throw in the tofu and stir-fry for a minute. Add the garlic and cook for a minute more. Add half the tamarind sauce and transfer the noodles into the wok. Stir-fry until the noodles just soften, adding a splash of water if they stick. Taste and add some or all of the remaining sauce, as needed. Push the noodles to the side of the wok and add the remaining oil. Crack the eggs into the base, stirring to scramble before letting them set into a makeshift omelet. Tumble the noodles and eggs together, throwing in half the peanuts, the preserved radish, if using, bean sprouts and chives at the same time.

6 Toss through until the bean sprouts lose their raw look and serve immediately, with the remaining peanuts on top and lime wedges on the side.

Hor Fun Noodles with Many Mushrooms

Serves 2

- 4 scallions
- 1 teaspoon cornstarch
- ⅔ cup (150 ml) vegetable stock
- 1 tablespoon light soy sauce
- 1 tablespoon mushroom ketchup, vegetarian oyster sauce or Worcestershire sauce
- 1 tablespoon Shaoxing rice wine
- 2 teaspoons sesame oil
- 1 teaspoon brown sugar
- Fat pinch of sea salt
- 3 tablespoons rice bran or peanut oil
- 7 ounces (200 g) fresh hor fun noodles, or 3.5 ounces (100 g) dried rice noodles
- 1 small onion, sliced
- ½- to 1-inch (1.3 to 2.5 cm) piece fresh ginger root, peeled and sliced into matchsticks
- 1 garlic clove, finely chopped
- 2 cups (150 g) torn shiitake or oyster mushrooms
- 3 cups (200 g) roughly chopped white or green cabbage
- ½ cup (50 g) bean sprouts
- 1 red chile, finely sliced

or fun are the flat, wide rice noodles sold in fresh form in the refrigerated cases of Vietnamese, Chinese and Thai food shops. If you have a Chinatown near you, you'll be in luck, but you can always use half the weight of readily available dried, flat rice noodles instead. Soak the latter in plenty of just-boiled water for about 10 minutes, or according to the package instructions, before using.

1 Set the oven at a very low warming setting.

2 Slice the scallions thinly, keeping the pale green and white parts separate from the dark green.

3 Put the cornstarch in a container and gradually stir in the stock, soy sauce, mushroom ketchup, rice wine, sesame oil, sugar and salt.

4 Have all the remaining ingredients prepared and sitting next to the stove. This is a quick stir-fry.

5 Heat 1 tablespoon of the rice bran oil in a large wok over over high heat until smoking hot. Add the noodles and stir-fry briskly for a minute or so, using a spatula to separate them as they cook (it doesn't matter if they break up a bit). Transfer out on a plate and return the wok to the high heat. Keep the noodles warm in the low oven.

6 Add the remaining 2 tablespoons of oil to the wok and warm through. Throw in the onion and fry for 1 minute. Push to the side of the wok and add the ginger, garlic and pale parts of the scallion, cooking for a few seconds before adding the mushrooms. After barely 1 minute, add the cabbage and stir-fry for 20 seconds or so. Stir the cornstarch mixture and transfer into the wok, stirring well. Bring to a boil, then reduce the heat and simmer briskly for 3 to 4 minutes. Stir in the bean sprouts and warm through until they just wilt.

7 Ladle over the warm noodles and scatter with the sliced chile and reserved, dark green scallion tops to serve.

Roasted Cauliflower and Carrots with Lime Sambal and Cilantro Chutney

Serves 4 with rice

- 2 bunches of carrots, trimmed, any leafy tops reserved
- 1 cauliflower, trimmed and separated into florets
- 2 tablespoons coconut butter, melted, or peanut oil
- Sea salt and freshly ground black pepper
- 2 limes
- 1 cup (90 g) coarsely grated fresh coconut
- 2 handfuls of cilantro, roughly chopped
- 2 green chiles, deseeded and finely chopped
- 1 to 2 teaspoons palm sugar or brown sugar, to taste
- 1 small garlic clove, crushed
- 1 tablespoon desiccated coconut

tend to serve this with rice, simmered with a twinkle of coconut milk in the water and a scrunched-up lime leaf to scent, but pretty much any cooked grain or lentil would do. Or serve it as a starter without any accompaniment. And, of course, you don't need to seek out the purple cauliflower and multicolored carrots shown in the picture; I couldn't resist their garishness, but standard colors will taste the same.

1 Preheat the oven to 425°F (220°C).

2 On a large baking sheet, toss the carrots and cauliflower florets with the melted coconut butter. Season with salt and pepper, spread out well and roast for about 30 minutes, until soft and sweet.

3 Meanwhile, make a little sambal. Finely grate the zest of 1 of the limes, then pare the skin and pith from the sides and remove the segments, discarding the tough membranes holding them together. Roughly chop the flesh and transfer to a mixing bowl with the zest. Finely chop a handful of the reserved and rinsed carrot tops and add to the mixing bowl with the grated coconut, 1 handful of chopped cilantro and 1 finely chopped green chile. Season with salt, pepper and sugar to taste.

4 For the chutney, pulse the remaining cilantro in a mini food processor with the garlic, the juice of the second lime and a pinch of salt. Add a splash of water to get the blades moving; it should have a very loose consistency. Stir in the desiccated coconut and season to taste.

5 Serve the roasted vegetables with all the sambal and some of the cilantro chutney spooned over. The remaining chutney can sit on the side, ready to add as wanted.

Penne with Asparagus Pesto and White Beans

Serves 4

- 10.5 ounces (300 g; 1 large bunch) asparagus
- Sea salt and freshly ground black pepper
- 12 ounces (350 g) whole wheat dried penne, or other short pasta shape
- Olive oil
- 1 garlic clove, chopped
- ¼ cup (25 g) almonds
- 2 small bunches of basil
- Finely grated zest and juice of 1 unwaxed lemon
- 3 tablespoons extra virgin olive oil
- ½ cup (50 g) finely grated vegetarian Parmesan cheese, plus more to serve
- One 15-ounce (400 g) can lima or cannellini beans, drained and rinsed

Replace half the basil used in this recipe with mint leaves, if you like; this is a summery affair, intended to coincide with the latter part of asparagus season when the spears are plentiful and cheap. Use any almonds you have in the pesto: Sliced, blanched, chopped or whole with skins all work well. Never drain pasta too thoroughly, as the starchy cooking water helps to form a sauce.

1 Trim the very ends from each asparagus spear, only removing more if they are woody. Cut off the tips with about a thumb's length of stalk. Set aside.

2 Bring a medium saucepan of water to a boil, add the trimmed asparagus stalks (not the tips) with a good seasoning of salt and boil for 5 minutes, or until tender. Scoop the stalks out and into a colander with a slotted spoon, leaving the water behind in the pan. Give the stalks a brief rinse under cool water, just to take their temperature down a little, and transfer into the bowl of a food processor.

3 Return the pan of asparagus water to the heat, topping it up if needed. Bring to a boil and add the pasta, cooking according to the package instructions, or until al dente.

4 Set a griddle pan over high heat until smoking, toss the asparagus tips with a little regular olive oil to coat lightly and griddle for 4 minutes, turning now and then, until colored and soft. Set aside in the pan.

5 Put the garlic, almonds, almost all the basil (reserving a few leaves to serve), a squeeze of lemon juice and the extra virgin olive oil into the food processor with the asparagus stalks and blend to a rough purée, stopping to scrape down the sides a couple of times. Stir in the lemon zest and Parmesan. Taste and season, stirring in more lemon juice if you like.

6 Drain the pasta—not too well—and return to the hot pan with the beans and the asparagus pesto. Warm through very gently, then divide between warmed bowls or plates with the griddled asparagus tips, the reserved basil leaves and more cheese.

Spinach Gnocchi with Parmesan and Samphire

Serves 4 / Makes about 40

- 2 pounds 10 ounces (1.2 kg; about 4) baking potatoes
- Sea salt and freshly ground black pepper
- 1 pound (450 g) spinach
- 1 cup (130 g) spelt flour, or as needed, plus more to dust
- 3 tablespoons finely grated vegetarian Parmesan cheese, plus more to serve
- Good grating of nutmeg
- 1 egg, lightly beaten
- 2 tablespoons olive oil, plus more for the tray
- 1¾ cups (250 g) halved cherry tomatoes
- 1 garlic clove, finely chopped
- 2.5 ounces (75 g) tender samphire or baby asparagus, rinsed
- Handful of basil leaves

Your aim, when making toothsome gnocchi, is to extrude water from the dough at every stage. The more you can remove, the less flour you will have to add . . . which gives a light result. Ricing the potatoes when hot does give slightly airier dumplings, but, really, you can get away with baking the spuds in advance and ricing them when cool if that works better for you, time-wise.

1 Preheat the oven to 400°F (200°C). Prick the potatoes a few times with a knife and bake for 50 to 60 minutes, depending on size, until tender. Gingerly slice the cooked spuds in half, being careful not to burn yourself. Scoop the insides out with a spoon, leaving the empty skins behind. (Toss these with olive oil, season and bake until crisp. Cook's treat.) Using a potato ricer—failing that, a masher—rice the potato flesh into a bowl. Let cool for 5 minutes so it doesn't scramble the egg when you add it.

2 Meanwhile, bring a large saucepan of salted water to a boil. Submerge the spinach in it, reduce the heat and simmer for a minute or so to wilt. Drain in a colander, refresh briefly under the cool tap and drain again. Squeeze the leaves out over the sink, then transfer into a clean kitchen towel and twist for all you're worth to squeeze out excess water. Chop the dry spinach leaves very finely.

3 Add the spinach, flour and Parmesan to the potato with a generous seasoning of nutmeg, salt and pepper. Mix lightly, then add the egg and combine to form a dough. If it is very sticky, add a little more flour, but only if strictly necessary. Divide into 4 pieces. Roll each piece into a 1-inch (3 cm) thick cylinder on a lightly floured surface. Cut each into about 10 gnocchi.

4 Bring a large saucepan of salted water to a boil (again) and gently add the gnocchi in 3 batches, cooking each until they float to the surface and simmer there for 2 minutes. Fish out to an oiled tray with a slotted spoon and cook the next batch until they are all done.

5 Put a large frying pan over medium-high heat and add the 2 tablespoons of olive oil. Throw in the tomatoes and garlic and cook for a few minutes until the tomatoes begin to break down. Stir in the samphire and cook for a minute or so, followed by the gnocchi, basil and plenty of black pepper. Toss the pan cautiously to coat the gnocchi in sauce, heating everything through, but being gentle. Serve immediately with more cheese, if you like.

Ziti with Broccoli and Toasted Pine Nuts

Serves 4

- 6 cups (400 g) broccoli florets
- 12 ounces (350 g) dried ziti pasta, or other long pasta shape
- Sea salt and freshly ground black pepper
- 2 tablespoons salted butter
- 1 fat garlic clove, crushed
- 2 tablespoons mascarpone, optional
- ⅔ cup (100 g) roughly chopped vegetarian blue cheese, such as gorgonzola
- 1⅓ cups (100 g) pine nuts, toasted until golden (see page 58)
- Vegetarian Parmesan cheese, finely grated, to serve, optional

Don't be scared of cooking the broccoli here until truly soft; it doesn't take long, and, as you want it to form a sauce for the pasta; this is not the time for fancy al dente vegetables. It is also the authentic Italian way, when using broccoli as part of a pasta dressing. If you are after a rich sauce, include the mascarpone but, if you prefer a lighter pasta, feel free to leave it out.

1 Blanch the broccoli in plenty of boiling water for 3 minutes or so. Drain in a colander and refresh under ice-cold water to preserve its color. Drain again and roughly chop.

2 Cook the pasta in plenty of boiling salted water for 10 to 12 minutes, or according to the package instructions, until al dente.

3 Meanwhile, put the butter and garlic into a cold large frying pan, place over medium heat and cook for a minute or so, until the garlic is fragrant but not browned. Add the broccoli, cover with a lid or baking sheet and cook very gently for a few minutes. The broccoli should be very soft and yield easily to a wooden spoon pressed on it. Stir in the mascarpone, if using, and blue cheese and heat through to form a sauce. Season with salt and lots of pepper to taste. Stir in the pine nuts.

4 Drain the pasta, but don't be too precious about draining off every drop of water. Transfer the pasta straight into the broccoli pan and mix well. Serve in warmed bowls, with vegetarian Parmesan cheese grated over, if you like.

chapter four

thrifty

T CAN BE A RELATIVE CHALLENGE to make vegetarian cooking particularly expensive—unless you have a penchant for the finest saffron and fresh produce from far-flung lands—but when you combine seasonal and local vegetables with cheap staples, such as dried beans, peas, lentils and whole grains, you can eat extremely well for very little indeed.

This is as much about where and when (in the year, that is) you shop as about what you buy. It's a message often repeated these days, but I can't stress it enough: Buy produce at the peak of its season. Make, say, my loose incarnation of the sunny Tunisian salad, *mechouia*, at the end of the summer when there is a veritable glut of the ripest tomatoes, peppers, eggplants and zucchini and you will pay far less, and be rewarded with terrific flavor. If repeated six months later, with imported vegetables, it will have none of the intensity, but will have an inflated price tag. Buy a privileged pear or cosseted mushroom, shrouded in layers of packaging, and, again, you will pay an inevitable premium. If you can seek out loose produce at times of abundance, you are bound to make significant savings.

Much of the time, the same packaging point can be made about dried spices. I try my best to avoid buying expensive jars when whole spices, bought in packages from Asian shops, are cheaper and usually fresher. Resist the temptation to buy large quantities unless you know you will race through them; the fresher the better when it comes to spice, so I recommend buying small amounts of whole spices to toast and grind at home. Musty, dusty ground spices make a poor substitute and won't make your food sing.

A disclaimer when it comes to investing in spices, oils, vinegars and the like: I have assumed that the keen cook will have a decent pantry and spice drawer. The humble and filling ingredients on which this chapter focuses— think protein-packed legumes, roots, brassicas and the like—can take some serious spice, so be prepared to exercise a liberal hand.

We modern cooks waste food. In fact, the statistics on food waste in Western countries are downright frightening, so if you can weave shopping little and often into your week, planning your cooking according to what's cheap and plentiful, you will inevitably throw less away. Weekly meal planning is admirable, but in practice, few people I know have the organizational skills to plan seven days' worth of food in one outing. A few small shops might be slightly more time consuming, but they will keep you in touch with seasonal produce, allowing you to snap up bargains and cultivate the habit of buying only the fresh ingredients you need.

For years, I struggled with a miniscule, iced-up glove compartment masquerading as a freezer, so if you are in that same boat, I realize it can be frustrating to be advised to batch cook and freeze the extras. But, as the old adage goes, "two can live as cheaply as one," and making double quantities of, say, soups and stews to freeze costs little more and will furnish you with future dinners. Having a larger freezer to store gluts of cheap fruit and (well-labeled) leftovers has been a revelation.

Rather than letting unused, soft herbs, kales and peppery salads go to waste, blend any leaves on the point of wilting with a little good oil and some nuts or seeds, if you have them. This rudimentary pesto can be frozen as is, ready to defrost and adapt when needed. Cilantro-based purées can be transformed into fresh curry pastes; basil, mint and parsley mixtures will either turn to pesto with some vegetarian Parmesan cheese stirred in, or a form of salsa verde with chopped capers and olives. If you can get into the habit of preserving these odds and ends as you cook other recipes—a form of good stock rotation, really—you won't just cut down on food waste and spend less, you will become a better, more imaginative and resourceful cook, too.

Nowhere is a thoughtful flourish of pesto or herb oil more welcome than when spooned over a modest soup. Surely, a bowl of soup with bread is the ultimate frugal food, and you will find many variations here. I hope you find them worthy of cooking for friends when you don't have much cash, as well as filling, nutritious and almost always suitable for freezing.

Lentils, beans and grains are perfect thrifty foundations. The cooked legumes and grains sold in fancy packages are, comparatively, very expensive and far less versatile. Better to buy the dried and, where relevant, whole-grain version and reap the nutritional benefits. If you remember to soak legumes you can shave a few pennies off, but I've generally opted for canned beans as they are still a good value and take less forethought.

Herbs, an ingredient I use in quantity across the board, are expensive when bought in tiny supermarket packages, but worth the outlay for their transformative effect on humble recipes. I recommend buying herbs in the far cheaper, loose bunches from markets and grocery stores. Growing your own in pots, window boxes or flowerbeds is obviously cheaper still. Or buy one of those stingy pots of growing herbs and replant a single plant in a larger pot or, thriftier still, split it into two or three and repot each. This will create a "cut and come again" herb garden on your windowsill in return for a few days' watering, making that single plant a worthwhile investment.

Zucchini, Ricotta and Dill Tart with Spelt-Rye Pastry

Serves 8

A deep tart, packed with a light, summery mix of vegetables and a touch of buttermilk. Do squeeze as much moisture as possible from the zucchini or the filling will be watery. The pastry is a cinch, nutty and sweet from rye, but use any pie crust pastry, store-bought or not. If you don't have a deep enough pan (2 inch/5 to 6 cm is ideal), use a 10-inch (25 cm) tart pan. A shallower tart will cook in 20 to 25 minutes.

For the pastry
- 2¾ cups (325 g) whole-grain spelt flour
- ⅔ cup (100 g) whole-grain rye flour
- ½ cup plus 6 tablespoons (200 g) chilled salted butter, chopped

For the filling
- 3 zucchini, shredded or coarsely grated
- Sea salt and freshly ground black pepper
- 1 cup (150 g) peas, defrosted if frozen
- Small bunch of dill, finely chopped
- 2 tablespoons capers, rinsed and drained
- Finely grated zest and juice of 1 unwaxed lemon
- ¾ cup (200 ml) buttermilk
- 1 cup (250 g) drained ricotta cheese
- 4 large eggs, lightly beaten

For the salad
- 1 pound (500 g) tomatoes, sliced or halved
- Small handful of oregano leaves
- Extra virgin olive oil

1 Start with the pastry (at least an hour ahead). Put both flours in a food processor, or, if making this by hand, a large bowl. Add the butter and pulse in the food processor, or rub in by hand, until it resembles fine bread crumbs. Add enough ice water to bring the mixture together in a ball, starting with 1½ tablespoons and working up to no more than 3 tablespoons, as needed. Again, either use a food processor here, being careful not to overwork the dough, or cut the water in with a table knife. Form the pastry into a flattened disc and roll out between sheets of parchment or wax paper until it is about ⅛ inch (3 mm) thick. Unpeel the top sheet of paper and flip the pastry on to a 2-inch (5 to 6 cm) deep, 9-inch (23 cm) pie dish or tart pan. Unpeel the second sheet of paper (now on top) and press the pastry into the pan, trimming the edges flush with the dish. Keep the paper. Cover with plastic wrap and chill for 30 minutes, or up to 48 hours.

2 Preheat the oven to 400°F (200°C). Line the pastry with a saved paper sheet and fill with baking beans or raw rice. Bake for 15 minutes until the pastry is set and no longer looks wet. Remove the paper and beans and return to the oven for 5 to 6 minutes, until lightly colored.

3 Reduce the oven temperature to 350°F (180°C). Put the zucchini in a sieve and sprinkle with a generous pinch of salt, tossing to distribute evenly. Set aside for 10 minutes, then press down on them to drain. Put into a clean kitchen towel and wring out any remaining liquid very forcefully.

4 Combine the zucchini, peas, dill, capers and lemon zest in a bowl. In a separate bowl, whisk the buttermilk, half the ricotta and the eggs with a little salt and a lot of pepper. Fold the 2 mixtures together. Pour into the crust and dot with the remaining ricotta. Bake for 25 to 30 minutes, until just set. Set aside for 15 minutes so the filling can settle.

5 Toss the tomatoes with the oregano, lemon juice and extra virgin olive oil to taste. Season and serve the salad with slices of the warm or cold tart.

Roasted Broccoli Tart with a Cauliflower Crust

Serves 4 to 6

- 4 cups (250 g) broccoli florets
- 7 ounces (200 g) small tomatoes
- 2 tablespoons olive oil, plus more for the dish
- Leaves from 3 sprigs of rosemary, finely chopped
- 3 cups (450 g) cauliflower florets
- ½ cup (50 g) almond meal
- 4 eggs
- ⅓ cup (30 g) finely grated vegetarian Parmesan cheese
- Sea salt and freshly ground black pepper
- 5 ounces (150 g) salted ricotta cheese, finely sliced
- ¾ cup (200 ml) light cream
- ¼ cup (30 g) sliced almonds

Despite my initial skepticism, I admit that vegetable pastry is a fantastic invention for those keeping an eye on carbs, gluten or both. Salted ricotta is a cheeky addition for a thrifty chapter, although a little goes a long way. Substitute feta for a cheaper alternative. Stretch this out to feed six smaller appetites (or four large) with roasted roots or a big salad; it is surprisingly filling.

1 Preheat the oven to 375°F (190°C).

2 Toss the broccoli and tomatoes with the oil and half the rosemary, spread out in a large roasting pan and roast for 30 to 35 minutes, until just browning.

3 Chop the cauliflower florets roughly. Blend half at a time in a food processor, until finely chopped, or grate the whole lot with a box grater; either way it should look like pale couscous. Transfer to a large baking sheet lined with nonstick parchment paper and spread out in an even layer. Slide into the oven for 15 minutes to dry out. Let cool for 10 minutes, then transfer into a clean kitchen towel, bring up the edges and twist. Squeeze as hard as you can to force as much water out as possible. Transfer the now-dry cauliflower to a mixing bowl.

4 Stir in the almond meal, 1 egg, the remaining rosemary, Parmesan cheese and plenty of salt and pepper. Line a 2-inch (5 to 6 cm) deep, 9-inch (23 cm) pie dish or tart pan with a circle of parchment paper to come right up the sides, and brush it lightly with olive oil (you can dispense with the paper, but it does make the tart easier to unmold). Mound the cauliflower mix into the dish, then press firmly and evenly over and up the sides, to make a crust.

5 Bake for 8 to 10 minutes directly on the oven floor, until just beginning to brown at the edges.

6 Arrange the roasted broccoli and tomatoes and the salted ricotta in the cauliflower crust. Beat the remaining 3 eggs with the cream, pour into the case and top with the sliced almonds. Return to the oven floor, reducing the temperature to 350°F (180°C). Bake for 25 minutes, or until just set with barely a wobble in the center when jiggled. Rest for at least 15 minutes before slicing, so the filling can set. Serve warm or cold.

Beet Soup with Horseradish

Serves 4 to 6

- 2 pounds 10 ounces (1.2 kg; 7 to 8 medium) beets
- 4 shallots, skins on
- 1 fennel bulb, quartered
- A few sprigs of thyme
- 2 tablespoons olive oil
- Sea salt and freshly ground black pepper
- ½ teaspoon fennel seeds
- 1 quart (1 L) vegetable stock
- ½ cup (100 ml) red wine
- 1 tablespoon plus 1 teaspoon grated horseradish, fresh or jarred
- ⅓ cup (75 g) Greek yogurt
- Handful of store-bought beet chips, optional

A little red wine balances the depth and sweetness of all the roasted vegetables here, rounding out the raucousness of beets in particular. I have given instructions to serve this soup hot as a bracing winter number, but it can also be a delicious and unexpected cold dish for warmer days, in which case whisk or swirl half the cold yogurt into the chilled soup just before serving.

1 Preheat the oven to 375°F (190°C).

2 Rinse the beets, trimming any stalks and leaves. (Save any nice baby leaves for a garnish.) Put the beets, still wet from rinsing, in a roasting pan with the shallots, fennel, thyme, olive oil and a seasoning of salt and pepper. Cover the pan tightly with foil and roast for 50 minutes. By this time, the beets should be tender and sweet and the shallots soft.

3 Meanwhile, cook the fennel seeds in a dry frying pan set over medium heat. They should take about 45 seconds to become fragrant and lightly toasted. Transfer into a mortar and crush with the pestle.

4 Set the roasted vegetables aside to cool for 10 minutes with the foil on, or, if you can't wait, don rubber gloves and remove the foil immediately. Peel the skin from the beets and chop the insides roughly. Put the fennel seeds and beets into a large saucepan with the roasted fennel, discarding the thyme. Squeeze the shallot flesh into the pan, too, discarding the skins. Add the stock and red wine and bring to a boil slowly. Once boiling, reduce the heat to a gentle simmer for 15 minutes.

5 Stir the horseradish into the yogurt and season to taste.

6 Blend the soup, preferably in the pan with a hand blender for ease, until very smooth. Check the seasoning and reheat gently. Remove from the heat and immediately whisk in half the horseradish yogurt.

7 Divide the hot soup between warmed bowls, topping with spoonfuls of the remaining horseradish yogurt, a couple of reserved, well-washed beet leaves, if you have them, and a few beet chips for crunch, if you like.

Yogurt Soup with Lentils, Barley and Mint

Serves 4 generously

- 3 tablespoons salted butter
- 1 onion, finely chopped
- 3 leeks, washed, trimmed and thinly sliced
- 2 green chiles, halved, deseeded if you prefer, finely chopped
- 2 teaspoons cumin seeds
- ⅔ cup (100 g) pot or Scotch barley or pearl barley
- 1 tablespoon unbleached all-purpose flour
- 5½ cups (1.3 L) vegetable stock
- ½ cinnamon stick
- One 15-ounce (400 g) can chickpeas, drained and rinsed
- ⅓ cup (75 g) brown lentils
- 3½ cups (100 g) baby spinach
- ¾ cup (200 g) full-fat Greek yogurt
- Juice of 1 lemon
- Sea salt and freshly ground black pepper
- 4 very fresh eggs, optional
- ½ garlic clove, crushed
- 1 teaspoon dried mint
- ½ teaspoon sweet smoked paprika
- Pinch of chile flakes

have tweaked this old, Turkish-style favorite over the years, but the original belongs to the food writer and owner of the Ginger and White cafes, Tonia George. It makes a soothing, unusual and exceptionally delicious soup. Finish it with a poached egg if you are very hungry. Pot or Scotch barley has a nicer chew than the more common pearl barley, so do try to get hold of it; you will find it in health food shops.

1 In a large saucepan or casserole set over low heat, melt half the butter and add the onion, leeks, chiles and cumin seeds. Cook for 10 minutes, stirring occasionally, until the vegetables are very soft.

2 Add the barley and flour, stirring for 1 minute to cook out the flour. Stir in the stock and cinnamon stick and simmer for 25 minutes. Add the chickpeas and lentils and simmer for 20 minutes more, until the lentils are cooked and the barley is just tender but still has a bite. Stir in the spinach, remove from the heat and fish out the cinnamon stick.

3 If you will be including the poached eggs, half-fill a deep frying pan with water and bring to a boil over high heat. Reduce the heat and leave to simmer gently.

4 In a separate bowl, whisk the yogurt and half the lemon juice with a ladleful of hot liquid from the soup pan. Stir this mixture back into the soup off the heat, then return it to a low flame. Stir gently for a couple of minutes; do not let it boil at any point or the soup will curdle. Taste and adjust with salt or pepper as you wish, remembering the butter added at the end will be quite salty.

5 Crack the eggs into the simmering water, spacing them out well. Poach very gently for 2½ to 3 minutes; the water should have barely a blip reaching its surface. Remove to a paper-towel-lined plate with a slotted spoon.

6 Melt the remaining butter in a small pan until foaming. Add the remaining lemon juice, the garlic, mint, paprika and chile flakes and cook until the butter turns a pale amber and smells nutty. Remove from the heat. Spoon most of the hot butter over the soup, then divide between warmed bowls, topping each with a poached egg, if using, and the rest of the butter.

Roasted Carrot Soup with Flatbread Ribbons

Serves 4

- 3½ pounds (1.6 kg) carrots, scrubbed and sliced
- 1 sweet white onion, sliced
- 2 tablespoons sunflower oil
- 2 unpeeled garlic cloves
- 1 red chile, halved and deseeded
- 5½ cups (1.3 L) vegetable stock
- ½- to 1-inch (1.3 to 2.5 cm) piece fresh turmeric, peeled and finely chopped
- 1 teaspoon nigella seeds
- 1 thin, round flatbread
- ¼ cup (60 g) crème fraîche or Greek yogurt
- Scant handful of chive sprouts, or chives, chopped

A sonorous soup, first roasted then slowly simmered, elevated with a flourish of toasted nigella seeds and fine strips of griddled flatbread. Fresh turmeric, long renowned for aiding digestion and calming inflammation, intensifies the deep golden hue of the soup. If you can't find the fresh root—though larger supermarkets should have it—use ½ teaspoon ground turmeric instead, or replace it with fresh ginger root.

1 Preheat the oven to 375°F (190°C).

2 Put the carrots and onion in a large baking pan and toss with the oil. Roast for about 20 minutes, then add the whole garlic cloves and halved chile, stirring everything thoroughly. Return to the oven for 20 minutes more, until the vegetables are soft and browned. Remove the papery skins from the soft garlic cloves.

3 Put the roasted vegetables in a large saucepan with the stock and turmeric. Bring to a boil, reduce the heat and simmer gently for 15 minutes, then purée, in batches if necessary, until completely smooth.

4 Toast the nigella seeds in a small frying pan set over medium heat until fragrant. Crush slightly with a mortar and pestle.

5 Put a griddle or frying pan over the heat and wait until it's smoking hot. Add the flatbread. Cook for a few seconds on each side, until warmed through. Remove to a chopping board and slice into fine ribbons.

6 Gently reheat the soup over low heat. Divide between warmed bowls and serve with a spoonful of crème fraîche, the toasted nigella seeds, chive sprouts and flatbread ribbons.

Tarka Dal Soup

Serves 4 generously

- 1¼ cups (250 g) chana dal, or dried yellow split peas, rinsed
- 3 garlic cloves, peeled
- 2 green chiles
- 3 tablespoons rice bran or peanut oil, or other flavorless oil
- 2 tablespoons cumin seeds
- Pinch of asafetida (hing), optional
- 3 shallots, sliced
- 1-inch (2.5 cm) piece fresh ginger root, peeled and finely chopped or grated
- 1½ teaspoons ground coriander
- 1 teaspoon garam masala
- ¾ teaspoon ground turmeric
- One 15-ounce (400 g) can plum tomatoes
- 1¼ cups (300 ml) vegetable stock, or as needed
- Sea salt and freshly ground black pepper
- 1 teaspoon brown mustard seeds

This substantial soup is made with chana dal (split, dried chickpeas) or the more common yellow dried split peas, which will make a slightly smoother soup. Chana dal, like all legumes, are famously good at balancing blood sugar and are also high in valuable protein, making this a nutritious as well as a filling supper for very little outlay. Add less stock to make a thicker dal, if you prefer.

1 Put the chana dal in a large saucepan with 1 quart (1 L) of water. Bring to a boil, skim to remove any foam from the surface, then reduce the heat and simmer for 30 to 45 minutes, or until tender. Beat well with a wooden spoon to break down the legumes. Set aside.

2 Meanwhile, crush 2 of the garlic cloves and slice the third finely. Pierce 1 chile with a knife, leaving it whole. Deseed and finely slice the second chile and add to the sliced garlic.

3 Heat 2 tablespoons of the oil in a second large saucepan or Dutch oven over medium heat. Add half the cumin seeds and cook for 30 seconds. Stir in the asafetida, if using, with 2 of the sliced shallots and the whole chile. Cook, stirring, for 5 minutes. Add the ginger, crushed garlic, coriander, garam masala and turmeric. Cook for a minute or so.

4 Snip the tomatoes in their opened can with scissors and transfer into the pan with ¾ cup (200 ml) of the stock. Bring to a boil, then reduce the heat and simmer for 10 minutes. Stir in the cooked chana dal and add the remaining ½ cup (100 ml) stock, as needed, to make a thick soup. At this stage, you can blend the soup with a hand blender if you would prefer it to be smooth. Season with salt and pepper to taste and leave to simmer while you make the tarka.

5 In a small frying pan, heat the remaining 1 tablespoon of oil over medium heat. Add the mustard seeds and cook for 30 seconds or so, until they fizz and crackle. Stir in the remaining sliced shallot, sliced chile and garlic, remaining cumin seeds and a pinch of salt. Cook through for 5 minutes, reducing the heat if it begins to catch. Divide the soupy dal between warmed bowls and spoon the tarka over to finish.

Split Pea Soup with Caraway Brussels Sprouts

Serves 4 to 6

- 1 large onion, finely chopped
- 2 tablespoons unsalted butter
- Sea salt and freshly ground black pepper
- 1 large parsnip, scrubbed
- 2 large carrots, scrubbed
- ½ teaspoon caraway seeds
- Sprig of rosemary
- 1 cup (200 g) dried yellow split peas, rinsed
- 1½ quarts (1.5 L) vegetable stock
- 1 cup (75 g) brussels sprouts
- Squeeze of lemon juice
- 1 teaspoon olive oil

n terms of soothing soups, yellow split peas are hard to beat, softening to velvet here as they cook with sweet vegetables. If you want more crunch at the end, be a little more generous with the butter used to cook the final flourish of brussels, throwing in a handful of small rye bread cubes halfway through. Keep them moving in the pan and they will turn crisp and golden by the time the sprout leaves are done.

1 Put the onion in a large saucepan or Dutch overn with 1½ tablespoons of the butter and a pinch of salt. Set over low-ish heat to cook, stirring now and then.

2 Chop the parsnip and carrots into small cubes—this is largely an unblended soup—and add to the onion pan with half the caraway seeds and the rosemary, stirring to coat in the butter. The onion should be translucent by now, so increase the heat slightly and cook for a further 5 minutes, until the roots begin to soften. Stir in the split peas, followed by the stock and another good pinch of salt. Bring to a boil and skim to remove any foam from the surface.

3 Reduce the heat and leave the peas to simmer for 35 to 40 minutes, until very soft. This cooking time will largely depend on the age of the split peas so start to check after 30 minutes, being prepared to let them cook for anything up to an hour, if needed. Splash in water to prevent the mixture sticking toward the end of the cooking time if they take longer than planned.

4 Meanwhile, prepare the sprouts by slicing off their bases and separating the leaves, slicing any tightly packed middles that won't unfurl.

5 Remove the rosemary sprig from the soup and blend about one third of it (easiest using a hand blender directly in the pan). Return to the heat, adjusting the consistency and seasoning with salt and pepper to taste. A squeeze of lemon juice should give the flavors a lift. Keep warm.

6 Put a large frying pan (you want the sprouts to have plenty of room) over high heat and add the remaining butter with the oil. Once foaming, throw in the remaining caraway seeds and the brussels sprouts, stir-frying for a few minutes until browned in places and just tender. Season. Divide the soup between warmed bowls and top with the charred sprout leaves.

Stuffed Baby Squash with Mujaddara

Serves 4

- 4 baby winter squash, about 5 inches (12 cm) in diameter or 1½ pounds (700 g) each
- ¼ cup (60 ml) sunflower oil, plus more for the squash
- Sea salt and freshly ground black pepper
- 4 fresh bay leaves
- 2 large onions, finely sliced
- 2 tablespoons coriander seeds
- 2 teaspoons cumin seeds
- 1¼ cups (200 g) brown basmati rice
- ½ teaspoon ground turmeric
- Pinch of chile flakes
- 2¼ cups (520 ml) vegetable stock
- ¾ cup (150 g) green or brown lentils
- 7 cups (200 g) baby spinach leaves
- ¼ cup (60 g) plain yogurt

Assuming you have spices on hand already, this is, dare I say it, a dinner-party-worthy supper for very little outlay. It may seem fussy to cook the lentil component of the stuffing separately from the rice, but lentils are a strange beast, cooking very quickly or obstinately refusing to soften, depending on age and storage conditions. Cooking them solo means they cook perfectly without affecting the rice.

1 Preheat the oven to 375°F (190°C).

2 Cut the squash tops off about one quarter of the way down. Using a sturdy soup spoon, hollow out the centers, including all the seeds. (Please don't attempt this with a knife; it is the fastest way to an injury.) Rub the squash with oil and season the insides generously with salt and pepper. Nestle into a roasting pan, large enough to hold all 4 squash, tucking the lids in wherever they will fit. Put a bay leaf into each hollow and roast for 1 hour.

3 Meanwhile, use your largest frying pan to cook the onions in 2 tablespoons of the oil with a large pinch of salt over medium heat. Stir often for 10 minutes, until softened and turning brown. Reduce the heat slightly and continue to cook for 10 minutes or so, stirring whenever the onions begin to catch. They should be soft, sweet and sizzling in places.

4 Put the coriander and cumin seeds in a medium saucepan with the remaining 2 tablespoons of oil. Cook over low heat for a couple of minutes until the seeds are fizzing gently. Stir in the rice, turmeric and chile flakes, followed by the stock. Bring to a boil, cover, reduce the heat and simmer for 25 minutes until the rice is tender. Set aside for a few minutes to finish cooking.

5 In a separate pan, cover the lentils with plenty of water, bring to a boil, then reduce the heat and simmer briskly for about 20 minutes, or until just tender (start checking after 15 minutes, though they might take up to 30). Drain well.

6 Add the spinach to the hot rice pan and stir through to wilt. Add half the fried onions and all the lentils, stirring well and seasoning to taste. Divide this mixture between the roasted squash, removing the bay leaves first. Top with the reserved onions and a spoonful of yogurt to stir in as you eat, accompanying with the roasted squash lids.

Soba Noodle Soup with Duck Egg and Greens

Serves 4

- 4 radishes, trimmed and sliced or quartered
- 2 tablespoons rice wine vinegar
- Pinch of sea salt
- Pinch of sugar
- 1 sheet dried kombu seaweed (about 2 × 4 inches/5 × 10 cm)
- Handful of fresh shiitake mushrooms, stalks separated, caps sliced
- 1 leek, washed and sliced
- 7 ounces (200 g) soba noodles
- 2 duck eggs
- ¾ cup (75 g) bean sprouts
- Large handful of seasonal greens, such as radish tops, kale, chard or spinach
- 1 to 2 tablespoons soy sauce, or to taste
- 1 to 2 tablespoons white or pale yellow mirin, or to taste
- 2 to 3 tablespoons white or yellow miso, or to taste
- 2 scallions, finely sliced

This started life as a ramen-style soup, but it didn't take many tries to conclude that getting depth and richness into a vegetarian ramen would take many hours. Cue a change of tack and a light, fresh, but no less pleasing noodle soup, with plenty of interest from pickles and vegetable goodies. Seek out a white or pale yellow miso for this, as anything darker will be too spiky; you need mellow and sweet.

1 Pickle the radishes by tossing them in the vinegar, salt and sugar. Set aside in a cool place for at least 2 hours, or chill for up to 2 weeks.

2 If you have time, soak the seaweed and the mushroom stalks in 1½ quarts (1.4 L) of water in a large saucepan for 30 minutes. Soaked or not, place the saucepan over low heat and heat through (don't boil) for 30 minutes to infuse the broth.

3 Strain the broth to remove the now-soft kombu piece and mushroom stalks, pressing down to extract all the flavor, including any gelatinous liquid clinging to the seaweed. Return the broth to the pan, adding the mushroom caps and the leek. Bring to a boil slowly, then cover and reduce the heat to simmer for anything from 20 minutes to 4 hours, depending on how savory and concentrated you want the broth to be and how much time you have.

4 While the broth simmers, cook the extras: In a separate pan, boil the soba noodles according to the package instructions. Drain and set aside. Use the same pan to simmer the duck eggs in plenty of boiling water for 9 to 10 minutes. Refresh under cool water and peel when cool enough to handle. Again, refill the pan with water and return to a boil. Blanch the bean sprouts for 30 seconds. Refresh under cool water and drain.

5 Add the greens to the simmering broth and let wilt for a minute. Season with the soy sauce, mirin and enough miso to cloud the broth. Taste and adjust as required. Add the noodles and warm through. Divide the soup between warmed bowls. Top each with scallions, a halved duck egg, blanched bean sprouts and a few slices of pickled radish for a bit of poke.

Winter Cabbage Rolls

Serves 4

- 2 tablespoons unsalted butter or ghee
- 1 large red onion, finely chopped
- Sea salt and freshly ground black pepper
- 1- to 1½-inch (1.3 to 2.5 cm) piece fresh ginger root, peeled and finely grated
- 1 teaspoon ground turmeric
- Fat pinch of chile flakes
- 2¼ cups (500 g) passata (tomato purée), sieved
- 2 leeks, washed and finely sliced
- 1 teaspoon cumin seeds
- 2 medium parsnips (11 ounces/320 g in total), grated
- 1 cup (200 g) red lentils
- 1 teaspoon garam masala
- 2¾ cups (650 ml) strong vegetable stock
- 12 large sweetheart (pointed or hispi) cabbage or other green leaves
- Small handful of cilantro, roughly chopped
- Squeeze of lemon juice
- Flavorless oil, for the dish
- ⅔ cup (100 g) crumbled feta
- 3 tablespoons chopped pistachios
- 3 soft dates, pitted and chopped

ron-rich cabbage leaves stuffed with a spiced leek, parsnip and red lentil mixture, rolled up and cloaked in a rich tomato sauce . . . not your average gratin, perhaps, but it really works. Less conventional still is the topping of crumbled feta, pistachios and dates. You could leave this out to keep costs down, but it adds so much to the flavor and texture that I highly recommend stretching to it, if you can.

1 Have 2 medium saucepans ready. Put the butter, red onion and a pinch of salt in a pan and cook over medium heat, stirring often, for 8 to 10 minutes, until softened. Add the ginger, turmeric and chile flakes and cook for a further minute. Now transfer half of this mixture to the second pan and add the passata. Simmer very gently for 15 to 20 minutes. Remove from the heat.

2 Go back to the first pan. Keeping it over medium heat, add the leeks and cumin seeds to the remaining onion mixture, stirring for 5 minutes until softened. Stir in the parsnips, lentils and garam masala, followed by the stock. Bring to a boil, then cover and reduce the heat to simmer gently for 25 minutes, stirring now and then, until the lentils are just cooked and the mixture is thick. (Boil down, uncovered, for a minute if any visible liquid remains on the base of the pan.) Remove from the heat and season generously with salt and pepper.

3 Blanch the green leaves in plenty of boiling water for about 1 minute, drain in a colander and refresh under cool tap water, then pat dry.

4 Preheat the broiler to medium. Stir most of the cilantro and the lemon juice into the lentils. Taste. Season, or add lemon to brighten, if needed.

5 Oil a medium gratin dish (about 12 × 8-inch/30 × 20 cm is ideal). Lay a greens leaf out on a chopping board. Place 1 heaping tablespoon of lentil mixture on the base and roll up to form a sealed cylinder, folding over both sides to close. Sit in the dish, seam side down, and repeat with the remaining leaves and filling. Pour the tomato sauce over and slide under the broiler for 10 minutes.

6 Combine the feta, pistachios, dates and remaining cilantro, seasoning well with black pepper. Scatter this mixture over the gratin as soon as it emerges from the broiler and let it sit for 5 minutes before serving, so the cheese can melt and the mixture can settle. Even better the next day, baked in a moderate oven until piping hot.

Northern-Style Pho

Serves 4

- 2 parsnips
- 2 large carrots
- 2 celery stalks
- 2 sweet white onions
- 4 cups (300 g) shiitake or field mushrooms
- 2 tablespoons peanut oil
- 1 teaspoon palm sugar or brown sugar
- 4 unpeeled garlic cloves
- 1 red chile
- 1- to 1½-inch (2.5 to 4 cm) piece fresh ginger root
- 2 tablespoons light soy sauce
- 1 star anise
- 1 small cinnamon stick
- 1 clove
- 6 white peppercorns
- Handful of cilantro with stalks
- 5 scallions, sliced
- 7 ounces (200 g) dried flat rice noodles
- Sea salt
- 1 cup (100 g) bean sprouts
- Chile or Sriracha sauce, to serve
- Lime wedges

The very idea of vegetarian pho might ruffle the aficionado's feathers. . . . Obviously, this incarnation of the famous noodle soup is made without bones, but it has resonance. Why northern-style? Because I find that they are less sweet and noticeably spiced. Of course, you can offer the whole gamut of herbs, bean sprouts and even hoisin sauce alongside, as you find in summery Saigon-style interpretations.

1 Preheat the oven to 400°F (200°C). Thickly slice the parsnips, carrots, celery, 1 of the sweet onions and half the mushrooms. In a large roasting pan, toss them with the oil, sugar, garlic and chile, spreading out in 1 layer (use 2 pans if there isn't enough room; they must roast, not steam). Roast for 50 minutes, stirring twice, until sticky and soft, but not burned.

2 Meanwhile, halve the remaining onion. Slice half paper-thin with a mandoline or very sharp knife. Cover with water in a bowl and set aside. Preheat the broiler to high, or turn a gas burner to high. Either broil the piece of ginger root and onion half, turning every minute until smoking and blackened in places, or spear both with large forks and hold directly over a gas flame until lightly charred all over. This will add a smoky depth.

3 Get a large saucepan or stockpot ready. Fill it with 7½ cups (1.8 L) of water. Add all the roasted vegetables, the charred ginger and onion, soy sauce and whole spices. Cut the stalks from the cilantro and add these, with the roots if present. Bring to a boil, partially cover and reduce the heat to simmer for 45 minutes, until the broth is reduced by one quarter. Carefully strain it through a sieve into a large bowl, pressing down on the vegetables to get every last drop out of them. Empty the pan and return the strained broth to it with the remaining sliced mushrooms and the scallions. Return to a boil, reduce the heat and simmer, uncovered, for 10 minutes. Taste and reduce a little more if it tastes too weak (remembering it isn't seasoned yet).

4 When the broth is done, soak the noodles in plenty of just-boiled water for 8 minutes, then drain. They should be barely cooked. Taste the broth again and add salt to bring the flavors alive. Divide the noodles, drained onion slices and bean sprouts between 4 wide, warmed serving bowls, stir the cilantro leaves into the broth and ladle over the noodles. Serve with chile sauce and lime wedges for seasoning at the table.

Chickpea Crepes with Wild Garlic

Serves 4

- 1 cup (100 g) chickpea (gram) flour
- 2 wild garlic leaves, shredded, plus 2 handfuls (about 2 ounces/60 g) wild garlic leaves and stems, washed and roughly chopped
- 1 teaspoon fine salt
- 2 tablespoons hulled hemp seeds, or chopped almonds
- ¼ cup (25 g) finely grated vegetarian Parmesan cheese, optional
- ¼ cup plus 2 tablespoons (90 ml) extra virgin olive oil, plus more to cover if needed
- Sea salt and freshly ground black pepper
- 1 to 2 tablespoons lemon juice
- Olive oil
- 4 duck eggs
- Bunch of young or wild asparagus, woody ends snapped off

Chickpea crepes are common in Italian cuisine and I wonder that we don't eat more of them. This is a cheap recipe for late spring, when there is a glut of asparagus and wild garlic. (Please don't pay good money for an abundant, free herb. Substitute basil, watercress or arugula, or a combination, instead.) Make it cheaper by subbing chicken eggs for duck, or leave the eggs and cheese out for a vegan meal.

1 Put the chickpea flour in a large mixing bowl and gradually whisk in ⅔ cup plus or minus a few tablespoons (150 to 160 ml) of water to form a smooth batter with the consistency of light cream. Stir in the shredded garlic leaves and fine salt. Set aside at room temperature for 1 to 4 hours (or 30 minutes, in a pinch).

2 Meanwhile, make the wild garlic pesto. Using a mortar and pestle, or the small bowl of a food processor, pound or blend the hemp seeds with the remaining wild garlic and the cheese, if using. Gradually pound or blend in the extra virgin olive oil to form a rustic pesto, season to taste and brighten with lemon juice. If you're not using the pesto in this recipe, or are making it for something else in advance, cover with a film of extra virgin olive oil and chill for up to 4 days.

3 When ready to cook, wipe the surface of a large cast-iron or nonstick frying pan with paper towels dipped in regular olive oil and place over very high heat until smoking. Reduce the heat to medium-high. Spoon a ladleful of the batter into the pan, swirling gently to encourage it to spread into an even circle. Cook it for 10 seconds, then flip it over with a spatula and cook on the other side. Remove to a plate, keep warm, and repeat to make 4 crepes. You may have a little batter left if you didn't need to practice on a first, throwaway crepe to get the technique right.

4 In a separate pan, gently fry the duck eggs, 2 at a time, in 1 tablespoon or so of regular olive oil, until the whites are set and the lacy edges are golden. Give them room so they stay separate, and spoon a little hot oil over them as they cook. Drain on paper towels and keep warm. Steam the asparagus for 3 to 4 minutes, depending on thickness, until just tender.

5 To serve, lay one quarter of the asparagus and a fried egg on each crepe. Season, then top with a good spoonful of wild garlic pesto, fold the edges over and eat hot.

Spiced Paneer for Spring in Semolina Dosas

Serves 4

Store-bought paneer, a mild and low-fat Indian cheese, is good value, but can be bland. These subtly spiced dosas, with their spring-like filling of curried peas and pea shoots, will perk it up no end. You can use 7 ounces (200 g) of canned chopped tomatoes instead of the fresh and omit the fragrant, fresh curry leaves if you can't find them. Be careful while the paneer fries, as the moisture in the cheese can spit.

For the dosas

- ⅓ cup (50 g) fine semolina flour or cornmeal
- ⅓ cup (50 g) rice flour
- 3 tablespoons spelt flour
- 2 green chiles, deseeded and chopped
- ½ small onion, finely chopped
- 1-inch (3 cm) piece fresh ginger root, peeled and finely chopped
- 8 fresh curry leaves, chopped
- Generous pinch of sea salt

For the paneer curry

- 3 tablespoons peanut oil, plus more for the dosas
- 10.5 ounces (300 g) paneer, cubed
- 1 teaspoon cumin seeds
- 1¼ cups (200 g) chopped tomatoes
- 1- to 1½-inch (2.5 to 4 cm) piece fresh ginger root, peeled and finely grated
- ½ teaspoon ground turmeric
- Sea salt
- 1¾ cups (250 g) peas, defrosted if frozen
- Handful of cilantro, roughly chopped
- Pea shoots, to serve

1 Mix the flours in a bowl with half the chile, the onion, ginger, curry leaves and salt. Gradually whisk in 1 cup (220 ml) of water; the consistency should be a bit thicker than milk. Pour into a container and set aside for 30 minutes.

2 Make the curry. Put the 3 tablespoons of oil in a wok or large frying pan set over high heat. Gently add the paneer and fry for 2 minutes, turning often, until the cubes turn a pale, golden brown. Remove with a slotted spoon and drain on paper towels.

3 Pour most of the oil away, leaving about 1 tablespoon in the pan. Reduce the heat to medium and add the cumin seeds. When they become fragrant, stir in the tomatoes, ginger, remaining chopped chile, turmeric and a generous pinch of salt. Stir well and allow to cook for a minute, then return the paneer cubes to the pan with ½ cup (100 ml) water. Bring to a boil, partially cover with a lid, then reduce the heat and simmer for 5 minutes. Stir in the peas and cilantro, adding a splash of water if the mixture looks dry, and cook for a couple more minutes. Remove from the heat and set aside while you cook the dosas.

4 For the dosas, place a large nonstick frying pan over high heat and wipe it with a piece of paper towel generously dipped in peanut oil. Pour 1 medium ladleful of the batter into the hot pan, from the edges toward the center, swirling quickly to make a very thin lacy crepe. Sprinkle a few drops of oil over. Cook for 30 seconds to 1 minute, until the base is golden or crisp. Flip over and cook for a further 30 seconds or so. When both sides are lightly colored, remove the dosa to a plate. Prepare all the dosas this way, stacking them up on the plate separated by sheets of parchment paper. Cover the plate with foil and keep warm in a low oven.

5 Rewarm the paneer curry and serve, wrapped in the dosas with handfuls of pea shoots.

Dill, Carrot and Chickpea Curry with Beet Raita

Serves 4

For the raita
- 1 small beet, scrubbed
- ¼ cup (60 g) plain yogurt
- 3 tablespoons coconut cream
- 3 tablespoons desiccated coconut
- 2 tablespoons lime juice
- Sea salt and freshly ground black pepper

For the curry
- 1 teaspoon coriander seeds
- 1 teaspoon cumin seeds
- 2 tablespoons coconut oil
- 1 red onion, chopped
- 2⅓ cups (300 g) sliced carrots (cut into chubby matchsticks)
- 1 teaspoon hot chili powder
- 1 teaspoon ground turmeric
- 2 garlic cloves, crushed
- 1-inch (2.5 cm) piece fresh ginger root, peeled and finely grated
- 2 vine tomatoes, chopped
- 2 bunches of dill, finely chopped
- One 15-ounce (400 g) can chickpeas, drained and rinsed
- Steamed rice or flatbreads, to serve

An unusual, fragrant, dry-style curry, making full use of dill's affinity with chickpeas and sweet carrots. Use any mild oil in place of coconut butter if you don't have the latter or don't like its mild, coconut taste (in which case, you might want to swap the coconut cream in the bright purple raita for more yogurt and leave out the desiccated coconut). Rather not buy a single beet? Substitute a small carrot instead.

1 Start by making the raita. Coarsely grate the beet into a bowl, skin and all. Stir through the yogurt, coconut cream and desiccated coconut. Stir in 1 tablespoon of the lime juice and season well with salt and pepper. Cover and chill until needed.

2 Toast the coriander and cumin seeds in a small frying pan set over medium heat, stirring them often for about a minute, until fragrant and toasted. Crush with a mortar and pestle.

3 Melt the coconut oil in a medium saucepan over medium-low heat. Cook the onion, stirring often, for about 7 minutes. Stir in the carrots and cook for 5 minutes more, until the onion is soft and translucent. Add the chili powder with the toasted spices, turmeric, garlic and ginger, stirring and cooking for 2 minutes or so. Stir in the tomatoes, increase the heat by a notch and sauté for 5 minutes, until the tomatoes begin to break down.

4 Add the dill, chickpeas, ¼ cup (60 ml) water and a generous pinch of salt. Simmer, stirring now and then, for 6 to 8 minutes, until the dill is completely soft and the carrots are tender. Stir in the remaining 1 tablespoon of lime juice off the heat. Taste and add salt and pepper as needed. Serve with rice or flatbreads, spooning on the raita as you eat.

Mechouia

Serves 4

- 3 large sweet peppers (red, yellow or orange)
- 2 red chiles, 1 halved and deseeded, 1 finely sliced
- Olive oil
- 1 small eggplant
- 2 green zucchini, plus 1 yellow zucchini (ideally)
- 1 red onion, thickly sliced
- 7 ounces (200 g) baby plum tomatoes
- Sea salt and freshly ground black pepper
- 2 teaspoons coriander seeds
- 1½ teaspoons caraway seeds
- 1 teaspoon cumin seeds
- ¼ cup plus 1 tablespoon (75 ml) extra virgin olive oil
- 1 fat garlic clove, finely chopped
- Finely grated zest and juice of 1 unwaxed lemon
- 1 teaspoon sweet paprika
- Large handful of flat-leaf parsley, chopped

f you can, cook the veggies for this Tunisian-style salad—a spiced ratatouille of sorts—on a grill. Once charred and soft, roughly chop them. It is a frugal dish if made at the end of summer. You can eat it with quartered hard-boiled eggs and steamed couscous if you want to be more traditional. Or continue the rebellion by serving it with griddled halloumi slices or baked feta.

1 Preheat the oven to 425°F (220°C).

2 Halve the peppers, removing their stalks and seeds. Arrange in a single layer, skin side up, in a large roasting pan with the halved chile tucked under a pepper half. Drizzle with a little regular olive oil, slide into the top of the oven and roast for about 30 minutes, until highly colored and soft.

3 Destalk, trim and roughly chop the eggplant and zucchini and transfer into a second large roasting pan with the red onion and tomatoes. Toss with enough oil to coat lightly and season well with salt and pepper. The vegetables should have room to breathe rather than sitting on top of each other. Slide into the center of the oven to roast under the peppers. After 25 to 30 minutes they will be soft, burnished and sweet. Cover loosely with foil and set aside.

4 Retrieve the chile halves from the pepper pan and finely chop. Transfer the roasted peppers into a bowl and sit the now-empty roasting pan on top. Set aside for 10 minutes to steam before skinning the peppers and slicing finely with a knife (wear rubber gloves if you can't wait for them to cool first!).

5 Meanwhile, put the coriander, caraway and cumin seeds in a frying pan and toast over medium heat for about a minute, until fragrant and lightly toasted. Transfer into a mortar and crush lightly with the pestle. Return the pan to low heat with the extra virgin olive oil and the garlic. Cook extremely gently for 5 minutes, infusing the oil rather than browning the garlic. Add the chopped red chile, crushed spices, lemon zest and paprika. Remove from the heat and stir in the lemon juice, parsley and seasoning to taste.

6 Put all the roasted veggies in a warmed serving dish and douse with the dressing.

Roasted Carrot, Chickpea and Pomegranate Salad

Serves 4 to 6

- 1¼ cups (250 g) wheat berries
- Sea salt and freshly ground black pepper
- 2 bunches of baby carrots, reserving the leafy tops (or use some parsley or chervil if you don't have the tops)
- 1 tablespoon coriander seeds
- Olive oil
- One 15-ounce (400 g) can chickpeas, drained and rinsed
- 1 tablespoon cumin seeds
- 2 garlic cloves, skins on
- ⅔ cup (100 g) walnut halves
- ¼ cup plus 1 tablespoon (75 ml) extra virgin olive oil
- 2 tablespoons pomegranate molasses, or to taste
- Squeeze of lemon juice
- ½ pomegranate, seeds only
- Large handful of arugula leaves

You can find, or make, sweet-sharp pomegranate molasses without spending much. Firstly, buy it in Middle Eastern and Asian shops for far less than the supermarket or deli price; a bottle lasts for an age in a cool pantry. Secondly, substitute date syrup with a squeeze of lemon juice. In a pinch, juice the remaining pomegranate half, simmering it down with brown sugar until thick and syrupy.

1 Preheat the oven to 400°F (200°C).

2 Put the wheat berries in a large saucepan with a generous pinch of salt, cover with cool water and bring to a boil. Once boiling, reduce the heat to a gentle simmer, partially cover and leave to cook for 25 to 30 minutes, until the grains are just tender (they should still be chewy). Drain and set aside.

3 On a large baking sheet, toss the carrots with the coriander seeds and a generous drizzle of regular olive oil. Season with salt and pepper, spread out well and roast for about 40 minutes, until browned and soft. On a second baking sheet, toss the chickpeas, cumin seeds and garlic cloves with another generous drizzle of regular oil, season, spread out and roast, alongside the carrots, for 25 to 30 minutes, until the chickpeas turn golden and the garlic softens.

4 Toast the walnuts in the oven for 5 to 7 minutes, until they turn a couple of shades darker.

5 To make the dressing, crush the roasted garlic cloves from the chickpea tray with the back of a knife, discarding the skins. Put in a bowl and stir in the extra virgin olive oil, pomegranate molasses, lemon juice and seasoning to taste. Chop or crush half the walnuts quite finely and stir these in, too.

6 Chop about 2 tablespoons of the reserved green carrot tops and toss with the wheat berries, roasted carrots, roasted chickpeas, pomegranate seeds, arugula and half the dressing. Transfer to a platter, spoon the remaining dressing over and scatter with the remaining toasted walnuts.

Chipotle Scotch Eggs with Smoky Tomato Dip

Makes 4

- 6 medium eggs
- 1 teaspoon hot smoked paprika
- Sea salt and freshly ground black pepper
- ⅔ cup (100 g) mixed seeds (flax, pumpkin, sesame, sunflower seeds . . .)
- 1 large red onion, finely chopped
- 1 tablespoon sunflower oil, plus more for the pan
- One 14.5-ounce (400 g) can chopped tomatoes
- 4 teaspoons chipotle paste (or 1 large chipotle chile in adobo, finely chopped)
- Pinch of brown sugar
- Two 15-ounce (400 g) cans lima beans, drained and rinsed
- One 15-ounce (400 g) can chickpeas, drained and rinsed
- Finely grated zest of 1 unwaxed lemon
- Small handful of cilantro, chopped, plus more to serve

A baked, seed-coated and bean-based picnic egg. Or leave out any suggestion of egg to make the bean mixture into vegan burger patties. Take your time to crush the lima beans and chickpeas properly; they don't need to be smooth but should be smashed roughly for the mix to hold together. Chipotle chile, a favorite stalwart, adds depth, spice and sweet smoke to both bean coating and tomato dip.

1 Put 4 of the eggs in a small saucepan, cover with cool water and bring to a boil. From the moment the water boils, set the timer and simmer gently for 4½ minutes. Drain, gently crack the shells once and refresh under running water until cool enough to peel completely. Dry the peeled eggs with paper towels and dust with the paprika.

2 Preheat the oven to 350°F (180°C). Crack the remaining 2 eggs into a shallow bowl, season with salt and pepper and beat lightly to combine. Empty the mixed seeds into a second shallow bowl. Set aside.

3 Gently fry the chopped red onion in the oil for 8 to 10 minutes, stirring often, until very soft and turning brown. Transfer half into a bowl, keeping the rest in the pan. Stir the chopped tomatoes, 2 teaspoons of the chipotle paste and the sugar into the remaining chopped onion in the pan. Simmer over medium-high heat for 15 minutes, stirring often, until reduced and thick.

4 Meanwhile, add the lima beans and chickpeas to the cooked onion in the bowl and crush with a potato masher, taking care to crush every legume to make a textured mash. Stir in the lemon zest, remaining chipotle paste, cilantro and seasoning to taste, then stir in 1 tablespoon of the beaten egg to help the mixture bind. Mix thoroughly, mashing the mixture together. Pat the surface down and make a cross in the top to divide it into 4 even portions. Taking one quarter at a time, flatten the mixture in your hand, bringing the sides up to form a cup. Put a paprika-dusted egg in the center and seal the mixture to evenly and snugly enclose it with no air gaps. Repeat with the remaining bean mixture and boiled eggs.

5 Line a roasting pan with parchment paper and oil the paper lightly. Roll each sphere in beaten egg to coat lightly, then into the mixed seeds. Space them out in the pan and bake for 45 minutes, until golden. Rest for 10 minutes, then carefully remove from the pan with a spatula. Serve warm or cool, with the smoky tomato dip and more cilantro scattered over.

Miso-Orange Tofu Salad

Serves 2

- 1- to 1½-inch (2.5 to 4 cm) piece fresh ginger root
- 2½ cups (250 g) finely shredded Japanese, napa or white cabbage
- 1 carrot, shredded or grated
- 1 parsnip, shredded or grated
- 2 large oranges
- 2 tablespoons honey
- 2 tablespoons light soy sauce
- 1 tablespoon miso paste (a pale and mellow one)
- Pinch of chile flakes
- 2 tablespoons sesame seeds
- 2 tablespoons peanut oil
- 7 ounces (200 g) firm tofu, drained and cubed
- 2 teaspoons toasted sesame oil
- 1 tablespoon rice wine or white wine vinegar
- 4 scallions, sliced

Salads are normally pricey things to make, especially once you start adding nuts or herbs. This salad relies on a good pantry, a generous amount of tofu in a miso-orange glaze and plenty of crunchy vegetables. You might want to steam some rice to serve, or toss noodles through the mixture. If you have any in the fridge, a handful of cilantro or mint is lovely stirred through this.

1 Peel the ginger and slice it into fine matchsticks, or coarsely grate.

2 Put the shredded cabbage, carrot and parsnip in a large bowl and cover with ice-cold water. Add a handful of ice if you have any, then set aside for 20 minutes to crisp up.

3 Pare the zest and pith from 1 of the oranges with a sharp knife and cut the flesh into discs. Sweep any juice on the chopping board into a container. Halve the other orange, juice it and add to the container. Whisk in the honey, soy sauce, miso paste, chile flakes and ginger.

4 Put the sesame seeds in a large wok or frying pan and toast over medium heat until golden. Transfer out on to a plate, then return the pan to high heat and add the oil. Pat the tofu cubes with paper towels to dry them and fry in the pan until brown on all sides. Remove to the sesame seed plate and return the pan to the heat. Pour in all but 2 tablespoons of the orange juice mixture, giving it a good stir first. Bring to a rolling boil, reduce the heat a notch and slowly reduce the liquid for 15 minutes, until it forms a sticky glaze. Return the tofu and sesame seeds to the pan, turning carefully to coat all over and warm through.

5 Drain the cabbage and root vegetables very thoroughly, then toss with the orange slices, toasted sesame oil, rice vinegar and reserved orange juice mixture. Divide between 4 bowls and top with the sticky tofu and sesame seeds. Finish with the sliced scallions.

Cheddar Quesadillas with Kale and Black Beans

Serves 2

- 1 tablespoon sunflower oil
- 1 small red onion, chopped
- 2 garlic cloves, crushed
- One 15-ounce (400 g) can black beans, with their liquid
- 1 teaspoon chipotle paste, optional
- 2 limes, juice of 1½, remaining half cut into wedges
- Sea salt and freshly ground black pepper
- 1 cup (150 g) sweet corn kernels (1 large ear)
- ¼ red cabbage, shredded
- 1 red chile, deseeded and finely chopped
- Handful of cilantro, roughly chopped
- 8 small (4-inch/10 cm) corn tortillas
- ¾ cup (75 g) grated aged cheddar cheese
- Small handful of young kale leaves, finely shredded
- Hot sauce and sour cream, to serve

Cooking on a budget can include lots of fresh vegetables if you keep them unassuming and shop in season . . . hence this colorful and unabashedly inauthentic supper will be cheap to make in autumn, when sweet corn is plentiful and kale and cabbage are coming into their own. Hopefully, cilantro, chile and a fresh lime or two are permissible extras, though the first two could be left out in a pinch. This recipe is easily doubled.

1 Heat the oil in a medium saucepan over medium heat and add the onion. Cook for about 8 minutes, stirring often, until softened and golden. Stir in the garlic and fry for 2 minutes more. Add the beans and their liquid with the chipotle paste, if using. Cook gently for 4 to 5 minutes, until the beans have softened further. Remove from the heat and crush the beans with a potato masher to make a rough purée, seasoning to taste with lime juice, salt and pepper.

2 Put your largest frying pan over very high heat. Once smoking hot, add the corn kernels, spreading them out in a single layer. Cook for a few minutes, stirring only occasionally, until well charred in places. Watch out for popping corn! Transfer into a bowl and toss with the cabbage, chile and cilantro. Add lime juice and seasoning to taste. Set aside.

3 Place the rinsed-out frying pan over medium-low heat. Once dry, add 2 to 4 tortillas, depending on the size of your pan, and toast until lightly golden on one side. Flip and cover the new top of each with a scant layer of grated cheddar, a spoonful of beans, a layer of shredded kale and a final layer of cheddar. Cook for 2 minutes, or until the base layer of cheese begins to melt. Lay a second tortilla on top of each stack, pressing down gently. Carefully flip each quesadilla over with a spatula and continue to cook for 2 minutes or so, until the new base tortilla is crisp and the cheese melted. If your pan would only hold 2 tortillas at once, repeat the process to make 4 quesadillas in all, keeping the cooked portions warm.

4 Slice each little quesadilla in half and serve with the remaining black beans (there will be a good two spoonfuls leftover), the sweet corn salsa, lime wedges, hot sauce and sour cream.

Cauliflower and Barley Cheese

Serves 4 as a main course, or 6 to 8 as a side dish

- ½ cup (100 g) pearl barley or spelt
- Sea salt and freshly ground black pepper
- 4 small cauliflowers of any color, trimmed
- Olive oil
- 1 banana shallot or large shallot, finely chopped
- 3 tablespoons dry white wine
- 2½ cups (250 g) grated aged or extra sharp cheddar cheese
- 1⅔ cups (150 g) crème fraîche
- 1 teaspoon Dijon mustard
- Handful of stale bread crumbs
- Small handful of flat-leaf parsley, chopped, optional

Whole, roasted cauliflowers sit in a sharp sauce, singing with cheddar and rich in crème fraîche. Barley grains (or spelt, if that's what you have) are stirred through before the final bake, adding bolster and texture. Diet food this most certainly isn't, but then this is a cookbook, not a diet book, and sometimes a cold day demands something rich. A crisp salad of bitter leaves or steamed winter greens both work well alongside, if this is to be a main course dish.

1 Cook the barley in a saucepan over medium heat with enough water to cover generously and a pinch of salt, allowing the grains to simmer for 20 minutes, or until tender. Drain well and set aside.

2 Preheat the oven to 400°F (200°C). Cut a deep cross in the base of each cauliflower and make sure they sit flat. Toss them in a generous amount of oil to coat and place in an ovenproof dish (they should fit quite snugly as the sauce needs to collect around them later on). Cover loosely with foil and roast for 30 to 35 minutes, until tender to the point of a knife.

3 To make the sauce, heat a splash of olive oil in a heavy-based saucepan over medium heat, add the shallot and cook for 5 minutes or so, until translucent and softened. Add the wine and bubble down until only about 1 tablespoon remains. Reduce the heat to its lowest setting and add the cheddar, crème fraîche and mustard. Stir constantly until the cheese melts to a smooth sauce. Stir in the drained barley and season to taste; it is a very strong sauce so it shouldn't need much salt, if any.

4 Spoon the sauce over and around the cauliflower, concentrating the grains in the base of the dish where they won't catch. Moisten the bread crumbs with a drizzle more olive oil to scatter over the top. Return to the oven for 10 to 15 minutes, or until browned and bubbling. Throw the chopped parsley on before serving, if you like.

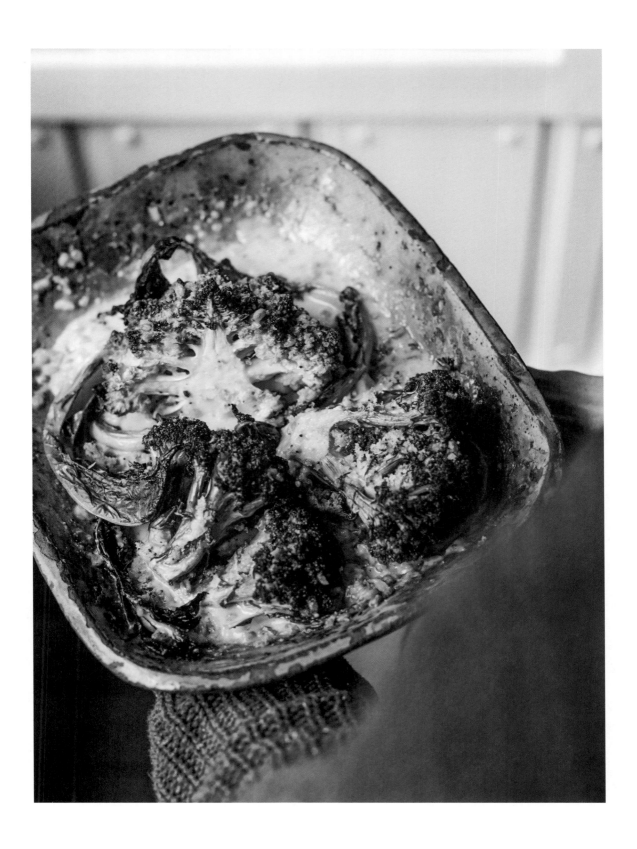

chapter five

gatherings

COOKING SPECTACULAR MODERN VEGETARIAN FOOD for larger dinners and parties is surprisingly easy. There is a balanced pitch to be found between overwrought and makeshift and—if you put beautiful vegetables center stage—it isn't a difficult note to hit. Keep the mantra "joyful, fresh and seasonal" uppermost in your mind when shopping and cooking for crowds, more than at any other time, and your food will follow suit (and needn't be expensive; a very real consideration when cooking for others).

The recipes here run the whole gamut from party snacks (sweet potato fries and raw vegetable platters with fresh dips, see pages 160 and 168), to quite involved suppers to make in advance (Baked Purple Goat Cheese Gnocchi, page 164), to summer lunches and barbecue food (a slow-baked frittata and Smoky Carrot and Millet Burgers, pages 170 and 158), all with a particular emphasis on bold flavors. This is confident food, full of texture and abundant in nature.

Large serving dishes create that sense of bounty and modernity, highlighting fresh ingredients and textures. It is hard to better the color of vibrant vegetables, so offer them casually with generous serving spoons tucked into a platter. A Nectarine, Tomato and Burrata Salad (page 163), with a basil dressing and baked sourdough, for example, is easy to put together, but manages to be one of the most vivid plates in the book because of the quality and color of the ingredients. It is simply stunning, both to look at and to eat.

If you build around a central dish—winter squash, olive and lentil tagine, say, or roasted roots on coriander salt (see pages 182 and 174)—you can bring it to the table last, having first amassed any accompanying grains, salads and sauces. It only takes one main dish to create drama; any extras really can be as simple as a bowl of leaves or a loaf. Having the confidence to pare the table back even further—serving just one or two humble recipes—can take courage if you are a natural over-caterer (as most keen cooks are), but, when the occasion fits, why not pull a bubbling and rich gratin of chard (see page 169) out of the oven to eat with, say, simple lentils and roasted carrots? Or a dish of richly sauced *gigantes* beans (see page 178), cooked the day before and simply reheated? Both are relaxed and frugal, but on a cold and wintry Sunday night, they are more than enough.

Incidentally, it's no accident that a page on cooking lentils falls in this chapter. Legumes are hard to better as a base to build from, accepting flavor as well as adding it and bringing high-quality protein at a low cost. I use them frequently as both accompaniment and star dish and, if you partner them with thoughtfully cooked ingredients—sticky roasted alliums, a vibrant gremolata and roasted cauliflower mash (see page 180), for example—they are most definitely both supper-party-worthy and refined.

Catering for groups or parties is as much about making it easy and enjoyable for you, the host, as making the food good, so it makes sense to prepare everything you can in advance. I don't mean that you should emulate restaurant chefs, who spend hours behind the scenes chopping and simmering, making flavorful stocks, bases and sauces before they are ready to start their dishes. This is home cooking, and, especially for those who get nervous when cooking for others, trying to replicate complicated restaurant dishes will set you on the road to fraught. The recipes in this chapter are relaxed and modern enough not to warrant endless sauces and garnishes. Be kind to yourself.

What I do mean is that, unless it's something particularly simple or thrown together, you will rarely find me making anything for a party or supper with friends that can't be at least partially prepared in advance. It's an unusual dressing, for example, that can't be made ahead of time, even if you add any herbs at the last minute to keep them from degrading in lemon juice or vinegar. Vegetables can be prepped at least a couple of hours ahead, gnocchi cooked, croutons baked. . . . Even better, in the case of slowly simmered recipes, tagines and the like, the entire recipe can be made a day ahead, save for the herbal flourishes thrown on at the very end, then gently reheated as your diners gather and mingle.

Where a recipe is a little more involved—the brown rice sushi (see page 151), for example—I suggest making everyone sing for their supper. Get the main components cooked or prepared (in that case the sushi rice, filling ingredients and pickled ginger, if you are making it), then put them out on the table so everyone can help with the rolling. The results won't look perfect, but that is hardly the point. And you could definitely double the recipe, as many hands would make a larger quantity of sushi achievable. Likewise, the Shiitake Mushroom Bun Noodle Bowls (page 154) can be served as a modern version of a buffet, ready for everyone to put their own bowls together. It's a relaxed way to serve supper, and that is what cooking for loved ones is all about: creating a convivial atmosphere with thoughtfully prepared, beautiful food.

I hope you'll see in this chapter that it is easier than you might think.

Rice Noodle Salad with Coconut Green Goddess Dressing

Serves 6

A celebration of spring herbs and vegetables, with a few noodles for substance and a delicate coconut dressing. You could just as well serve this hot from a wok as more of a stir-fry, adding the herbs and dressing right at the end. The deep purple (black before cooking) noodles I have used are for dramatic effect only. They taste exactly the same as standard rice noodles.

- ¾ cup (100 g) cashews
- 1 pound 5 ounces (600 g) mixed green vegetables, such as pak or bok choy, sugar snap peas, green beans, young pea pods, baby zucchini . . .
- One 13.5-ounce (400 ml) can coconut cream
- 1 plump garlic clove, crushed
- 1 or 2 green chiles, roughly chopped
- 1-inch (2.5 cm) piece fresh ginger root, peeled and finely grated
- 2 lemongrass stalks, trimmed and finely sliced
- 3 fresh or frozen makrut lime leaves, shredded
- 2 to 3 tablespoons tamari sauce
- 1 to 2 tablespoons palm sugar
- Juice of 2 limes
- Handful of cilantro leaves
- Handful of mint leaves
- Handful of Thai basil leaves
- Sea salt
- 9 ounces (250 g) fine, dried black or white rice noodles
- 6 ounces (160 g) store-bought marinated tofu cubes (ideally those in tamari)
- Handful of purple basil leaves, if in season

1 Preheat the oven to 375°F (190°C). Spread the cashews out on a baking sheet and roast for 6 to 8 minutes, until golden brown. Cool slightly, then crush or chop.

2 Carefully cut the green vegetables into bite-size pieces. Set aside.

3 To make the dressing, blend the coconut cream with the garlic, chiles, ginger, lemongrass and lime leaves. Add 2 tablespoons of the tamari, 1 tablespoon of the sugar and two thirds of the lime juice, along with half the herbs (excluding any purple basil, if using, purely to keep the dressing green). Blend again to finely chop. Taste and adjust the seasoning as needed: You may wish to add the extra tamari or sugar or lime juice . . . or you may not. Set the seasoned dressing aside.

4 Lightly blanch the vegetables in plenty of boiling, salted water for 2 to 3 minutes, or until barely tender. Immediately refresh under ice-cold water and drain well.

5 Simmer the noodles in plenty of boiling water for 2½ to 3 minutes, then refresh under ice-cold water and drain well.

6 Toss the dressing with the blanched vegetables, cooked noodles and marinated tofu pieces. Shower with the remaining herbs and the crushed cashews to finish.

Brown Rice Sushi with Quick-Pickled Ginger

Makes 24 pieces

For the quick-pickled ginger
- Two 1-inch (2.5 cm) pieces fresh ginger root, peeled and thinly sliced
- 1 slice of raw beet, optional (purely for color)
- 3 tablespoons rice wine vinegar
- 1 tablespoon unrefined sugar
- 1 teaspoon sea salt

For the sushi
- 1½ cups (250 g) brown sushi rice or black short-grain rice
- 3 tablespoons rice wine vinegar
- 2 tablespoons unrefined sugar
- Pinch of sea salt
- 4 nori seaweed sheets, toasted or untoasted
- Your chosen filling (see page 152)
- Tamari sauce, wasabi and steamed edamame beans, to serve

Plan on this serving two very hungry people, or four as a snack. Either make all four fillings—each makes enough for one roll or six pieces—or choose two variations and double the quantities, to make life simpler. A note on tamari: I have suggested using it to keep the recipe gluten-free (though check the bottle), but you could just as well use light soy sauce, if gluten isn't a consideration.

1 To make the quick-pickled ginger, put all the ingredients in a bowl and stir to coat the ginger. Leave at room temperature for 1 hour and drain well before eating. The ginger will keep, chilled, for a couple of weeks or so.

2 Rinse the rice well, then put it in a large saucepan with 3 cups (700 ml) of water and set aside to soak for 1 hour. Place over medium heat and bring to a boil. Reduce the heat, cover with a lid and simmer gently for 40 minutes until all the water has been absorbed and the rice is tender.

3 Meanwhile, gently heat the rice vinegar, sugar and salt in a saucepan, stirring until the sugar dissolves. Set aside until the rice is cooked.

4 Pour the vinegar mixture over the cooked rice, stirring to combine, then spread the rice out on a large plate to cool, fanning occasionally.

5 Place a sheet of nori, shiny side down, on a rolling mat or a piece of plastic wrap with a short side in front of you. Wet your hands and spread an even, thin layer of rice over three quarters of the sheet, positioning the uncovered section of nori furthest away from you. This will soften and stick the sushi rolls in place. Place the filling across the center of the rice in a neat line, then carefully and firmly roll up, using the mat or plastic wrap to help you. Leave in a cool place (do not refrigerate, or the rice will harden) for up to 1 hour until ready to slice.

6 Wet a sharp knife and slice each sushi roll into 6 pieces. Serve with tamari, wasabi, steamed edamame beans and the quick-pickled ginger.

recipe continues . . .

FILLING IDEAS

OMELET, KALE AND SESAME

Beat 1 egg with 1 teaspoon tamari sauce and a few drops of toasted sesame oil. Pour into a hot medium frying pan that you have first coated with flavorless oil. Reduce the heat and cook gently for 2 minutes until set, flip over and cook for 30 seconds more. Transfer onto a chopping board, roll up and shred into ribbons. Blanch a scant handful of shredded kale and drain well. Slice a trimmed scallion into fine strips. Arrange the omelet strips, kale and scallion across the sushi, sprinkling 1 teaspoon black sesame seeds over before rolling up.

AVOCADO, SESAME, SPROUTS AND RADISH

Cut a small, ripe avocado half into chubby strips and slice 2 red radishes very finely by hand or with a mandoline. Lay on the rice in a line, topping with 2 tablespoons purple radish sprouts and a generous pinch of toasted sesame seeds. Roll up.

ASPARAGUS, SWEET POTATO AND WASABI MAYONNAISE

Cut 1 cup (150 g) peeled sweet potato into small cubes and cook with 1 to 2 tablespoons flavorless oil in a frying pan over medium heat, stirring often until golden and tender. Season and set aside. Blanch 6 fine or 2 regular trimmed asparagus spears until just tender. Stir ½ teaspoon wasabi paste into 1 tablespoon (ideally Kewpie) mayonnaise and spoon in a line on the rice. Lay the sweet potato and asparagus spears on top in a line and roll up.

CUCUMBER, SMOKED TOFU, CILANTRO AND SUNFLOWER SPROUTS

Cut a piece of peeled cucumber the size of a small matchbox into batons. Do the same with a matchbox-sized piece of smoked tofu (the very firm variety with chopped almonds and sesame seeds is good here). Lay on top of the rice in a neat line, topping with a couple of tablespoons cilantro microgreens (coriander cress) or regular cilantro leaves and a tablespoon of sprouted sunflower seeds. Roll up, roll up.

Shiitake Mushroom Bun Noodle Bowls

Serves 4

There is no getting around this: Most Vietnamese food demands a bit of chopping and a few separate components. But once that chopping is done—and you can cheat with a mini food processor—the method is a cinch. Serve this in the warmer months as a light and summery supper. To save yourself the trouble of plating, arrange the ingredients on platters and ask everyone to build their own bowls.

For the mushrooms

- 3 garlic cloves
- 2 red chiles, halved
- Two 1-inch (2.5 cm) pieces fresh ginger root, peeled
- 2 lemongrass stalks, trimmed
- 3 tablespoons palm sugar or brown sugar, or to taste
- ¼ cup (60 ml) Vegetarian "Fish" Sauce (page 300) or tamari sauce
- 10.5 ounces (300 g) shiitake mushrooms or a mix of exotic mushrooms
- 7 ounces (200 g) firm tofu, cubed
- 1 teaspoon five-spice powder
- 3 tablespoons rice wine vinegar
- Juice of 1 or 2 limes, to taste
- Sea salt
- 2 tablespoons peanut oil

For the noodle bowls

- 5.3 ounces (150 g) dried fine rice noodles
- 1½ cups (150 g) bean sprouts
- ¼ cucumber, sliced
- Handful each of cilantro, mint and Thai basil leaves
- 1 head lettuce, leaves separated
- Quick Vietnamese Pickles (page 304)
- ¾ cup (100 g) roasted peanuts or cashews, crushed

1 Start by finely chopping the garlic, chiles (deseed first, if you wish to reduce the heat), ginger and lemongrass. You can do this in a mini food processor if you wish. Transfer to a large bowl and stir in the sugar and "fish" sauce. Remove half of this mixture to a small bowl, cover with plastic wrap and set aside for the moment.

2 To the original large bowl, add the mushrooms, tofu and five-spice, folding through to coat. Leave for at least 20 minutes or up to 1 hour.

3 Meanwhile, add the rice vinegar and the juice of 1 lime to the small bowlful with 1 tablespoon of just-boiled water. Stir well, taste and adjust with more lime juice, salt or sugar, to make a balanced sweet, salty, sour and hot dipping sauce. Cover and set aside until needed; the sugar should dissolve.

4 Cook the rice noodles according to the package instructions, then refresh in cold water and drain. To blanch the bean sprouts, have a bowl of ice water ready. Plunge the bean sprouts into a small saucepan of boiling water for 30 to 45 seconds. Transfer into a colander to drain and immediately submerge them in the ice water for a minute. Drain thoroughly.

5 Divide the bean sprouts, noodles, cucumber, herbs, lettuce leaves and pickles to taste between 4 large serving bowls, keeping everything in distinct piles. Set aside in a cool place for a few minutes.

6 Set a large frying pan over high heat until smoking hot and add the oil. Scoop up the tofu and mushroom mixture, leaving the liquid in the bowl. Cook for 4 to 5 minutes until well browned. Add the liquid and bubble down until all is richly glazed and highly colored.

7 Divide the tofu and mushrooms between the bowls. Spoon one quarter of the dipping sauce over each serving and scatter with the crushed nuts.

Griddled Halloumi Salad with Date Dressing

Serves 4 to 6

- 1 small red onion, sliced paper-thin
- Juice of 1 lemon
- ¼ cup plus 1 tablespoon (75 ml) extra virgin olive oil
- 12 Medjool dates, pitted and chopped
- 2 preserved lemons, rind only, cut into fine strips
- 1 red chile, finely sliced
- Handful of mint leaves, roughly chopped
- Small handful of parsley, finely chopped
- Sea salt and freshly ground black pepper
- 1 pound (500 g) halloumi cheese, cut into ⅜-inch (1 cm) slices
- 1 tablespoon mild olive oil
- 3⅓ cups (100 g) tender spinach leaves
- Flatbreads, toasted on the grill or warmed in a low oven, to serve, optional

A sweet, hot and sharp dressing, full of herbs, dates, preserved lemon and chile, makes an incredible contrast to hot, salty halloumi. Consider grilling it over hot coals. Make sure everyone is ready to eat before cooking the cheese; it tends to turn rubbery when it cools, so the magic lies in getting it from pan to plate as quickly as possible.

❶ Start by mixing the red onion and lemon juice together in a bowl. Set aside for 10 minutes or so; the onion should turn a lurid pink as it pickles.

❷ To make the dressing, add the extra virgin olive oil, dates, preserved lemon rind, chile, mint and parsley to the red onion and lemon juice bowl, making sure you crush some of the softer date pieces into the mix to add background sweetness (a foil for the salty halloumi). Taste and season with salt and pepper as needed, remembering the cheese will be salty.

❸ Place a frying or griddle pan over high heat until smoking hot. You could also cook the halloumi directly on the bars of a white-hot grill, in which case make sure there's no trace of flame and that the coals look ashen before beginning.

❹ Pat the halloumi slices dry with paper towels and coat with the regular olive oil. Dry-fry or griddle, in the hot pan or on the grill, until well marked. This should take 1 to 2 minutes per side. Be careful not to overcrowd the pan or everything will stew. The cheese will release itself from the pan or grill grate when it's browned and ready, so don't fiddle with it.

❺ Pile the spinach and cooked halloumi in a bowl or on a platter, spoon the dressing over and serve immediately with warmed flatbreads on the side, if you like.

Smoky Carrot and Millet Burgers

Serves 4

- 5 medium (1 pound/ 500 g) carrots, trimmed and scrubbed
- 2½ tablespoons olive oil
- 1 teaspoon hot smoked paprika
- Sea salt and freshly ground black pepper
- 2 shallots, finely chopped
- 1 fat garlic clove, crushed
- ½ teaspoon dried oregano
- 1 cup (100 g) millet flakes
- ¾ cup (200 ml) strong vegetable stock
- ¾ cup (50 g) walnuts, finely crushed
- 3 tablespoons finely grated vegetarian Parmesan cheese
- 4 brioche buns
- ¼ cup (60 g) mayonnaise
- 8 small lettuce leaves
- 1 avocado, sliced
- Large handful of store-bought carrot chips
- ½ small container mustard or garden cress, snipped

A sturdy burger, full of both roasted and grated carrots. Rendering this vegan would be easy; swap out the cheese for a couple of teaspoons of nutritional yeast flakes, or a tablespoon of seaweed seasoning, to mimic the umami notes. I like the sweet, rich flavor of brioche as a bun here, but sub with any roll you like, or leave out the bread completely in favor of the polenta fries (see next page) and a salad.

1 Preheat the oven to 400°F (200°C). Slice 4 of the carrots (about 14 ounces/400 g) on the diagonal to make ⅜-inch (1 cm) thick slices. Toss in a roasting pan with 1 tablespoon of the olive oil, half the paprika and salt and pepper. Spread out in an even layer and roast for 25 minutes or so, until very soft and slightly browned. Crush with a potato masher to make a rough paste and set aside.

2 Put 1 tablespoon olive oil in a medium saucepan with the shallots. Cook over medium-low heat for 8 to 10 minutes, stirring often, until soft and translucent. Add the garlic, dried oregano and millet flakes. Cook for a few minutes, until the millet begins to color, then stir in the stock and bring to a boil. Cover with a lid, reduce the heat and simmer briskly for 5 minutes, stirring once or twice, until the stock has been absorbed and the mixture looks like a very thick paste. Replace the lid and set aside to cool for 10 minutes.

3 Finely grate the remaining carrot and add to the millet pan with the crushed roasted carrots, walnuts and Parmesan. Mix really thoroughly, season to taste (it is fine to try the mixture at this stage) and firmly shape into 4 burgers. Chill for 30 minutes if you want to grill the burgers, or cook immediately if frying.

4 Put the remaining olive oil in a large frying pan set over medium heat, swirling to coat the pan. Add the burgers and cook for 2 to 3 minutes on each side, flipping with a spatula once well colored. If cooking on the grill, brush the burgers with oil before cooking for the same time, flipping very carefully only when colored enough to release from the grate easily. Split the buns and lightly toast in a toaster or under the broiler.

5 Cover the lower bun halves with a spoonful of mayonnaise, a shake of paprika and a couple of lettuce leaves each, followed by a few pieces of avocado. Put a burger on top and cover with a few carrot chips and a good hat of cress. Top with the bun lid and eat immediately.

Chubby Polenta Fries with Almond Za'atar Salt

*Serves 6 as a starter
or as part of a spread*

- ¼ cup (60 ml) olive oil
- 1¼ cups (250 g) coarse cornmeal or polenta
- 5 cups (1.2 L) vegetable stock
- ½ teaspoon plus 1 tablespoon sea salt
- Freshly ground black pepper
- Large handful of flat-leaf parsley, finely chopped
- ¾ cup (100 g) blanched almonds
- 1 batch Sesame Seed Za'atar (page 299)

Serve these chubby fries with drinks, or as part of a larger spread with antipasti-style vegetables and olives. Roasted Tomato and Pickled Lemon Relish (page 294) is excellent as a dip for them.

Baking the polenta before leaving it to set adds to the flavor significantly. It is a hands-off method but it takes time, so if you need these in a rush, stir 1¼ cups (250 g) quick polenta into 3½ cups (850 ml) simmering stock and cook, stirring, for a few minutes until very thick. Pour into the dish and leave to set for at least 2 hours, as below. Preparing the polenta can also be done up to 2 days in advance; keep it covered in the fridge until needed.

1 Preheat the oven to 350°F (180°C). Line an 8 × 12-inch (20 × 30 cm) baking pan or dish with plastic wrap and set aside. Use 1 tablespoon of the olive oil to grease a second medium-size pan or dish and add the polenta and vegetable stock. Stir in 1⅔ cups (400 ml) of water and the ½ teaspoon of sea salt. Bake, uncovered, for 40 minutes, then stir well and cook for 10 minutes more.

2 Immediately stir in half the chopped parsley and a really generous amount of black pepper. Pour into the lined pan or dish, quickly level the surface and set aside to cool completely, for at least 2 hours.

3 Preheat the oven to 400°F (200°C). Cut the polenta into chubby "fries" and carefully toss with the remaining 3 tablespoons of olive oil. Spread out on 2 lined baking sheets and bake for 25 minutes, turning halfway, until golden and crisp.

4 To make the za'atar salt, spread the almonds out on a baking sheet and roast alongside the polenta fries for 6 to 8 minutes, until golden brown. Blend or crush in a mini food processor, or with a mortar and pestle, with 2 tablespoons of the za'atar to form a lumpy mixture. It needs to be fine enough to dip into, but don't take it too far or the nuts will turn to butter. Stir in the remaining za'atar, the 1 tablespoon of sea salt and the remaining parsley.

5 Serve the za'atar salt in a couple of small bowls alongside the hot fries, ready to scatter over or use as a potent dip.

Sweet Potato Fries with a Green Herb Dip

Serves 4 as a starter,
side dish or snack

- 2¼ pounds (1 kg) sweet potatoes (about 4 medium), scrubbed
- 2 heaping teaspoons cornstarch
- 1 teaspoon fine cornmeal
- ½ to 1 teaspoon hot paprika, depending on heat tolerance
- ½ teaspoon dried garlic powder
- 3 tablespoons peanut or sunflower oil
- 1 small, ripe avocado, halved, pitted and flesh scooped out
- ¾ cup (200 g) Greek yogurt or crème fraîche
- Juice of ½ lime
- Sea salt and freshly ground black pepper
- 2 generous handfuls of soft summer herbs, such as basil, mint and cilantro in any combination, plus more herb leaves, sprouts or shoots, to serve

Truly crisp, baked sweet potato fries are an elusive beast. Soaking them draws out starch, which helps immensely. Add a generous hand when spreading the fries out (if in doubt, give them more space), a spiced cornmeal coating and a good seasoning after cooking, not before (it will only make them soggy), for caramel-edged results. Temper the sweetness with a soothing avocado dip, stuffed with herbs, for spooning over or dunking in.

1 Start by slicing the sweet potatoes from top to tail to create large oblongs, about ½ inch (1.5 cm) thick. Stacking a few at a time, slice lengthwise into long ½-inch (1.5 cm) thick batons. Submerge them in a large bowlful of cool water. Set aside for at least 1 to 2 hours; if you have more time, put the bowl in the fridge and leave for up to 12 hours.

2 When ready to cook, preheat the oven to 425°F (220°C) and line your largest 2 baking sheets with parchment paper (the fries really need this or they will stick). Combine the cornstarch, cornmeal, paprika and garlic powder in a small bowl.

3 Drain the sweet potatoes in a colander and transfer into a clean, dry kitchen towel. Rub and pat from all sides to get as much excess water off as possible.

4 Now transfer the fries into a large plastic bag or, failing that, a large mixing bowl. Either way, sprinkle with the cornstarch mixture and shake the bag or toss the fries to coat thinly and evenly. Transfer the oil into the bag or bowl and again, shake or toss to coat. Divide the fries between the baking sheets. If they don't sit in a single layer with space to breathe, use a third baking sheet, too (a bit bothersome, but overcrowding = soggy). Roast for 15 minutes, then rotate the pans and cook for 10 to 15 minutes more until browned.

5 Meanwhile, throw the avocado into a blender with the yogurt and lime juice. Blend until smooth, season with salt and pepper to taste and add the herbs. Pulse a couple of times, to roughly chop the leaves rather than purée them, then spoon the lot into a small bowl.

6 Allow the fries to cool for 5 minutes, then carefully remove from the pans. Shower with salt and pepper and serve with the dip and a fistful of herbs or shoots, such as the purple radish sprouts in the picture.

Nectarine, Tomato and Burrata Salad

Serves 4

- 7 or 8 slices (300 g) stale sourdough bread
- 2 tablespoons extra virgin olive oil, plus more for the dressing
- Sea salt and freshly ground black pepper
- 2 handfuls of basil leaves
- Small handful of mint leaves
- ½ small garlic clove, crushed
- Squeeze of lemon juice
- 4 ripe nectarines or peaches
- 12 ripe, heirloom tomatoes, depending on size
- 2 spheres of vegetarian burrata or mozzarella, drained
- Good balsamic vinegar, to drizzle

A beautiful salad for a summer lunch or outdoor supper, heavily inspired by a Skye Gyngell recipe using similar flavors. As with anything simple, this dish relies wholly on the quality of its components, so make it in late summer when ripe tomatoes, heady basil and the most fragrant nectarines or peaches are in season. I used blush-red nectarines with an incredible flavor for this photo.

1 Preheat the oven to 350°F (180°C). Slice the crusts from the bread and tear the remainder into generous bite-size pieces. Toss with the extra virgin olive oil. Season with salt and pepper and roast in the oven for about 15 minutes, turning at least once, until pale golden and crisp. Transfer into a bowl.

2 Put half the basil and all the mint into a mini food processor, or mortar and pestle, with the garlic, a generous pour of extra virgin oil and a good pinch of salt. Blend or pound to form a rough, sludgy purée, adding more oil if it needs loosening further. Stir in lemon juice to brighten, taste and adjust the seasoning. Spoon a couple of tablespoons into the bread bowl and toss to coat the bread lightly.

3 Halve and pit the nectarines, slicing them into thick wedges. Slice the tomatoes into wedges according to size; you want all the pieces to be easy to eat, but not so small they lose their identity.

4 Toss the nectarines and tomatoes with the remaining basil (tearing the larger leaves) in the bread bowl. Divide between serving plates with the burrata or mozzarella, loosely torn over the plates as you go. Spoon more basil and mint dressing over, season and finish with a few drops of good balsamic vinegar.

Baked Purple Goat Cheese Gnocchi

Serves 4

- 2 cups (500 g) ricotta cheese
- 1¼ pounds (600 g) smallish purple potatoes, scrubbed
- Sea salt and freshly ground black pepper
- 1 cup (100 g) finely grated vegetarian Parmesan cheese
- 2 medium eggs, lightly beaten
- Generous grating of nutmeg
- 1¾ to 2 cups (225 to 250 g) whole-grain spelt flour, plus more to dust
- 1 tablespoon olive oil, plus more for the tray
- 4 tablespoons unsalted butter
- Small bunch of fresh sage leaves
- 1 fat garlic clove, finely chopped
- Large bunch of lacinato kale (cavolo nero), coarse ribs removed, leaves roughly chopped
- 7 ounces (200 g) soft and fudgy goat cheese, chopped or broken up

The gnocchi can be formed and chilled—or boiled and chilled—before the final bake, if you want to get ahead. I tend to take the recipe right through to the point of baking, assembling it completely and chilling it for a day, ready to slide into the oven. You could also skip the final baking step and simply toss the ingredients in the hot pan to finish. It goes without saying that any floury potato will do, purple or not.

1 Put the ricotta on a plate lined with a double layer of muslin or cheesecloth. Put another couple of layers of muslin or cheesecloth on top, cover with a second plate and press down firmly for a couple of minutes, changing the cloths if needed. When the ricotta is firm and flattened, weigh it. You will need 1¼ cups (300 g) for the gnocchi dough. Any extra can be reserved and added to the goat cheese quantity later on in the recipe.

2 Cook the potatoes in their skins in a large saucepan of boiling salted water until tender. This will take 15 to 20 minutes, depending on their size. Drain and cool slightly.

3 Peel the spuds by scraping the skins off with a small knife. Pass through a potato ricer into a large bowl. (If you don't have a potato ricer, use a masher.) Beat in the drained ricotta, then add half the grated Parmesan, the eggs and nutmeg. Mix lightly to combine, seasoning and adding as much of the flour as needed to make a firmish, moldable dough. Do not overwork, or the gnocchi will be heavy.

4 Divide the dough into 6 even pieces and roll each out on a lightly floured work surface to make ¾-inch (2 cm) thick cylinders. Cut the cylinders into 1-inch (2.5 cm) lengths and roll each gnocchi over the well-floured tines of a fork to mark it, pushing your floured thumb into the other side to create an indent as you do so. Space out on lightly floured trays and chill for up to 1 hour if not cooking immediately.

5 Cook the gnocchi, in batches, in a large saucepan of gently simmering salted water. Remove them with a slotted spoon after they have floated to the surface and remained there for no more than 2 minutes. Transfer to a lightly oiled tray and set aside. At this stage the gnocchi can be cooled, covered and chilled for up to 1 day.

recipe continues . . .

6 Preheat the oven to 425°F (220°C).

7 Melt ½ tablespoon of the olive oil and 1 tablespoon of the butter together in a large frying pan set over medium heat. Working in 2 batches, add half the gnocchi to the pan and brown quickly on all sides. Remove to a large gratin dish or roasting pan (or you can use 2 medium dishes or pans) with a slotted spoon. Repeat, with more oil and butter, to brown the remaining gnocchi.

8 Reduce the heat under the now-empty pan slightly and add the remaining butter. Add the sage leaves and cook for a few seconds until just starting to brown. Remove and set aside. Stir in the garlic and kale and cook, stirring often, until the leaves are dark and wilted (3 to 4 minutes). Add to the gnocchi dish or dishes with the sage leaves, combine gently and dot any reserved ricotta and all the goat cheese on top, finishing with the rest of the grated Parmesan.

9 Bake for 15 minutes, or up to 20 minutes if the dish has been assembled and chilled in advance, until the goat cheese has melted and is bubbling.

Raw Vegetable Platter with Avocado-Pistachio Dip

Serves 6 to 8 as party
food or a starter

- A selection of raw vegetables and leaves (a good handful, prepped, per person): such as chicory and endive, crisp lettuce leaves, radishes, baby carrots, young asparagus, green beans, sugar snaps, cucumber, cherry tomatoes, cauliflower, celery, fennel, kohlrabi . . .
- 1 large, very ripe avocado
- 1½ cups (150 g) unsalted (shelled) pistachios
- 1 fat garlic clove, chopped
- 1 green chile, chopped
- ¼ cup (60 ml) cold-pressed avocado or extra virgin olive oil
- Small handful of cilantro, roughly chopped
- Finely grated zest and juice of 1 large lime
- Sea salt and freshly ground black pepper

The idea here is to take a selection of really beautiful seasonal vegetables and salads, carefully prepared, ready to dunk first in the buttery-smooth dip and second into a pistachio-lime blend. Plan on a good handful of prepared veggies for every person. Both pistachios and avocados are expensive, so pumpkin seeds are a good (and tonal) alternative for half or all the pistachios, if you would rather.

1 Take the time to gently scrub your crisp and colorful vegetables, removing any mud or grit. Halve, quarter or slice them as needed to make them easy to eat, but try to keep any decent leaves or green stalks in place on, say, radishes or baby carrots, to pick them up with. Halve, pit and scoop the flesh from the avocado. It needs to be perfectly ripe to blend smoothly.

2 Put the pistachios in the small bowl of a powerful food processor or blender and blend to a rough mixture using the pulse button. Transfer into a bowl.

3 Now take out the most finely ground third and set aside. Return the remaining two thirds of pistachios to the food processor with the garlic, chile and avocado. Blend on a high speed, stopping to scrape down the sides. Add the oil, cilantro, lime juice, a pinch of salt and 3 tablespoons of water. Blend again until buttery-smooth (this is when a powerful blender will really come into its own), then taste and adjust the seasoning with salt and pepper as needed. Divide between a couple of small serving bowls.

4 Combine the reserved pistachio mixture with the lime zest and a pinch of salt and transfer into a third small bowl.

5 Arrange the vegetables on an abundant platter and nestle the 3 dip bowls among them.

Chard Gratin with Gruyère

Serves 6 as a main course,
or 8 as a side dish

- 2¼ cups (500 ml) vegetable stock
- 1 fresh bay leaf
- 1¼ cups (300 ml) heavy cream
- 3½ tablespoons unsalted butter
- 2 tablespoons whole-grain plain or spelt flour
- ¾ teaspoon freshly grated nutmeg
- 1½ cups (150 g) grated vegetarian Gruyère cheese
- 2 egg yolks
- 2¼ pounds (1 kg) Swiss or rainbow chard
- 2 garlic cloves, crushed

rarely cook with cream these days, preferring bright flavors to shine through unfettered . . . but when it's worth doing, the results can be incredibly luxurious. Serve this velvet-textured and buttery chard gratin as a convivial winter's supper in itself; a simple treat, with braised lentils or excellent bread and an easy side dish, such as a bowl of roasted carrots, to accompany.

1 Preheat the oven to 350°F (180°C).

2 Put the stock in a small pan with the bay leaf and simmer until reduced by one third. Add the cream and keep warm.

3 Melt half the butter in a medium saucepan over medium heat, stir in the flour and continue to cook for 1 to 2 minutes, stirring constantly. Reduce the heat to low. Slowly add the cream mixture, whisking all the time with a balloon whisk, until smooth, thickened and silky. Keep simmering gently for 5 minutes to cook out the flour. Remove from the heat and stir in the nutmeg and half the Gruyère, continuing to stir until it has melted. Whisk in the egg yolks. Cover the surface with plastic wrap to prevent a skin forming and set aside.

4 Slice the chard stalks from the leaves. Shred the leaves into ⅜-inch (1 cm) thick ribbons and set aside. Cut the stems into 1-inch (3 cm) pieces and keep separate.

5 Put the garlic and remaining butter in a large frying pan, place over low heat and fry very gently for a couple of minutes, until softened but not colored. Stir in the chard stems and cover with a lid or baking sheet. Continue to cook for 5 minutes until the stems are translucent and soft. Uncover, increase the heat and stir in the leaves, cooking briskly for a couple more minutes until the leaves have wilted and the liquid in the pan has evaporated.

6 Transfer into a large gratin dish and cover with the sauce, tossing to combine slightly. Scatter with the remaining Gruyère and bake for 25 minutes, until golden and bubbling.

Slow-Baked Artichoke Frittata, Watercress Pesto and Slow-Roasted Tomatoes

Serves 4 to 6

- 1 pound (500 g) flavorful tomatoes, halved if larger than a walnut
- 1 cup (200 g) charred artichoke hearts in olive oil, drained (oil reserved)
- Sea salt and freshly ground black pepper
- 2 garlic cloves, roughly chopped
- Large pinch of chile flakes
- ¼ cup (30 g) roughly chopped almonds
- 2 bunches of watercress
- ½ to ¾ cup (120 to 200 ml) extra virgin olive oil, or other cold-pressed oil, plus more to serve
- ½ cup (50 g) finely grated vegetarian Parmesan cheese
- Lemon juice, to taste
- 1 red onion, finely sliced
- 12 eggs

Cooking a frittata slowly and gently, as you would a quiche, makes perfect sense if you have ever tried cooking one under the broiler—as I have—and cut into it only to find an unwelcome layer of runny egg hiding under a beautifully browned top. You won't have that problem here. Use any almonds you like in the watercress pesto: Skin on, blanched or sliced will all do perfectly.

1 Preheat the oven to 350°F (180°C). Put the tomatoes on a baking sheet, drizzle with a little oil drained from the artichokes, season with salt and pepper and put in the oven to roast slowly; they'll be ready at the same time as the frittata.

2 Pound or blend the garlic, chile flakes and a pinch of salt with a mortar and pestle or in the bowl of a mini food processor. Add the almonds and pulverize by hand or machine until roughly chopped. Reserving a handful of the prettiest watercress sprigs for later, add the rest of 1 bunch of watercress to the mortar or food processor bowl. Again, pound or blend, adding enough extra virgin olive oil to loosen and get the pesto running freely, starting with ½ cup/120 ml. Stir in half the grated Parmesan and check the seasoning, using a little lemon juice to brighten, if you like.

3 In a large, heavy-based frying pan (ideally 10 inches/25 cm in diameter), cook the sliced onion in 2 tablespoons more drained artichoke oil with a pinch of salt over low heat for 10 minutes, until softened and lightly browned.

4 Lightly whisk the eggs with the remaining Parmesan and some salt and pepper in a mixing bowl.

5 Increase the heat under the onion pan. Add the artichokes and remaining watercress (except the reserved sprigs), stirring over the heat for 30 seconds to wilt the greens. Pour in the egg mixture and cook for a further 30 seconds. Slide the pan into the oven and cook for 25 to 30 minutes, until the eggs are just set and the tomatoes look a bit shriveled (they will have had about 1 hour). Serve the frittata with a squeeze of lemon juice and a drizzle of extra virgin olive oil, the roasted tomatoes, watercress pesto and reserved watercress sprigs.

Baked Squash, Ricotta and Sage

Serves 4 to 6

- 2½ pounds (1.1 kg) firm and dense winter squash, such as butternut, peeled and deseeded (prepared weight)
- 3 tablespoons olive oil
- ½ teaspoon chile flakes
- 12 medium-size fresh sage leaves
- 2 cups (500 g) ricotta cheese, drained
- 3 eggs, lightly beaten
- 1 cup (50g) finely grated vegetarian Parmesan cheese
- ½ cup (75 g) pine nuts, toasted (see page 58)
- Sea salt and freshly ground black pepper
- 1 tablespoon small capers, rinsed and dried

t is a relief, I find, to accept that food for friends or family doesn't always have to be served piping hot. As it cools slightly, this layered bake of squash- and sage-spiked ricotta firms up enough to turn out and slice. I suggest a round cake pan here, as most people have one, but a loaf pan would also work well. Serve it just warm, or even at room temperature, as an alternative to pâté, with sourdough bread, a drizzle of balsamic vinegar and dressed salad leaves, or roasted pepper antipasti.

1 Preheat the oven to 425°F (220°C). Carefully slice the squash into ½- to ¾-inch (1.5 to 2 cm) thick slices, making them as long and even as possible. Toss the slices with 2 tablespoons of the olive oil and the chile flakes and divide between 2 large baking sheets, so they sit in a single layer with no overlapping and roast quickly without steaming. Roast for 20 minutes, until softened and beginning to brown. Set aside to cool slightly.

2 Reduce the oven temperature to 350°F (180°C). Finely chop half the sage leaves. Mix the ricotta, eggs, grated Parmesan, chopped sage, pine nuts and plenty of salt and pepper in a mixing bowl.

3 Line a deep 8-inch (20 cm) cake pan with parchment paper. Cut an extra sheet of parchment to cover the pan later. Line the base with a double layer of roasted squash slices, making sure there are no gaps. Cover the sides with squash slices as best you can. Spoon half the ricotta mixture over evenly. Repeat the layers of squash and ricotta, finishing with a final layer of squash slices to cover completely. Bake for 50 minutes to 1 hour, until slightly risen and springy to the touch.

4 If you want to turn this out, cover with the reserved sheet of parchment and weigh down with a couple of unopened cans. Set aside to cool for 30 to 40 minutes. (Or leave it in the fridge overnight and serve cold.) When ready, remove the unopened cans and paper, top with a serving plate and flip the whole lot over.

5 Heat the remaining 1 tablespoon of olive oil in a frying pan over medium heat and add the capers and whole sage leaves. Cook for 1 to 2 minutes, until beginning to sizzle. Drain on paper towels, season with pepper and spoon onto the strata.

6 Slice into wedges and serve.

Salt and Coriander Roasted Roots with Smoky Yogurt

Serves 6 to 8 with salad

- 6½ pounds (3 kg) rock salt
- Finely grated zest of 2 unwaxed lemons, plus 1 tablespoon juice
- ¼ cup (20 g) coriander seeds, roughly crushed
- Handful of thyme sprigs, plus thyme leaves to serve
- 3¼ pounds (1.5 kg) baby or small root vegetables in their scrubbed skins, such as multicolored beets, multicolored carrots, parsnips, orange and purple sweet potatoes, new potatoes . . .
- 1⅓ cups (300 g) mild Greek yogurt
- 1 small garlic clove, crushed
- Freshly ground black pepper
- 2 or 3 chipotle chiles in adobo, crushed, or 2 teaspoons chipotle paste
- ½ teaspoon hot smoked paprika
- Cold-pressed oil (olive, canola, pumpkin seed, hemp . . .), to drizzle
- Seasonal greens, to serve

A bed of spiced salt adds theater to an easy roast; it intensifies the vegetables' flavors, too. I haven't added egg white to the salt crust to make a paste, as I didn't find it necessary and because, with such a large quantity of salt, it seemed a shame to make it unusable a second time. This way, it can be reused as a seasoning, if you don't mind the odd zip of zest or coriander seed, or even used to bake more roots.

1 Preheat the oven to 400°F (200°C).

2 Combine the salt with the lemon zest, crushed coriander seeds and thyme sprigs. Spread half this mixture out across a very large roasting pan (or divide between 2 smaller pans). Nestle the roots into this mixture, making sure any larger ones aren't touching to give the heat a chance to circulate around them properly. Spread the rest of the salt on top, mounding it up to cover every vegetable. Slide into the oven and cook for 50 minutes to 1 hour, until a skewer slides into the center of the largest vegetable easily (stick it in, right through the salt). Spoon the top layer of salt away, but keep the roots nestled in the salt to serve (everyone can peel or split their own veggies as they eat).

3 Combine the yogurt with the crushed garlic, lemon juice and pepper to taste in a serving bowl. Swirl in the crushed chipotle and dust with the paprika. Drizzle with the cold-pressed oil, shower with extra thyme leaves and serve alongside the roots and a large pile of salad leaves, spooning over the yogurt as you eat.

Baked Giant Beans with Dill

Serves 8

- 1 pound (500 g) dried gigantes beans or lima beans
- 2 carrots
- 2 celery stalks
- 2 onions
- 5 garlic cloves
- ¾ cup (200 ml) extra virgin olive oil
- 2 teaspoons dried oregano
- Two 14.5-ounce (400 g) cans plum tomatoes
- Sea salt and freshly ground black pepper
- Bunch of dill, finely chopped
- 1⅓ cups (200 g) crumbled feta, optional

These are incredible. It really is worth tracking down dried gigantes beans. You could, I suppose, make this with 2¼ pounds (1 kg) of luscious, jarred, ready-made gigantes, but it would be very expensive and the beans are already tender, so you'd have to reduce both liquid and baking time, taking great care when stirring. Cooking your own keeps costs low, and means you can control the firmness of the beans. Serve them with an arugula salad—dressed with lemon juice and olive oil—and rice, roasted vegetables or toasted pita breads.

❶ Cover the beans with cool water in a very large bowl and soak overnight, or for at least 8 hours. If you don't have the time, put the beans in a very large saucepan, cover generously with cool water and bring to a boil. Simmer for 2 minutes and skim the foam off. Turn the heat off and set aside for 3 hours. Either way, drain the beans in a colander and rinse well.

❷ Again, cover the beans with fresh water—this time in a very large saucepan—and bring to a boil. Skim off any foam with a large spoon (keep this nearby to skim regularly) and simmer for 45 to 50 minutes, until very nearly cooked. Start checking after 40 minutes, as cooking time can vary. Strain the beans, reserving 2¼ cups (500 ml) of the cooking liquid.

❸ Preheat the oven to 340°F (170°C). Finely chop the carrots, celery, onions and garlic. Add to the rinsed-out pan with about 3 tablespoons of the olive oil and the dried oregano. Cook very slowly and gently for 15 minutes or so, stirring often, until soft and sweet. Don't let them brown. Open the tomato cans and snip the tomatoes with scissors to chop roughly. Pour into the pan and increase the heat to medium. Cook for 5 to 10 minutes, until the oil separates. Stir in the reserved bean-cooking liquid and remove from the heat. Add the remaining olive oil and season generously.

❹ Put the beans in a large baking dish and pour the tomato mixture over. It will look very liquid. Carefully slide into the oven and bake for 1 hour 45 minutes, or until the sauce looks thick and rich. Stir every 30 minutes while they cook. Keep an extra ¾ cup (200 ml) water on hand and, if the beans look at all dry after the first hour, add a little. Once finished, the beans should be cloaked in a thick, rich sauce. Remove from the oven, leave to sit for 10 minutes, then gently stir in the dill. Scatter with feta, if using, and leave for 5 more minutes for the cheese to soften before serving.

HOW TO COOK LENTILS BEAUTIFULLY

Cooking for groups can be costly, so a cheap, nutritious lentil base, ready to soak up and enhance aromatic additions, is a valuable tool. Every variety teems with insoluble fiber, sustaining protein, folic acid, iron and useful levels of potassium, among other minerals and vitamins. As a rough guide, stick to a lentil classically used with the flavors you want. Red lentils, for example, combine perfectly with Asian spices, tomato, coconut and greens, collapsing to form a dal, but a small French-style lentil would need hours of cooking to do the same.

A basic, beautifully cooked pan of lentils will provide many satisfying suppers. A sturdy type—say a Puy lentil, black Beluga or humble brown—will do well. As a guide, 1½ cups (300 g) will feed four to six, depending on appetite.

So, how to cook them? First, place your lentils into a sieve to check for stones. Hold them under cold running water for a quick rinse, too, removing any grit or dirt. Transfer to a saucepan and add scrubbed vegetables freely. I nestle in a whole carrot, a celery stalk, a halved onion and half a garlic bulb. This is also a good place to add flavorful parsley stalks. Essentially, you are creating stock in the pan. As lentils simmer, they swell, absorbing liquid and, if you let them, aromatics. A judicious hand with woody herbs (rosemary, bay, thyme) will pay dividends if it will suit your end flavors; simply fish out the stalks before serving. Similarly, toasted spices (cumin, caraway, coriander, black pepper . . .) will infuse lentils with warmth, but you can always stir them in after a quick sauté with a chopped onion.

The issue of salting lentils is contentious. I dare say that boiling a lentil in sea water might give it a tough jacket, but I have not found that a meager amount of salt makes any difference. So, cover the lentils with a generous layer of water, adding a pinch of salt. I always include a bay leaf. (I once read that bay, added to lentil cooking water, helps to neutralize unwanted effects after eating. However, bay's sharp, peppery notes enhance lentils beautifully, so the habit is as much for flavor as anything else.)

Bring to a boil, reduce the heat and simmer gently for 25 minutes. Begin to check after this time, but expect to cook them for up to 30 minutes more. Season and let them rest for five minutes to settle before draining well. Keep the lentils—chilled—for a few days before eating as is, or add further character with oils, sautéed vegetables, spices or herbs to skew the flavor and feel to pretty much any region of the world. They could be the foundation to a salad, vegetarian patty, curry or braise, or, cooked down further, as a soup or mash. A panful of possibilities.

Sticky Alliums with Lentils and Hazelnut Gremolata

Serves 6 as a light main course

For the dish

- 1 cup (200 g) Puy lentils
- Sea salt and freshly ground black pepper
- 4 to 5 tablespoons extra virgin olive oil, plus more for drizzling
- Squeeze of lemon juice
- 14 ounces (400 g) banana shallots or large shallots, peeled and halved
- 1 sweet onion, peeled and quartered
- ¼ cup (60 ml) balsamic vinegar
- 1 large cauliflower head, cut into small florets
- 2 garlic cloves, peeled

For the gremolata

- Large bunch of flat-leaf parsley, finely chopped
- ¾ cup (75 g) shelled hazelnuts, toasted and crushed
- 3 garlic cloves, finely chopped
- Finely grated zest of 2 unwaxed lemons

A zesty gremolata, more commonly scattered over Italian braises, lifts this unpretentious dish—based on roasted cauliflower, lentils and mellow balsamic shallots—into sophisticated, main course territory. If your bottle of balsamic vinegar is a good-quality version, you could drizzle a little extra over each plate at the end.

1 Cover the lentils with plenty of cool water, bring to a boil, add a generous pinch of salt, reduce the heat and leave to simmer gently for 25 to 30 minutes, until tender. Drain and dress with a dash of olive oil and lemon juice.

2 Preheat the oven to 400°F (200°C). Put the shallots and onion in a small roasting pan, season with salt and pepper and drizzle with 2 tablespoons of the olive oil. Cover tightly with foil and roast for 40 minutes until very soft. Uncover, drizzle with the balsamic vinegar and return to the oven for 5 to 10 minutes, stirring once or twice, until caramelized and sticky.

3 Toss the cauliflower and whole garlic cloves with 2 to 3 more tablespoons olive oil, as needed to coat. Spread out in a roasting pan and roast for 20 to 25 minutes, until the cauliflower is very tender and just beginning to brown. Transfer the cauliflower to a food processor with an extra drizzle of olive oil. Blend until smoothish. Alternatively, mash the cauliflower and garlic by hand with a potato masher. Season with salt and pepper.

4 To make the gremolata, combine all the ingredients in a bowl, cover and set aside in a cool place until needed.

5 Serve a generous spoonful of warm cauliflower mash with a spoonful of lentils on top, followed by the sticky alliums. Scatter with gremolata and drizzle lightly with olive oil to finish.

Squash, Green Olive and Lentil Tagine

Serves 6

- 1 cup (200g) Puy lentils
- Pinch of saffron threads
- 2 pounds 10 ounces (1.2 kg) firm winter squash, peeled and deseeded
- 4 tablespoons unsalted butter
- 1 tablespoon olive oil
- ¾ cup (100 g) blanched almonds
- 1 red onion, sliced
- 1½ teaspoons cumin seeds
- Large cinnamon stick
- 1-inch (2.5 cm) piece fresh ginger root, peeled and finely grated
- 3 plump garlic cloves, finely chopped
- 2 preserved lemons, rind only, roughly chopped
- 3 cups (700 ml) weak vegetable stock
- 1 tablespoon honey
- ¾ cup (120 g) pitted green olives
- Sea salt and freshly ground black pepper
- Handful of cilantro, chopped

This celebratory tagine, made with inauthentic Puy lentils, is even better made the day before you want to serve it, giving the flavors time to round out and settle. If you do make it in advance, be sure to add the cilantro only just before serving; and be mindful not to overcook the squash first time round, as it will cook a little more when you reheat the tagine. Serve this with a steamed grain or couscous with plenty of herbs and lemon zest stirred through.

1 Rinse the lentils in a sieve, checking for any stones. Transfer to a saucepan, cover with plenty of cool water and bring to a boil. Simmer for 20 to 25 minutes, until only just tender. Drain well.

2 Boil a kettle and put the saffron in a small bowl. Pour a couple of tablespoons of boiling water onto the threads and set aside for 5 minutes.

3 Cut the squash into large pieces (about 2 inches/5 cm square, if you're counting).

4 Heat the butter and olive oil in a large Dutch oven or saucepan over medium heat and add the almonds. Cook for a few minutes, stirring occasionally, until the nuts are golden all over. Scoop on to a plate with a slotted spoon and set aside.

5 Add the onion to the pan and cook for 5 minutes. Stir in the cumin and cinnamon and cook for 1 minute or so, followed by the squash pieces. Cook, stirring occasionally, for a few minutes, until the squash begins to brown, then stir in the ginger, garlic, preserved lemon rinds, stock, honey and saffron (with its soaking water). Bring to a boil, then cover. Reduce the heat and simmer very gently for 20 to 25 minutes, or until the squash is just tender. Stir in the lentils, being careful not to break the squash down.

6 Plunge the olives into a separate saucepan of boiling water, to remove some of their salt. Drain after 20 seconds and add to the simmering tagine with the golden almonds. Cook for a further 5 minutes or so, until the squash is very tender but still holding its shape. Taste and season with salt and pepper; it should only need a little salt, if any, due to the preserved lemons, stock and olives. Scatter with the cilantro to serve.

Caramelized Fennel Tagliatelle

Serves 4

- 2 large fennel bulbs
- 4 tablespoons unsalted butter
- 1 tablespoon olive oil
- 1 garlic clove, finely chopped
- Fat pinch of chile flakes
- Scant ½ cup (100 ml) white wine
- Scant ½ cup (100 ml) vegetable stock
- ⅓ cup (50 g) walnut halves
- 12 ounces (350 g) dried whole wheat tagliatelle
- Sea salt
- Finely grated vegetarian Parmesan cheese, to serve, optional

There's a good amount of toasted sweet butter here. If the quantity offends you, cut it by half, or replace it with olive oil . . . but a little butter here and there is celebratory and adds richness to a simple dish. The sauce is spectacular folded through braised lentils, with or without goat cheese, as a warm salad. Look for the plump, round female fennel bulbs rather than their slim, tall brothers, who tend to be stringy.

1 Trim any woody stalks from the fennel bulbs, also trimming the bases and removing the entire outer layers if they are very woody or tough. Slice the bulbs in half and cut out most of the solid cores. Slice across the bulbs very finely, as you would an onion (easiest on a mandoline, if you have it). Roughly chop and reserve any fronds.

2 Heat the butter and oil in a large Dutch oven or deep frying pan set over medium-high heat. Add the fennel slices, spread out well and cook for 15 minutes, stirring occasionally, until browned and sweet. Stir in the garlic and chile flakes and cook for 1 minute, then pour in the wine and stock. Bubble for 1 minute, then reduce the heat to as low as it will go. Simmer for 15 to 20 minutes, stirring often, until the liquid has been absorbed and the fennel is very tender. Add a little water if it sticks at any point.

3 Meanwhile, preheat the oven to 375°F (190°C). Spread the walnuts out in a roasting pan and cook for about 8 minutes, until toasted and fragrant. (You can toast the nuts in a dry frying pan if you would rather not turn the oven on, but roasting them gently brings out more flavor.) Place on a chopping board and, when cool enough, roughly chop the nuts. Some should be chopped fine, some a little larger.

4 Cook the pasta until al dente in plenty of boiling salted water, according to the package instructions. Drain in a colander, reserving a few tablespoons of cooking water. Place the drained pasta into the fennel pan with the nuts and reserved pasta water to emulsify the butter. Turn the pasta with tongs to coat in the sauce and serve as is, or with grated Parmesan, if you like.

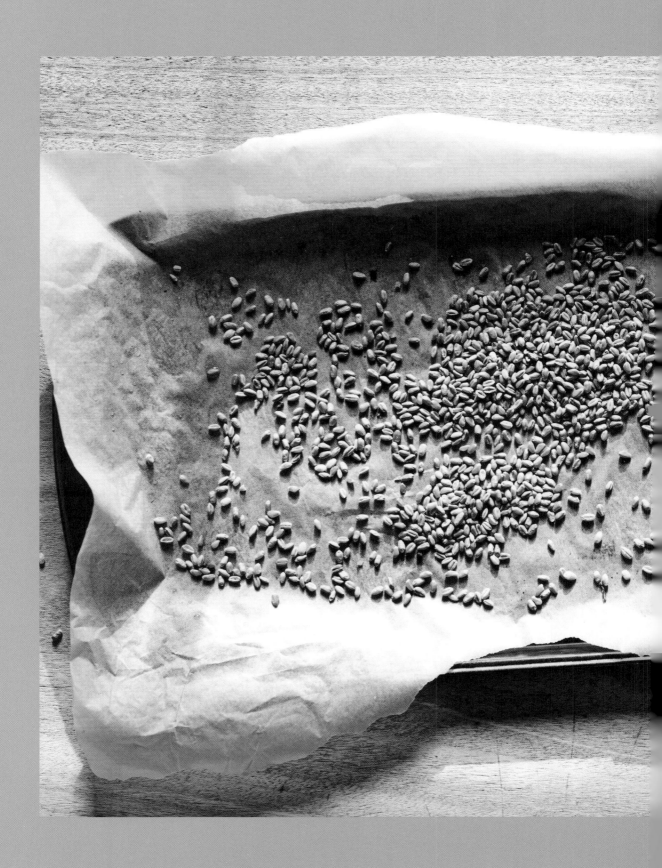

chapter six

grains

A MASS OF GRASSLIKE PLANTS huddles under the great grain umbrella. My scientific terminology isn't entirely correct, I grant you, but, as I know of no other term to encompass the whole gamut of grains, grasses and cereals that we eat, "grains" will do as my shorthand.

Vegetables, even when they take center stage, often need the balance and bolster of grains. And, yet, the nutritious whole forms are today often lambasted with the same "bad carbohydrate" brush usually reserved for cheap white bread and cakes. I wonder if we are in danger of losing our way completely and forgetting that eating is about giving ourselves energy, pleasure, balance and sustenance, not about achieving weight loss. Unless you have an allergy, I have seen no good evidence to avoid grains; in fact, I feel that a daily diet without them would be restrictive and lacking. Eating whole grains, for flavor as well as complete nutrition, couldn't be further from mainlining sliced white bread and jam. And it certainly won't make you fat.

There are many levels of processing where grains are concerned, a veritable minefield of them in fact. Pearled barley and spelt, for example, are not whole grains, because the fibrous bran has been polished away, but rolled oats—even whole-grain flour—are in the club with their brans intact. A whole grain is just that: the outer bran, the starchy endosperm and the protein- and oil-rich germ all present together. Your body can glean B vitamins, iron and omega-3 fatty acids (and more) from the germ, and has to work harder to break through the bran layer. Hence whole grain's status as a darling of low glycemic index (GI) eating: They sustain steady blood sugar levels for a long time. All told, they are a notable source of energy for very little outlay and they bring flavor in spades. If you eat whole grains where possible, but cook any grain—whole or occasionally not—in a modern way, for texture as well as taste, combining them with vegetables and high-quality protein, I don't feel any concern is warranted.

The breadth of grains at our fingertips is magnificent, ranging from lesser-known amaranth, kasha, millet and teff, through still-quite-exotic buckwheat, farro, quinoa and rye, to mainstream barley, corn, oats, spelt, wheat and wild rice (in fact all rices).

Dry roasting—or roasting or sautéing grains in flavor-rich fat—is the best way to impart a rounded, nutty flavor to grains. After that initial toast, intense enough to turn them a shade or two darker, and making them smell toasted, they are ready to be simmered as usual. They will be a better, more confident version of themselves, once cooked.

If you aren't planning on dry-roasting or toasting grains, soaking them in cool water for an hour or two will lessen cooking times. And here, on that all-important simmer, you can alter the direction of a grain-based dish significantly. Add umami with vegetable or mushroom stock, lend comfort with coconut milk, or boost aromatic qualities with bay, thyme, cinnamon or star anise. Leave well alone to cook, or stir constantly to coax out starches, thickening to a risotto-like end.

Any grain portion of a recipe doesn't have to be the main, or even side, event, it can be the finishing touch . . . so I'd always recommend cooking more than you need, in order to have extra in the fridge or freezer. It is easy to use it up: Throw cooked grains into or onto rustic soups and stews; fold them into sweet, roasted roots with legumes and a mustard dressing; add herbs, seeds and nuts with a generous hand. . . .

And you can toast grains at the end as well as at the start of cooking. In the fava bean tostadas in this chapter (see page 208), I suggest frying a small amount of cooked quinoa to spoon over at the end. The cooked grains shrink down in a hot frying pan, turning crunchy and intensifying in flavor. They are there for texture as much as taste. Similarly, raw rice can be toasted in a dry pan until golden, then pounded to a gritty dust, with or without spices, to throw over East Asian salads. A small spoonful adds great texture contrast and flavor.

To take the texture in a different direction, try sprouting grains such as rye, wheat and oat groats just as you would seeds or legumes: Cover a handful of grains with plenty of cool water and leave to soak overnight. Rinse and drain well and transfer to a clear jar with a square of muslin or cheesecloth fastened over the top with an elastic band. Invert the jar and prop it up at an angle in a bowl or similar. Now leave the jarred grains in a cool place to sprout, filling the jar with cool water, rinsing out and draining through the muslin or cheesecloth twice a day (return it to its inverted, angled position after each rinse). When you see little sprouts growing, which could take two to five days, rinse the grains well and eat immediately, or keep in the fridge for about three days. They are milky and slightly crisp, packed with nutrients and excellent on salads or blended into pesto, hummus, or even smoothies.

Lastly, a note. Gluten-free readers will know this, but, for the rest of us, it is useful—essential even—to know which grains and grasses are safe for those with an allergy. Amaranth, buckwheat, corn, millet, oats, quinoa, rice, teff and wild rice—if from a certified gluten-free source—are all fine.

Quinoa and Fava Bean Falafel with Lemon

Serves 4 to 6 / Makes about 36

- 1½ cups (300 g) split, dried fava beans
- 1⅓ cups (150 g) quinoa
- Sea salt and freshly ground black pepper
- 1 teaspoon coriander seeds
- 1 teaspoon cumin seeds
- ½ red onion, chopped
- 1 plump garlic clove, chopped
- 1 preserved lemon, rind only, chopped
- Handful each of parsley, cilantro and mint leaves
- Pinch of cayenne pepper
- Pinch of baking powder
- 1 quart (1 L) canola oil
- Handful of pea shoots or watercress
- 1¼ cups (200 g) fava beans, lightly steamed and double shelled
- 4 tablespoons Roasted Tomato and Pickled Lemon Relish (page 294)

P lease make these; they are incredible. They have a delightful crunch from the quinoa—I used black for the picture—and a fresh quality from the herbs. Do buy the peeled or skinless dried fava beans, or you'll spend a good 20 minutes slipping soaked beans from their brown skins. Try health food shops and anywhere selling North African food if you can't find them in the supermarket.

1 The day or night before, cover the dried fava beans with plenty of cold water in a bowl and leave to soak in a cool place for 10 to 24 hours. Drain thoroughly.

2 Put the quinoa in a saucepan, add 1¼ cups (290 ml) of water and a pinch of salt and bring to a boil. Partially cover with a lid, reduce the heat and simmer for 15 minutes, or until no liquid remains in the pan. Set aside to cool slightly.

3 Toast the coriander and cumin seeds in a dry pan over medium heat until just fragrant. Crush roughly and add to a food processor with the soaked beans, red onion, garlic, preserved lemon rind, herbs and cayenne. Blend to make a rough, moldable paste, stopping to scrape down the sides and mix through every now and then and adding the quinoa near the end of blending time. Transfer to a bowl, stir in the baking powder, season generously with salt and pepper, cover with plastic wrap and chill for 1 hour to make the mixture easier to shape.

4 Form into walnut-sized balls, scooping out spoonfuls and rolling them firmly between your palms. Wet your hands lightly if they stick at all. Have them all ready on a tray.

5 Put the oil in a medium saucepan and heat gently until a scrap of the falafel mixture sizzles gently when dropped into the oil.

6 Deep-fry in batches until golden, keeping a close watch and turning the falafel regularly so that they color evenly. Remove with a slotted spoon and drain on a plate lined with paper towels, keeping the fried falafel warm in a low oven.

7 Serve with a little salad of the pea shoots and fresh beans, with spoonfuls of the Roasted Tomato and Pickled Lemon Relish.

Fragrant Carrot, Mandarin and Onion Red Rice Pilaf

Serves 4

- 1½ cups (300 g) red rice
- 1 large mandarin, halved
- 4 to 5 tablespoons olive oil
- 2 tablespoons unsalted butter, optional
- 3 large onions, halved and finely sliced
- 1 teaspoon coriander seeds
- 1 teaspoon cumin seeds
- 4 green cardamom pods
- 1 large cinnamon stick
- 2 large carrots, coarsely grated
- 2½ cups (600 ml) vegetable stock
- ¾ cup (100 g) sliced almonds, toasted
- Large handful of fennel fronds or dill, chopped
- Large handful of mint leaves, roughly chopped
- Sea salt and freshly ground black pepper

Much can be made from an onion or two, and this beautiful red pilaf, with its gently spiced rice and colored-at-the-edges onion-mandarin hat, relies on cooking them slowly and patiently to release their natural sugars. It won't attain the heights of fluffiness because of the grated carrot, but it's no less delicious for that. Serve this with roasted roots on the side and perhaps some yogurt.

1 Start by rinsing the rice in a bowl of water held under the cool tap, swishing the grains and draining, then refilling, until the water runs clear. Drain the rice well and set aside.

2 Squeeze a little of the mandarin juice into a cup and finely slice the mandarin halves. Set aside.

3 Put 2 tablespoons of the olive oil and the butter, if using, in a large frying pan and set it over medium-low heat. Add the onions and cook gently for 15 minutes, stirring often, until they are very soft and beginning to turn golden. At this point, transfer one third of the onions to a large saucepan and return the frying pan to medium heat, stirring in the mandarin slices and a little more oil. Cook, stirring often, until both onions and mandarins begin to color at the edges. Set aside.

4 Meanwhile, lightly crush the coriander and cumin seeds with a mortar and pestle. Add the cardamom pods and crush to split them open. Stir all these spices, along with the cinnamon stick, into the smaller amount of onions in the saucepan over gentle heat and cook for 5 minutes more. Stir in the drained rice and grated carrots, coating with the fat. Add the stock, bring to a boil, then reduce the heat to a gentle simmer. Cover the pan and cook for about 30 minutes, until the liquid has been absorbed.

5 Remove the rice pan from the heat, cover with a kitchen towel, replace the lid and leave to steam for 10 minutes. Stir the almonds, fennel fronds and mint into the rice. Season with the reserved mandarin juice, salt and pepper and spoon the golden onion and mandarin mixture over to finish.

Fennel and Lima Bean Tabbouleh

Serves 4

- 1 teaspoon fennel seeds
- 1 cup (150 g) freekeh (green wheat)
- ¼ cup plus 2 tablespoons (90 ml) extra virgin olive oil
- Leaves from 2 large bunches of flat-leaf parsley
- Leaves from 1 large bunch of mint
- 1 large fennel bulb, halved
- 1¾ cups (300 g) cooked, drained lima beans (or one 15-ounce/400 g can)
- 1 bunch of scallions, trimmed and finely sliced
- Juice of 1 large lemon
- 1 garlic clove, crushed
- Sea salt and freshly ground black pepper
- 2 tablespoons Sesame Seed Za'atar (page 299)

This is not an authentic tabbouleh by any stretch; I have simply borrowed the idea of an exuberant and herb-rich grain salad. *Herb-rich* means positively singing with green herbs, so don't stint; these simple flavors rely on their vibrancy to pull the dish off. Replace the toasted freekeh (green wheat) with any grain or grass you like. The slight crunch of quinoa works particularly well as an alternative.

1 Lightly crush the fennel seeds. Put the freekeh and fennel seeds in a saucepan with 1 tablespoon of the olive oil. Toast over medium heat, stirring often, until the grains begin to darken slightly and smell nutty. Add 2 cups (450 ml) of water, bring to a boil and partially cover with a lid. Reduce the heat and simmer briskly for 10 minutes or so, until the water has been absorbed. The freekeh should still have texture and bite. Set aside to cool.

2 Finely chop the parsley and mint leaves, along with any fennel fronds. You should have a very generous amount, far more herb than grain. Combine with the freekeh in a large bowl.

3 If you have a mandoline, use it to slice the halved fennel bulb very finely. Otherwise, use a sharp knife and have patience. Add to the freekeh with the lima beans and most of the scallions, keeping a small handful back for the end.

4 Combine the lemon juice and remaining olive oil with the crushed garlic. Season well with salt and pepper to make a dressing and pour most of it over the freekeh mixture. Taste and adjust the seasoning as needed, then spoon onto a serving plate. Finish with the rest of the dressing, the remaining scallions and the za'atar.

Turkish Peppers

Serves 4

- ¾ cup (150 g) wheat berries
- Sea salt and freshly ground black pepper
- 4 red, yellow or orange peppers
- 5 scallions, trimmed
- Small bunch of dill
- 2 garlic cloves, finely sliced
- Handful of mixed olives, pitted and halved
- 16 sun-dried tomato quarters, drained
- Olive oil
- ⅔ cup (100 g) crumbled feta
- ½ cup (100 g) Greek yogurt
- 2 tablespoons pine nuts
- ½ teaspoon sumac, optional

Bouncy wheat grains are ideal spooned into these Mediterranean-inspired peppers, adding sustenance and texture to the sweetly roasted vegetables. The baked peppers are finished with a light dill and feta yogurt and plenty of golden pine nuts. There is a lot going on, but the premise owes more than a nod to the well-known Piedmont peppers Elizabeth David first wrote about more than half a century ago.

1 Preheat the oven to 350°F (180°C).

2 Put the wheat berries in a large saucepan with a generous pinch of salt, cover with cool water and bring to a boil. Once boiling, reduce the heat to a gentle simmer, partially cover and leave to cook for 25 to 30 minutes, until the grains are just tender (they should still be slightly chewy). Drain and set aside.

3 Slice the peppers in half from stalk to base and remove the pale ribs and seeds. Arrange in a single layer in a roasting pan, cut sides up. Finely slice the green scallion tops and set aside. Cut the remainder of the scallions into thirds and finely chop half the dill, keeping the rest in sprig form. Tuck a few slices of garlic, a few olive halves, a couple of sun-dried tomato quarters, a sprig of dill and 1 or 2 scallion lengths into each pepper half. Drizzle with olive oil—be generous—and roast for 35 to 40 minutes, until tender.

4 While the peppers cook, beat the feta and Greek yogurt together with the chopped dill and plenty of black pepper until light. Cook the pine nuts in a frying pan with another drizzle of olive oil over medium heat. They'll need a couple of minutes, with frequent stirring, to turn golden brown all over. Transfer to a plate.

5 Gently stir 1 heaping tablespoon of cooked wheat into each pepper half, coating it with the garlicky, olive-y, peppery juices that have pooled there. At this stage you can leave the peppers to cool if you like, but I think they are best when warm. Either way, top with a spoonful of the whipped feta, sliced scallion tops and a final scattering of golden pine nuts, sprigs of dill and sour sumac, if you have any.

Eggplant and Sweet Potato Lasagna with Walnuts

Serves 4

- Two 14.5-ounce (400 g) cans plum tomatoes
- 2 garlic cloves, crushed
- Pinch of chile flakes
- 3 tablespoons red wine
- 2 tablespoons olive oil, plus more for roasting
- Sea salt and freshly ground black pepper
- 1 pound (450 g) sweet potatoes, peeled
- 2 tablespoons chopped thyme leaves
- 2 medium eggplants
- 5.3 ounces (150 g; about 7) lasagna sheets
- Three 5.3-ounce (150 g) spheres of vegetarian mozzarella, drained and sliced
- Handful of basil leaves, torn
- ⅔ cup (100 g) chopped walnuts

will leave the type of pasta up to you; there are some pretty good dried whole-grain varieties around now, beyond the standard durum wheat. When developing this recipe, I used whole-grain spelt lasagna sheets and was impressed with their flavor and texture after baking. Serve this with salad and red wine.

1 Put the tomatoes, half the garlic, the chile flakes, wine and 2 tablespoons of olive oil in a saucepan with a pinch of salt. Set over medium heat. Bring to a boil, stirring often, then reduce the heat to low. Simmer for 50 minutes, stirring now and then, until rich and thick, not watery.

2 Preheat the oven to 400°F (200°C). Slice the sweet potatoes into ⅜-inch (1 cm) discs. Toss with a good pinch of the thyme and enough olive oil to coat. Season with salt and pepper and spread out in a roasting pan. Roast at the base of the oven for 30 minutes, until tender.

3 Trim the eggplants and slice from top to bottom, making each slice about ¼ inch (5 mm) thick. Brush with oil, season and lay out on 2 large baking sheets, in single layers. Roast at the top of the oven for 20 minutes, swapping the trays around halfway, until tender and beginning to brown.

4 To assemble the lasagna, spread one quarter of the tomato sauce into an 8 × 12-inch (20 × 30 cm) ovenproof dish. Cover with a single layer of lasagna sheets, topping these with one quarter more of the sauce. Now add half the sweet potato in a single layer, followed by an overlapping layer of about half the eggplant slices. Cover with half the mozzarella slices and torn basil leaves. Repeat the layers once more, finishing with the remaining tomato sauce in an even layer. Bake for 25 to 30 minutes, until bubbling.

5 While the lasagna bakes, combine the remaining crushed garlic clove, walnuts and remaining thyme in a bowl with a drizzle of oil and plenty of seasoning. When there are 10 minutes until the lasagna is ready, scatter evenly with the walnut mixture. Set aside to rest and settle for a final 10 minutes before attempting to slice and serve.

Farro and Squash Kofta in a Roasted Tomato Sauce

Serves 4 / Makes about 20

- 2 sweet white onions, finely chopped
- 3 garlic cloves, chopped
- ½ teaspoon dried oregano
- Sea salt and freshly ground black pepper
- Olive oil
- 2½ pounds (1.2 kg) ripe tomatoes, halved
- 1 pound 3 ounces (550 g) firm winter squash, peeled deseeded and cut into ¾-inch (2 cm) cubes
- 1⅓ cups (200 g) farro or spelt
- 1 celery stalk, finely chopped
- 2 tablespoons tomato paste
- 2 teaspoons chopped rosemary leaves
- 1½ cups (150 g) sourdough bread crumbs
- 1 egg, lightly beaten
- ⅓ cup (30 g) finely grated vegetarian Parmesan cheese, plus more, shaved, to serve
- Large handful of basil leaves, chopped, plus more to serve

These plump little kofta—as close as I could get to meatless meatballs, really—are as delicious with braised lentils or beans as they are with peppery salads. Because they are so rich in grains, I'd opt for serving them with "zucchini noodles" or other vegetables that are blanched and shredded into strands instead of pasta (more grains), though of course you can serve them just as suggested below, with their smoky-rich tomato sauce, basil and cheese.

1 Preheat the oven to 400°F (200°C). Scatter half the onions into a roasting pan with the garlic. Sprinkle with the oregano, season with salt and pepper and drizzle generously with olive oil. Cover the whole lot with the tomatoes in a single layer, cut sides down. Slide into the oven and roast for about 45 minutes, until completely tender. Set aside to cool slightly, then remove the tomato skins by pulling them off. Blend to make a rich, smooth sauce.

2 Meanwhile, toss the squash with oil to coat and spread out in a roasting pan with plenty of salt and pepper. Roast for 45 minutes, or until tender. Transfer into a large bowl and set aside. Cover the farro with water in a saucepan, add a pinch of salt and bring to a boil. Reduce the heat and simmer merrily for 25 minutes, or until just tender. Drain thoroughly and add to the squash.

3 Put 1 tablespoon of olive oil in a frying pan and set over medium-low heat. Add the remaining onion and the celery with a pinch of salt and sauté gently for 10 minutes, until soft and just beginning to brown. Add the tomato purée and rosemary and cook, stirring, for a couple of minutes. Transfer into the bowl with the farro. Using the back of a spoon, crush the squash to make a rough mash—you don't need to overdo it—combining all the ingredients. Stir in the bread crumbs, egg, grated Parmesan and chopped basil. Season with lots of black pepper and a little salt. Cover and chill for 30 minutes or up to 24 hours to firm up.

4 Preheat the oven to 400°F (200°C). Scoop out a heaping tablespoon of the mixture and roll into kofta, each slightly smaller than a golf ball. They can be chilled again for up to 24 hours at this point. Put your largest frying pan over medium heat and add enough oil to form a film over the surface. Fry the kofta gently for 8 minutes, until golden brown all over. Spoon the tomato sauce into the pan, giving it a shake to redistribute. Bring to a simmer, then slide into the oven and bake for 10 minutes. Scatter with basil leaves and Parmesan before serving.

Idli with Coconut Chutney

Serves 4 / Makes about 18

For the idli

- ½ cup (120 g) urad dal
- ¼ teaspoon fenugreek seeds
- 1 cup (210 g) ground rice (also known as cream of rice)
- 1 cup (175 g) cooked brown basmati rice
- 1 scant teaspoon fine salt
- Sunflower oil, for the molds

For the coconut chutney

- 1 tablespoon sunflower oil
- Small handful of mint leaves
- ½- to 1-inch (1.3 to 2.5 cm) piece fresh ginger root, peeled and chopped
- Handful of curry leaves
- 1 green chile, roughly chopped
- 1¼ cups (100 g) grated fresh coconut
- Sea salt
- ½ teaspoon mustard seeds

f you have spent any time in south India, you will have tried these fluffy, slightly sour rice cakes with sambal. Though the batter takes a while to ferment, they're easy to make with a powerful blender. Track down *urad dal* (black gram) in Asian shops; you want the skinned, white ones. The ground rice is good old cream of rice, found in the baking section of supermarkets. You could always soak, dry and grind white basmati instead.

1 At least 14 hours before you want to eat the idli (in practice, this will be more like 2 days), soak the urad dal and fenugreek seeds in a bowl of cool water for at least 4 hours or overnight. Put the ground rice in a second bowl and cover generously with cool water. It will look cloudy; don't worry, it will settle. Leave the rice to soak for 2 hours. I usually leave both bowls to soak overnight with no ill effects.

2 Strain the urad dal and fenugreek through a fine sieve, but save the soaking water. Strain the ground rice, too. The sieve needs to be very fine here, so line with a piece of muslin or cheesecloth if needed; there is no need to save any of this soaking water. Put both in a powerful blender with the cooked rice.

3 Add 2 tablespoons of the reserved dal-soaking water and begin to blend. When the mixture begins to break down, stop the motor and stir, then blend again to make a paste. Add a further ⅔ cup (150 ml) of the reserved soaking water and continue to blend until completely smooth. The mixture should be bubbling on top and silky, not gritty (check by rubbing a little between your fingers). If your blender is too small, divide the mixture—and the liquid to be added—in half and blend in two batches.

4 Pour into a large bowl and stir in the salt. Cover with plastic wrap or a plate and set aside in a warm place (an airing pantry, or next to the oven in a warm kitchen, are both ideal) to ferment for 10 to 12 hours, until the batter smells pleasantly sour and has risen and bubbled dramatically. If it hasn't fermented properly, the idli won't rise or turn out fluffy, so be patient and let the batter sit for up to 10 hours longer if needed, making sure the room isn't too cold, as this will slow fermentation drastically.

5 To make the chutney, put half the oil in a frying pan set over medium heat. Add the mint leaves, ginger, half the curry leaves and the green chile. Cook for a few minutes, until the leaves turn dark and fragrant. Transfer into the blender with the coconut and 3 tablespoons of water. Blend until smooth, stirring in salt to taste; it should make quite a loose mixture. Wipe out the pan and return to high heat with the remaining oil. Add the remaining curry leaves and the mustard seeds and cook, stirring, until the seeds begin to pop. Pour this temper over the chutney.

6 Assuming you don't own an idli mold, oil 6 heatproof ramekins or dessert molds (about 2¾ inches/7 cm in diameter). Arrange in a steamer, fill each mold with 1½ tablespoons of idli batter and steam, covered, over simmering water for 8 to 10 minutes until puffed and springy to the touch. Flip the cooked idli out of the molds, wrap in a kitchen towel and keep warm while you cook the remaining 12 in the same way. Serve with the chutney.

Sweet Potato, Buckwheat and Herb Muffins

Makes 6 large muffins

- ⅓ cup (75 ml) fruity olive oil, plus more for the pan, optional
- 1⅓ cups (200 g) grated sweet potatoes
- ⅔ cup (100 g) mixed seeds (flax, pumpkin, sesame, sunflower seeds . . .)
- Large handful of soft herbs, finely chopped
- Finely grated zest of 1 unwaxed lemon
- 2 tablespoons chia seeds
- ¼ teaspoon fine salt
- 2 eggs, lightly beaten
- 1 heaping tablespoon Greek yogurt
- ½ cup (60 g) buckwheat flour
- ½ cup (60 g) whole-grain spelt or unbleached all-purpose flour
- ¾ teaspoon baking powder
- ¼ teaspoon baking soda

ike most recipes in this book, these wholesome savory muffins contain a generous hit of vegetable. So much grated sweet potato means they will never be elegant, but that's not to their detriment. They are well suited to buttering or spreading with cream cheese to go with soup. And should you want a muffin for breakfast, make a batch the night before and reheat them. They also freeze well, once baked.

1 Preheat the oven to 350°F (180°C). Line 6 holes of a 12-hole muffin pan with paper baking cups, or just oil the pan.

2 Stir together thoroughly the grated sweet potatoes, two thirds of the mixed seeds, the herbs, lemon zest, chia seeds, salt, oil, eggs and yogurt and set aside for 5 minutes, so that the chia seeds swell up a little. Sift the flours, baking powder and baking soda into a second bowl.

3 Stir the sweet potato mixture into the dry ingredients to form a very dense batter; be careful not to overmix. Divide between the muffin cups, sprinkle the tops with the reserved seeds and bake for 20 minutes or so, until risen and springy to the touch. Leave to cool for 5 minutes before turning out to cool completely on a wire rack.

Grain Supper Bowls . . . Principles and Variations

The idea of today's "bowl food" is to create informal and relaxed meals. They don't need to be slovenly; in fact, they are the ideal opportunity to put personality and care into your food, considering balance and texture in particular.

GRAIN OR GRASS

The nutritious base. Let your mood guide you. Robust buckwheat and rye overpower timid flavors and jar with spices, so combine them with pesto, dairy and roasted veggies. Any rice, or quinoa, takes well to Asian or South American spice. Nutty grains—the wheat, spelt, farro and pot or Scotch barley tribe—mix well with strong dressings. Summery grain bowls can be a showcase for sprouted grains (especially good for you).

VEGGIES . . .

Don't hold back; these are the stars. Spike them with spices and herbs. Roast, grill, steam or sauté, balancing their textures with other additions.

. . . OR SALAD

I include handfuls of soft herbs and young brassicas in the salad bracket. Don't forget cutting techniques make a real difference: Shaved fennel or carrot, perked up in ice water for a minute, will add another element.

HUNGRY?

Add good-quality protein. Tofu, tempeh, seitan, dairy, eggs in any form, legumes, even mushrooms, nuts and seeds will do the job.

SWEET NOTES

Naturally sweet alliums and peppers, cooked slowly to coax their sugars out, add another layer, especially when balanced with vinegar or citrus.

POKE

Think pickled. Kimchi or quick pickles of radish, carrot or cucumber lend crisp crunch and sour contrast.

DRESS

Sauces, dressings, pestos and relishes to stir through as you eat are of pivotal importance. Try a miso seaweed relish (see page 301) with rice bowls, or spoon on serious spice with a Thai-style chile paste (see page 309).

TO FINISH

A chance to add charm and texture. Sprouts; nuts and seeds (soaked or toasted); herbs; fried shallots; cold-pressed oil; matchsticks of ginger . . .

Whole Eggplants, Couscous and Confit Peppers

Serves 4

- 4 large, sweet peppers
- 4 garlic cloves
- 1 red onion, halved and sliced
- ½ cup plus 1 tablespoon (135 ml) extra virgin olive oil
- 3 tablespoons good sherry vinegar
- ½ teaspoon sweet smoked paprika
- Sea salt and freshly ground black pepper
- 3 tablespoons ras el hanout
- 4 large, long eggplants
- Good squeeze of lemon juice
- Small handful of mint leaves, chopped, plus more to serve
- ¾ cup (150 g) Israeli whole-grain couscous
- 1½ cups (350 ml) vegetable stock or water
- 4 heaping tablespoons labneh, store-bought or homemade (see page 26)

A stunner. Sweet peppers, charred eggplants, toasted giant couscous, a spiced dressing, mint and spoonfuls of cool labneh. It is important to choose the longest eggplants you can find. Plump eggplants will need to be sliced in half, or given a good 10 minutes longer if left whole. You could forgo the broiler entirely in favor of a grill; the extra smokiness would be very welcome.

1 Up to a week ahead of time, make the pepper confit. Deseed the peppers, cutting them into chubby strips and removing any pale ribs from the insides as you do so. Finely slice 3 of the garlic cloves and add to a frying pan with the peppers, red onion and 2 tablespoons of the olive oil. Sauté over medium-low heat, stirring frequently, for 20 minutes, until softened. Once they have started to color at the edges, add 1 tablespoon of the sherry vinegar and stir well, scraping at the pan with a wooden spoon to deglaze. Stir in the paprika, reduce the heat to low and cover. Leave to cook, stirring now and then, for a further 15 minutes, until sweet and very soft. Season with salt and pepper to taste. Use immediately, or cover and chill for up to 7 days.

2 To cook the eggplants, preheat the broiler to medium. Combine 1 tablespoon of the ras el hanout with 3 tablespoons of the olive oil. Prick the eggplants all over with a fork. Rub with the spiced oil, turning to coat; the hope is that each eggplant absorbs oil and spice through the holes. Arrange on a baking sheet and broil for 25 to 30 minutes, turning with tongs every 10 minutes.

3 To make the dressing, crush the remaining garlic clove with a fat pinch of salt to make a paste. Combine it with the remaining ¼ cup (60 ml) of olive oil, remaining vinegar and ras el hanout, lemon juice and chopped mint. Make the dressing directly with a mortar and pestle if you have one, muddling the mint slightly. Otherwise, just combine everything in a bowl.

4 Toast the couscous until golden in a dry frying pan set over medium heat, stirring. Add the stock, cover and cook for 15 minutes, stirring often, until the liquid is absorbed and the couscous is cooked through. Fold half the dressing through and season to taste.

5 Serve the whole eggplants and confit peppers with the couscous, pouring the remaining dressing over with spoonfuls of the labneh. Scatter more mint leaves over the top.

Coconut Sevai Rice

Serves 4 as a side dish

- 1⅓ cups (250 g) whole-grain basmati rice
- ⅔ cup (160 ml) coconut milk
- 2 tablespoons coconut oil
- 1¼ cups (100 g) grated fresh coconut (or see recipe introduction)
- Handful of fresh curry leaves
- ½ green chile, sliced
- 1 teaspoon black mustard seeds
- Pinch of chile flakes
- Sea salt
- ¼ cup (30 g) broken cashews
- ¼ cup (30 g) golden raisins

can't recommend this gentle rice highly enough as a simple, soothing supper with stir-fried greens, or as a rice bowl with spiced roasted vegetables and a tangle of fried onions. If you don't have fresh coconut, soak ⅓ cup (25 g) unsweetened desiccated coconut in boiling water for 15 minutes and replace some of the 2 cups (500 ml) rice-cooking water with the soaking water. I suggest using broken cashews, as they are cheaper.

1 Start by rinsing the rice in a bowl of water held under the cool tap, swishing the grains and draining, then refilling, until the water runs clear. Drain the rice well and set aside.

2 Combine the coconut milk with 2 cups (500 ml) of water and pour into a medium saucepan. Add the rinsed rice and bring slowly to a boil. Partially cover with a lid, reduce the heat and simmer for about 25 minutes, until the rice is just tender and the liquid no longer present. Cover with a kitchen towel and the lid and set aside to rest for 5 minutes.

3 While the rice rests, put 1½ tablespoons of the coconut oil in a frying pan. Melt over medium heat and add the grated coconut, curry leaves, green chile slices, mustard seeds and chile flakes. Season with salt and cook for a few minutes, stirring constantly, until the mixture sizzles slightly. Fold through the rice. Wipe the pan out and return to the heat with the remaining ½ tablespoon of coconut oil. Add the broken cashews and cook until golden all over. Remove from the heat and stir in the raisins with a little more salt. Spoon the coconut rice into a serving bowl, or divide between individual plates or bowls, and top with the cashew and raisin mixture.

Brown Rice Bibimbap Bowls with Smoky Peppers

Serves 4

For the bibimbap

- 1 cup (200 g) brown short-grain rice
- Sea salt
- 4 red peppers, halved
- Peanut oil
- Toasted sesame oil
- Toasted sesame seeds
- Tamari or light soy sauce
- 3 tablespoons gochujang
- 2 tablespoons unrefined brown sugar
- 1 garlic clove, crushed
- 1 tablespoon rice wine vinegar
- 1 carrot, sliced into matchsticks
- 1¼ cups (100 g) sliced shiitake mushrooms
- 1-inch (2.5 cm) piece fresh ginger root, peeled and finely chopped
- 2 handfuls of kale, shredded
- 1 cup (100 g) bean sprouts
- 4 very fresh eggs

To serve

- Pickled ginger, finely sliced
- Scallions, finely sliced
- Rehydrated seaweed or nori strips

An exercise in organization if ever there was one, this Korean-inspired dish isn't hard to make, but it does involve spinning a few plates. Drop one or more of the vegetable elements to make it easier, or get a friend to help you, dividing the cooking between you. Gochujang is a fiery Korean chile paste. Find it online or in East Asian shops or, in a pinch, substitute Thai-Style Roasted Chile Paste (page 309).

1 Start by rinsing the rice in a bowl of water held under the cool tap, swishing the grains and draining, then refilling, until the water runs clear. Drain the rice well and transfer into a saucepan. Cover with 2 cups (450 ml) of water and add a pinch of salt. Bring to a boil, cover, reduce the heat and simmer for 25 minutes, until the water has evaporated and the rice is tender.

2 Preheat the oven to 425°F (220°C). Arrange the pepper halves on a baking sheet, skin sides up. Drizzle with a little peanut oil and roast for 25 to 30 minutes, until soft and blackened. Transfer into a bowl and cover with a plate. Leave for 10 minutes, then peel and roughly slice. Season the pepper ribbons with sesame oil, sesame seeds and tamari.

3 Meanwhile, make the bibimbap sauce by combining the gochujang, sugar, garlic and vinegar with 2 tablespoons each of water, sesame oil and sesame seeds in a small bowl. Season with salt and set aside.

4 To cook the carrot, heat a whisper of peanut oil in a wok over high heat. Add the carrot and stir-fry for 1 to 2 minutes until just tender. Season with salt and set aside. Wipe the wok clean before returning it to the heat. Cook the mushrooms in a little oil in the same way, keeping the heat high and the pan moving until the mushrooms are cooked. Season with tamari.

5 Again, wipe out the wok. Add a little more oil followed by the ginger and the kale and a splash of water, stir-frying for a few minutes until wilted. Toss with a drizzle of sesame oil, 1 teaspoon of sesame seeds and salt to taste.

6 Blanch the bean sprouts in boiling salted water for a few seconds, until just wilted. Scoop out with a slotted spoon, refresh under cool water and drain well.

recipe continues . . .

7 To fry the eggs, pour a thin film of peanut oil into a wok or frying pan set over medium heat. Crack the eggs in separately and fry gently, flicking a little oil over the tops, until they are golden and lacy underneath and the whites have set.

8 To serve, divide the warm rice between generous warmed serving bowls. Spoon each distinct element on top in a roughly circular pattern: peppers, carrots, mushrooms, greens and bean sprouts. Lay the fried egg on top and add pickled ginger, sliced scallions, seaweed, toasted sesame oil and toasted sesame seeds to taste. Add a generous spoonful of the bibimbap sauce, putting the rest on the table to spoon over as you mix everything together and eat.

Dill and Celery Wild Rice with Roasted Fennel

Serves 4

- 1 cup (100 g) pecans
- 3 celery stalks
- 1 tablespoon unsalted butter
- 3 tablespoons olive oil
- 2 teaspoons coriander seeds, lightly crushed
- 1 small red onion, halved and finely sliced
- 1⅓ cups (250 g) wild rice
- 3¾ cups (900 ml) vegetable stock
- Sea salt and freshly ground black pepper
- 2 fennel bulbs, trimmed
- ½ cup chopped (100 g) dried apricots
- Small bunch of dill, chopped

Celery, fennel and onion all cook down to become soft and sweet. Celery in particular, I feel, is vastly underrated as a cooked vegetable; it is excellent braised or slowly roasted. All that natural sweetness, further enhanced by dried apricots and pecans, makes this baked pilaf of sorts the perfect candidate to accompany a salty slab of baked feta (see page 89) and perhaps a crisp salad of bitter chicory, endive or dandelion greens.

1 Preheat the oven to 375°F (190°C). Spread the pecans out on a baking sheet and roast for 8 to 10 minutes, until golden and toasted. Cool and roughly chop.

2 Slice 1 celery stalk. Heat the butter and 1 tablespoon of the olive oil in a large Dutch oven set over medium heat. Add the crushed coriander seeds and cook for a minute or so. Stir in the sliced red onion and sliced celery and cook for 5 minutes, until beginning to soften. Now add the wild rice, stirring well to coat with the fat, and pour in the stock. Season lightly with salt and pepper (you can always adjust the seasoning later), cover with a lid and bake for 40 minutes.

3 Cut the remaining celery stalks into thirds. Trim the bases from the fennel bulbs and cut each into 8 slim wedges. Toss the celery and fennel pieces with the remaining 2 tablespoons of olive oil, spread out in a roasting pan and roast alongside the wild rice for about 30 minutes, until soft and sweet. Set aside.

4 Uncover the pilaf and cook for 15 minutes, then remove from the oven to fold in the roasted vegetables, apricots, toasted pecans and chopped dill. Return to the oven—still uncovered—for 10 to 15 minutes, until no liquid remains. Taste and adjust the seasoning as needed.

Fava Bean and Asparagus Tostadas with Refried Beans

Serves 4

- ½ cup (50 g) black quinoa
- Sea salt and freshly ground black pepper
- 1 red onion, halved
- ¼ cup (60 ml) plus 2 tablespoons sunflower oil
- 1 scant teaspoon cumin seeds
- 1 tablespoon oregano leaves
- 2 cups (300 g) cooked black beans, plus ½ to ⅔ cup (100 to 150 ml) bean cooking liquid (or use one 15-ounce/400 g can and its liquid)
- 1 garlic clove, finely chopped
- 1 bunch of asparagus, trimmed and chopped
- 1 cup (150 g) shelled fresh fava beans
- 8 small corn tortillas
- 1 cup (100 g) coarsely grated Wensleydale or feta

Grains don't always have to form the basis of a dish. Here, a little quinoa—strictly a grass and not a grain—is flashed through a frying pan until crisp, adding a clever hit of texture to these tostadas. The refried beans will be better made with freshly cooked beans, but canned are absolutely fine to use, in which case, drain them, but reserve the canning liquid to add as needed.

1 Cover the quinoa with ½ cup (125 ml) of water in a small saucepan, add a fat pinch of salt and bring to a boil. Cover, reduce the heat and simmer for 15 minutes, until the grains have unfurled slightly. Set aside.

2 Finely slice half the red onion and set aside. Finely chop the remaining half. Add 1 tablespoon of the sunflower oil to a saucepan and set over medium heat. Add the chopped onion with a pinch of salt and cook for 5 minutes, until softening. Stir in the cumin seeds and half the oregano and cook until the onion is golden. Stir in the black beans and cook for a minute to warm through, then stir in ½ cup (100 ml) of their cooking or canning liquid and cook for 5 minutes. Remove from the heat and, using a potato masher, crush the beans roughly, seasoning generously with salt and pepper and adding more liquid if they are too thick, or simmering down a little if they seem thin. You want a soft, spoonable purée. Cover and keep warm.

3 Put a frying pan over high heat and add 1 tablespoon of sunflower oil. Add the sliced onion, garlic and asparagus. Season and stir-fry for 3 to 4 minutes, until the asparagus is almost tender. Add the fava beans and cook for 2 minutes. Transfer to a bowl and keep warm.

4 Wipe out the pan and return to the heat with the remaining ¼ cup (60 ml) oil. Flick a drop of water at the pan: If it dances and spits, it is hot enough. Add half the tortillas and cook for 30 seconds on each side, turning with tongs when pale golden and crisp. Drain on paper towels and repeat, topping up the oil if needed. Keep the pan on the heat (there should be about 1 tablespoon of oil left, drain any excess away) and quickly add the quinoa, stirring, for 3 to 4 minutes, until each sphere has reduced in size, turning crunchy. Add the remaining oregano, season and remove from the heat.

5 Spoon refried beans onto each crisp tostada, top with the asparagus mixture and spoon over the crisp quinoa and grated Wensleydale.

Very Green Spelt "Risotto"

Serves 4 generously

- One 21-ounce (600 g) piece of firm winter squash, deseeded
- 3 tablespoons olive oil
- A few sprigs of thyme
- 1½ quarts (1.5 L) vegetable stock
- 1 tablespoon unsalted butter
- 4 shallots, finely chopped
- 1¾ cups (375 g) pearled spelt
- ½ cup (125 ml) dry white wine
- 10 cups (300 g) spinach leaves, plus more to serve
- Extra virgin olive oil, to taste
- ½ cup (50 g) finely grated vegetarian Parmesan cheese, plus more, shaved, to serve
- ¼ cup (60 g) crème fraîche
- Finely grated zest and 1 tablespoon juice of 1 unwaxed lemon
- Sea salt and freshly ground black pepper

This verdant "risotto" is particularly elegant served as I have described below, with more spinach leaves, roasted winter squash and a lemon and thyme crème fraîche, but you could always substitute celery root or even plump tomatoes for the squash, if you prefer. Or forget the embellishments and serve the risotto just as it is, with the extra cheese pared over the top with a vegetable peeler.

1 Preheat the oven to 400°F (200°C). Slice the squash into 4 wedges. Toss them in a roasting pan with 2 tablespoons of the regular olive oil and all but 2 of the thyme sprigs. Roast for 30 minutes or so, until browned and soft.

2 You will need a grand total of 3 pans here, so bear with me. Put the stock in a saucepan and bring it to a simmer. Reduce the heat and keep it hot.

3 Heat the butter and remaining 1 tablespoon of regular olive oil in a second saucepan over low heat. Add the shallots and cook for 5 minutes, until translucent, but not colored. Spoon half into a bowl and set aside. Increase the heat slightly and stir in the spelt. Add the wine and stir until it has nearly all evaporated. Add a ladleful of hot stock and stir until it has nearly evaporated before adding another. Continue in this way, adding stock and stirring constantly, for about 20 minutes, until the spelt is almost cooked. Make sure you have about ½ cup (100 ml) of stock left.

4 Transfer the reserved shallots to a deep-sided frying pan. Set it over medium heat and add the spinach with the remaining stock. Heat until the spinach wilts. Transfer to a blender with a good drizzle of extra virgin olive oil and blend to make a velvet-textured purée.

5 The spelt grains should still have a little bite and the overall consistency should be thicker than a standard risotto. Stir in the spinach purée with the finely grated Parmesan. Cover and leave to settle for a few minutes. Strip the leaves from the remaining sprigs of thyme and stir through the crème fraîche with the lemon zest and juice and seasoning to taste with salt and pepper.

6 Divide the risotto between serving bowls (it won't sit on a plate), topping with roasted squash, a few extra spinach leaves, spoonfuls of thyme and lemon cream and Parmesan shavings. Finish with a little extra virgin olive oil, if you like.

Cress, Millet and Beet Salad with Cilantro Yogurt

Serves 4

- 12 multicolored beets, scrubbed and cut into wedges
- A few sprigs of thyme
- ¼ cup (60 ml) olive or canola oil
- 1 cup (200 g) millet
- 2 cups (450 ml) vegetable stock
- 2 preserved lemons, rind only, roughly chopped
- 1 green chile, deseeded if you like, roughly chopped
- Large handful of cilantro, half finely chopped
- ¾ cup (200 g) mild Greek or plain yogurt
- Sea salt and freshly ground black pepper
- 3 small containers cress, snipped
- Handful of sprouts or microherbs, such as cilantro microgreens (coriander cress)
- Extra virgin olive oil or pumpkin seed oil, to drizzle
- Squeeze of lemon juice

This is an excellent opportunity to use up any cold-pressed oil you might have sitting in the fridge. It will add great flavor to the fluffy millet grain, as well as precious polyunsaturated fatty acids. I love pumpkin seed oil, but you could use any nut oil or avocado, canola or hemp. Substitute more cilantro or more cress for the microherbs, if you can't get them easily or cheaply.

1 Preheat the oven to 400°F (200°C). Coat the beets and sprigs of thyme in 2 tablespoons of the regular olive or canola oil, spread out in a baking pan and roast for 40 to 45 minutes, stirring halfway, until soft and tinged with brown.

2 Rinse the millet in a sieve held under a cool running tap. Drain well. Put the remaining 2 tablespoons of the regular olive or canola oil in a large frying pan set over medium-high heat. Add the rinsed millet and toast it, stirring often, for 6 minutes or so, until the water evaporates and the grains turn an even, pale golden color and smell fragrant.

3 Add the stock, bring to a boil, partially cover with a lid, reduce the heat and simmer for 25 to 30 minutes, until all the liquid has been absorbed and the millet is fluffy and soft. Set aside to steam off the heat for 10 minutes. After this time the grains should no longer have a mealy texture (as does only partially cooked millet).

4 Pound the preserved lemon rind and green chile together with a mortar and pestle until pulverized. Stir the finely chopped cilantro into the yogurt with this pounded lemon-chile mixture and season with salt and pepper to taste. Serve the roasted beets on the millet with the cress and sprouts, reserved cilantro leaves and spoonfuls of cilantro yogurt, all drizzled with extra virgin olive and a good squeeze of lemon juice.

Roasted Cauliflower and Sesame Bowls with Miso

Serves 2

- ½ cup (100 g) grains (see recipe introduction)
- 1¼ cups (250 ml) vegetable stock
- 3¾ cups (400 g) cauliflower florets
- 2 tablespoons sunflower oil
- 1 teaspoon ground turmeric
- ½ teaspoon chile flakes
- Sea salt and freshly ground black pepper
- 5 tablespoons sesame seeds
- 2 tablespoons mellow miso paste
- 2 tablespoons rice wine vinegar
- 2 teaspoons maple syrup
- ½-inch (1.5 cm) piece fresh ginger root, peeled and finely grated
- 2 teaspoons toasted sesame oil, plus more to serve
- 4 scallions, finely sliced
- Handful of cilantro, roughly chopped
- Handful of baby kale leaves
- 2 tablespoons sprouts or cress
- Sambal Oelek (page 304), or chile sauce, to serve

Comfort food can appear in many guises. This bowl of thoughtfully spiced and dressed grains, vegetables and leaves is simple to throw together if you are feeling fragile. Use any grain you like, though I suggest choosing similarly sized grains or groats to suit the cooking times below. Farro, kamut, oat (groats), pot or Scotch barley, rye, spelt and wheat all have great character and respond well to a bout of oven-toasting.

1 Preheat the oven to 400°F (200°C). Spread the grains out in a roasting pan and roast for 12 to 15 minutes, shaking the pan partway through, until the grains turn a couple of shades darker and smell nutty. Transfer into a saucepan and pour in the stock. Bring to a boil, cover, reduce the heat and simmer for 25 minutes or so, until the grains are just tender but still retain a touch of bite. Different grains will vary, so check the pan every now and then, splashing in more water if the pan looks dry.

2 In a second roasting pan, toss the cauliflower with the sunflower oil, turmeric and chile flakes. Season generously with salt and pepper and spread out in a single layer. Roast for 15 minutes, then scatter with 2 tablespoons of the sesame seeds and roast for 5 minutes more, until tender and deeply golden.

3 Toast the remaining 3 tablespoons of sesame seeds in a dry pan over medium-low heat until golden.

4 To make the dressing, put 2 tablespoons of the toasted sesame seeds in a powerful blender with the miso, vinegar, maple syrup, ginger, 2 teaspoons of toasted sesame oil and ¼ cup (60 ml) of water. Blend until smooth. Taste and season as needed.

5 Toss a spoonful of the dressing through the cooked grains with nearly all the scallions and chopped cilantro. Divide between 2 serving bowls with the baby kale and the cauliflower. Drizzle with the rest of the dressing and scatter with the remaining scallions and cilantro and the sprouts. Finish with a final scattering of sesame seeds, a drizzle of sesame oil and a spoonful of sambal, if you like.

Brown Rice Congee with Asian Greens

Serves 4

- 1¼ cups (200 g) long-grain brown rice
- Sea salt
- 2 tablespoons coconut oil
- 2 garlic cloves, finely chopped
- 1-inch (2.5 cm) piece fresh ginger root, peeled and finely grated
- 1 red chile, sliced
- ½- to 1-inch (1.5 to 2.5 cm) piece fresh turmeric, peeled and finely grated, optional
- 1 large carrot, coarsely grated
- 1⅓ cups (120 g) sliced mushrooms, such as shiitake
- 1 quart (1 L) weak vegetable stock, plus more if needed
- Large handful of tender Asian greens, such as mizuna, mustard greens, or tatsoi
- 2 teaspoons toasted sesame oil
- Small handful of cilantro, roughly chopped
- Your choice of toasted sesame seeds, crisp fried shallots or sliced scallions, or all 3, to serve

Cooking the rice separately at first makes its second simmer shorter, keeping the flavors fresh and true but still allowing it time to break down slightly into a magnificent savory porridge. Swap in another sweet root such as celery root or parsnip for the carrot, if you like, or add a halved (boiled) or whole (fried or poached) egg on top. Use any tender Asian leaves here, or substitute watercress, spinach or young kale.

1 If you can, soak the rice in plenty of cool water for at least 4 hours or overnight. This will lessen the cooking time dramatically and make for a more porridge-like congee. Rinse the rice in a sieve held under cold running water. Drain well, transfer into a large saucepan and add 2⅓ cups (550 ml) cool water and a pinch of salt. Bring to a boil, cover with a lid—set very slightly ajar—and reduce the heat to low-ish. Cook for 35 minutes or so, until no liquid remains and the rice is extremely tender. Remove from the heat.

2 When the rice is nearly done, put the coconut oil, garlic, ginger, chile and turmeric, if using, in a large wok or saucepan. Set over high heat and stir-fry until the mixture begins to fizz, but not color. Once softened (about 30 seconds), add the carrot and mushrooms and stir-fry for a couple of minutes. Transfer the cooked rice into the wok, pour the stock over and bring to a boil. Adjust the heat to keep the mixture simmering merrily and leave to cook for 35 minutes or so, stirring occasionally. The rice should break down a little to form a porridge-like consistency, but it will take a long time to become completely smooth (so be aware if you want a smoother congee). Adjust the consistency as you wish: For a thicker result, continue to simmer; or add extra stock or water to thin the mixture down. When you are roughly happy with the consistency, add the greens and cook for 3 minutes. Remove from the heat and season with salt to taste.

3 Stir in the sesame oil and serve scattered with cilantro and your choice of sesame seeds, fried shallots or sliced scallions (or all 3).

chapter seven

raw-ish

THIS IS A CHAPTER OF sprightly recipes with pure, clean flavors. It relies heavily on fresh, often raw, vegetables, as well as seaweeds and naturally fermented foods. The hope is that they will make you feel well nourished and lively rather than weighed down, or—worse— hungry. Any dishes that are on the light side have made the cut because they possess natural health benefits and, most importantly, taste wonderful as they are, not because I tried to bend, strip or twist them to fit. In essence, this chapter isn't about denial; rather, it is about balance, big flavors and considered eating with health in mind. Many of the recipes are naturally gluten-free, if that's a consideration for you, while dairy is also a rarity. Lots of the food here—minus any eggs—happens to be vegan, too.

You will find cold-pressed oils, avocados, nuts and seeds used with a free hand, and I have tried, unlike in other chapters, not to roast the latter groups unless the recipe begged for a toasted flavor, keeping the ethos raw-ish. So-called "good fats" and natural oils are everywhere you look in fresh ingredients, making it easy to avoid the hydrogenated vegetable oils (sometimes incorrectly known as trans fats) found in store-bought cakes and cookies, ready-made meals and their ilk. When cheap oils are processed at high temperatures to prolong shelf life, they harden and are known to raise "bad" LDL or low density lipoprotein levels in the body. (Contrary to popular belief, it is the lipoproteins carrying cholesterol around our bloodstream, rather than the cholesterol itself, that possess the "good" or "bad" traits.)

The issue of saturated (solid at room temperature) versus unsaturated (liquid at room temperature) fat is less clear-cut. Saturated fat, found for example in dairy products and coconut oil, has been linked to high cholesterol, but that isn't necessarily a problem as the increase is due to raised levels of "good" HDL or high density lipoprotein carrying cholesterol around the body. Numerous studies have been unable to significantly link saturated fat to heart disease. Moreover, low-fat diets have been shown to cause no significant reduction in heart disease among healthy people, and, to add another twist, replacing saturated fats in the diet with vegetable oils has even been shown to increase the incidence of heart disease. Conclusion? Healthy people need to eat unsaturated and some saturated fat from natural sources, and to avoid processed oils and fats.

Natural fats will help you to feel satiated, as well as benefiting your body in myriad ways: balancing blood sugar levels and nourishing skin, hair and nails, for example. Use precious cold-pressed oils to drizzle and dip rather than to cook with, as heat destroys their antioxidant profiles and in most cases their flavors, too. I also use grass-fed butter to add rich flavor, but obviously that isn't an option for vegans. Hopefully, we have become less frightened of these good fats now that sugar is the devil du jour.

And what about sugar? Do we need to be *constantly* on guard against it? Well, no. Eating well, at least most of the time, can and should be simple. Personally, I choose to avoid the thickeners, emulsifiers or bulking agents that are usually present in low-fat and artificially flavored dairy products, in favor of unadulterated ingredients. In practice that means, say, passing over artificially thickened and low-fat yogurts to enjoy a spoonful or two of the natural, luscious and full-fat equivalent. On a similar note, I prefer to use a few crushed dates, fresh fruits, sweet vegetables or a spoonful of honey to sweeten where necessary, instead of relying on refined sugar. The exception that proves the rule—and one of the only instances, in fact, of its use in this whole book—being the kombucha tea recipe, where white sugar is essential to brew the probiotic tea simply and successfully at home.

To quite literally grow your own vitamins in concentrated form, try sprouting seeds or grains (see pages 232 to 233). These powerhouses require little more than a twice-daily rinse and a few days to grow, bringing texture and beauty to your plate. In this chapter, I also cover iodine- and umami-rich seaweeds, and fermented foods abundant in beneficial bacteria and flavor.

If you value exciting, fresh flavors, I'd urge you to gravitate toward cuisines and dishes that are naturally rich in vivid, fresh and often raw ingredients. Chase the sun to Asia. Southeast Asian food so frequently hits the vibrant notes that naturally healthy food needs to keep our interest. It is impossible to tire of those verdant herbs combined with contrasting textures and temperatures, light dressings and accents of chile heat.

Creating an authentic balance between salt, hot, sweet and sour, while also keeping an eye on the sugar content, is a challenge in Thai- and Vietnamese-style dressings, but there are ways around it. For instance, I find including a sweeter vegetable or fruit in a salad allows for a sharper dressing. Making sure there is a good amount of protein helps, too, as your body absorbs protein slowly and its presence—regardless of other ingredients—will help to prevent a spike in blood sugars.

I make no unscientific claims, in this chapter or elsewhere, about lemon juice detoxifying your body or the like. This is exciting, delicious and invigorating food. It just happens to be good for you.

A New Green Salad

Serves 4 to 6

- 1 large head soft, green lettuce
- 1 small head crunchy green lettuce, such as Cos or Little Gem, leaves separated
- Handful of peppery leaves such as frisée or wild arugula
- 1 cucumber, peeled, deseeded and sliced
- 2 ripe avocados, halved, pitted, peeled and cut into chunks
- Handful of soft seasonal herb leaves, any stalks removed
- 2 tablespoons mixed seeds (flax, pumpkin, sesame, sunflower seeds), toasted in a dry pan
- Handful of sprouts, such as alfalfa or purple radish
- One of the Four Essential Dressings (see page 221)

With a little care and forethought, a simple green salad can be exceptional. Think of this as a gentle reminder and guide, rather than an etched-in-stone recipe. Peppery, crunchy, soft and bitter leaves and herbs can be balanced to create interest, while crunchy vegetables, avocados, seeds and sprouts lend layers of substance. Vary the leaves all year round: In winter add delicate chicory, endive or dandelion greens; in summer, pea shoots.

1 Start by plunging the soft, crunchy and peppery leaves into a large bowl of ice water. Set aside for 5 to 10 minutes to crisp up, then drain thoroughly and spin the lettuce dry. If you don't own a salad spinner, put the leaves in a large kitchen towel, bring the edges together, go outside and whizz the towel in circles above your head for a minute.

2 Put the leaves in a serving bowl with the cucumber, avocados, herb leaves, toasted seeds and sprouts. Spoon the dressing over and toss lightly to coat every leaf. Serve immediately.

FOUR ESSENTIAL DRESSINGS

The combinations that follow—herb, yogurt, mustard and sesame-soy—will make easy dressings to fit most moods or ingredients. Each version will make enough to dress a salad or steamed vegetables for four to six people, depending on how generous you are with dressing. Do play with the sharp notes (vinegar) and any sweet elements (honey, sugar and so on), adjusting them to taste as you wish.

Herb

Serves 4 to 6

- Handful of soft herb leaves, such as basil, chervil chives, cilantro, dill or parsley, finely chopped
- 1 garlic clove, roughly chopped
- 1½ tablespoons cider vinegar
- 1 teaspoon Dijon mustard
- Pinch of unrefined sugar, if needed
- 5 to 6 tablespoons mild olive or canola oil
- Sea salt and freshly ground black pepper

Mustard

Serves 4 to 6

- 2 tablespoons red or white wine vinegar
- 1 tablespoon whole-grain mustard
- 1 to 2 teaspoons honey, to taste
- ¼ cup plus 2 tablespoons (90 ml) extra virgin olive oil
- Sea salt and freshly ground black pepper

Yogurt

Serves 4 to 6

- ¼ cup (60 g) mild plain yogurt
- ½ garlic clove, crushed
- 1 tablespoon finely chopped chive, cilantro or mint leaves, optional
- Squeeze of lemon juice
- 3 tablespoons olive oil
- Sea salt and freshly ground black pepper

Sesame-Soy

Serves 4 to 6

- 2 teaspoons finely grated fresh ginger root
- 1 small garlic clove, crushed
- 1 red or green chile, deseeded if you like, finely chopped
- 2 tablespoons light soy sauce
- 2 tablespoons toasted sesame oil
- 3 tablespoons peanut oil
- Sea salt and freshly ground black pepper

To make any of the 4 options, shake the ingredients together in a lidded jar to emulsify, adding 1 tablespoon of water to each. Alternatively, whisk everything together in a bowl with 1 tablespoon of water, adding the oil in a thin stream while whisking, and season to taste. The splash of water adds lightness.

In the case of the herb dressing, use a hand blender to blend the ingredients until smooth, if you like. You can then use this as a dip for crudités as well as a dressing.

Shaved Fennel Salad with Maple Dressing

Serves 4

A naturally sweet and crunchy salad without so much as a lettuce leaf in sight. It's a fabulous dish, popular with all, I find. If there was ever a time to buy a cheap Japanese-style mandoline (and a hand guard if you value your fingerprints), it would be to make this; the mandoline renders it very easy. Cooked and cooled spelt or farro grains go well here, folded through at the end. As does a slab of crumbled feta.

1 Halve the fennel bulbs and slice very finely using a mandoline or a sharp knife. Reserve any fennel fronds. Sweep the fennel slices into a bowl of ice water and set aside for 15 minutes to crisp up.

2 To make the dressing, shake all the ingredients together in a lidded jar with 1 tablespoon of water. Season to taste and adjust any of the components if you wish, remembering the apple and pecans are naturally sweet, so the dressing should be on the tart side.

3 Quarter and core the apples. Again, slice very finely with a mandoline or a sharp knife. Immediately toss with lemon juice to prevent browning. Finely shred the brussels sprouts and roughly shred the chicory heads.

4 Combine the drained fennel and sliced apple with the shredded sprouts, chicory and basil in a serving bowl. Chop any reserved fennel fronds and add these, too. Toss the dressing through and scatter with the crushed pecans to finish.

For the salad
- 2 large fennel bulbs, trimmed
- 2 dessert apples, such as Braeburn, Gala, Jonagold or Granny Smith
- Squeeze of lemon juice
- 2½ cups (200 g) trimmed brussels sprouts
- 2 heads red chicory or endive, trimmed
- Handful of Greek basil leaves, chopped (use Italian basil if Greek basil is not available)
- ½ cup (50 g) pecans, quite finely crushed

For the dressing
- ⅓ cup (75 ml) extra virgin olive oil or canola oil, or to taste
- 3 tablespoons red wine vinegar, or to taste
- 1 tablespoon maple syrup, or to taste
- 2 teaspoons whole-grain mustard, or to taste
- Sea salt and freshly ground black pepper

Puntarelle with a Black Olive Dressing

Serves 4

- 1 head puntarelle (see recipe introduction for substitutions)
- ½ head frisée
- 1 preserved lemon
- ¼ cup (60 ml) extra virgin olive oil
- 1¼ cups (150 g) pitted black olives
- 1 green chile, deseeded if you like, chopped
- 1 garlic clove, chopped
- Juice of 1 lemon
- Handful of flat-leaf parsley leaves, chopped
- Sea salt and freshly ground black pepper

Substitute shredded chicory or endive and fennel, or arugula and kohlrabi, for majestic Italian puntarelle, but it's worth buying if you see it. Look out for a large, chicory-like vegetable with whitish stems and flashes of green, jagged leaf. Inside these outer layers, the stumpy shoots are blanched white and crisp. For a more celebratory salad, serve a whole or—slightly less extravagantly—half burrata on each plate.

1 Trim the larger outer stems from the puntarelle, leaving the short, squat (and tender) stems in the center. You won't be using the outer leaves here, so save them for a stir-fry later. Cut or break the core up into single stems and slice these finely from top to bottom. Transfer to a bowl of ice water. Set aside for 40 minutes. The stems will curl up slightly. Drain and dry gently with a kitchen towel. Separate the frisée leaves, discarding any very dark or bitter outer leaves, then rinse and dry them.

2 To make the dressing, quarter the preserved lemon and slice the flesh and white pith away using a sharp knife. Roughly chop the rind and put it in the small bowl of a food processor. Add 2 tablespoons of water, the olive oil, one third of the olives, the chile and garlic. Blend, using the pulse button to roughly chop. Transfer to a bowl and stir in the lemon juice and parsley, seasoning with salt and pepper to taste. Arrange the puntarelle stems and frisée leaves on a large platter and spoon the dressing over. Toss through very gently to distribute evenly, then add the remaining olives.

Thai-Style Tofu Salad

Serves 2

Handfuls of summer herbs are one of my favorite salad ingredients, and a Thai-style recipe shows them off perfectly, making them a vital part rather than an accent. If you can't find Thai basil, use only cilantro and/or mint. By tamarind water, I mean the strained liquid from soaking one part seedless tamarind pulp in six parts boiling water. If you use jars of tamarind purée, dilute it with an equal amount of water.

For the dressing
- 2 or 3 green bird's eye chiles, thinly sliced
- 1 tablespoon palm sugar
- Juice of 1 lime
- 2 tablespoons tamarind water (see recipe introduction)
- 2 tablespoons Vegetarian "Fish" Sauce (page 300), or light soy sauce

For the salad
- 1 lemongrass stalk
- 1 fresh makrut lime leaf
- ½ cucumber
- 14 ounces (400 g) store-bought marinated tofu cubes (ideally those in tamari)
- 3 red Asian or regular shallots, thinly sliced
- Large handful of mixed cilantro, mint and Thai basil leaves
- 2 tablespoons unsalted peanuts, crushed

1 To make the dressing, pound the chiles and sugar with a mortar and pestle to form a rough paste. Stir in the lime juice, tamarind water and "fish" sauce and check the seasoning.

2 Remove the tough outer layers from the lemongrass stalk and finely chop the tender core, discarding the fibrous top part of the stalk. Roll the lime leaf into a cigar shape and slice into tiny shreds, avoiding the central stalk. Either shave the cucumber into wide ribbons with a vegetable peeler or slice it finely.

3 Toss the lemongrass, lime leaf, cucumber, tofu, shallots and herbs together in a bowl. Add the dressing and half the crushed peanuts, gently toss again and serve with the remaining crushed nuts scattered over.

Vietnamese Coconut and Pomelo Salad

Serves 3

For the dressing
- 1 tablespoon uncooked basmati rice
- ½ cup (60 g) chopped cashews
- 2 lemongrass stalks
- 3 tablespoons palm sugar or coconut sugar, or to taste
- 2 teaspoons peeled and finely chopped fresh ginger root
- 2 red chiles, finely chopped, or to taste
- ⅔ cup (160 ml) coconut milk
- 3 tablespoons Vegetarian "Fish" Sauce (page 300) or light soy sauce, or to taste
- Juice of 2 limes, or to taste

For the salad
- 1 large carrot, peeled
- ½ cucumber, peeled
- 1 pomelo or 2 large pink grapefruits
- ⅔ cup (50 g) unsweetened toasted coconut chips
- 2 Thai red shallots, halved and very finely sliced
- Large handful of mixed cilantro, mint and Thai basil leaves

The trouble and the beauty of East Asian salads lies in the preparation and, specifically, the chopping. The trick is to get the chopping done first, then make the dressing, concentrating on getting a good balance of hot, sweet, salty and sour. Putting the salad together then becomes a joy, and this one is particularly beautiful, with its luscious pomelo and a coconut dressing.

1 Start by making the dressing. Put the uncooked rice in a dry frying pan. Set it over medium heat and toast the rice, stirring, until it turns a pale golden color and smells nutty and fragrant. Transfer to a mortar and pestle and grind to a rough powder. Toast the chopped cashews in the same way, tossing the pan until they are burnished and fragrant. Transfer on to a plate.

2 Trim the woody ends from the lemongrass stalks and peel away the outer layers to reveal the softer core. Finely slice this.

3 Spoon the sugar into a frying pan with 2 tablespoons of water and place over medium heat. Once the sugar has dissolved and the pan begins to simmer briskly, add the chopped lemongrass, two thirds of the chopped cashews and the ginger and chiles. Continue to cook, without stirring, for a couple of minutes, then stir in the coconut milk and "fish" sauce. Simmer for a minute or so, then remove from the heat and stir in the lime juice. Taste the dressing. It should be hot, sweet, salty and sour and needs to pack quite a punch. Adjust the sugar, chile, "fish" sauce or lime juice to tweak it to your liking. Cover and set aside.

4 Use a vegetable peeler to pare the carrot into ribbons. Do the same with the cucumber, discarding the seedy, central core. Slice the top and bottom from the pomelo. Score it from top to bottom, then break it open, picking or peeling the pith and membrane away to reveal each clean segment. Break these into large pieces. If using grapefruit, use a sharp knife to pare off the skin, following the curve of the fruit to reveal the pink flesh. Cut between the membranes to release the segments. Either way, add the citrus to a bowl with the carrot and cucumber ribbons.

5 Throw in the coconut, shallots, herbs (reserving a few leaves) and the dressing. Toss to combine and pile onto serving plates. Finish with the remaining cashews, the toasted rice powder and reserved herb leaves.

Thistle Salad

Serves 4

For the dressing
- 3 tablespoons sunflower seeds
- Sea salt and freshly ground black pepper
- 1 garlic clove
- 1 shallot, finely chopped
- 1 tablespoon chopped tarragon leaves
- Juice of ½ lemon
- 1 teaspoon Dijon mustard
- ⅓ cup (75 ml) cold-pressed sunflower oil

For the salad
- 1 lemon, halved
- 14 ounces (400 g; about 10) tiny, tender artichokes
- 1 head romaine lettuce
- 4 fresh marigold flower heads, optional
- 3.5 ounces (100 g) hard goat cheese

To explain the name: Artichokes and sunflowers belong to the thistle family, which is a subfamily of asters, to which also belong lettuces and marigolds. It's a whimsical association but, regardless of name, this is a beautiful, light salad with a tarragon and toasted sunflower seed dressing. I have used tiny raw artichokes, but, outside their season, substitute store-bought marinated artichoke hearts to great effect.

1 To make the dressing, toast the sunflower seeds in a frying pan set over medium heat, shaking the pan often until the seeds are pale golden.

2 Add a good pinch of salt to a mortar and pestle with the whole garlic clove and crush to a paste. Add half the sunflower seeds and crush to a rough paste. Stir in the shallot, tarragon, lemon juice and mustard, then gradually whisk in the oil to make a dressing, seasoning with salt and pepper to taste and stirring in 1½ tablespoons water to lighten the texture.

3 For the salad, fill a bowl with cold water and squeeze the lemon juice in, dropping in the empty lemon halves.

4 Peel or snap the outer petals from the artichokes, paring any tough customers away with a knife. Slice off the tops of the leaves, leaving only tender parts behind. The artichokes should be too young to have formed any bristly choke. Peel and trim the stalks and pop the prepared artichokes into the lemon water bowl to stop any blackening. When they are all trimmed, drain the artichokes and dry with a kitchen towel. Using a mandoline or very sharp knife, finely slice the artichokes.

5 Trim the base of the romaine lettuce and thickly shred the head. Toss the artichoke slices with the lettuce in a serving bowl. Pull the petals from the marigold heads, if using, and toss most of them through the salad with the dressing. Shave the goat cheese over with a vegetable peeler and scatter with the reserved sunflower seeds and more marigold petals to finish.

Fresh Cheeses with Flowers and Herbs

Makes 6

- 42 ounces (1.2 kg) Greek yogurt
- 1 garlic clove, crushed
- Finely grated zest of 1 unwaxed lemon, optional
- Handful of parsley, chive or chervil leaves, chopped
- Sea salt
- Soft herbs, leaves and edible flowers, to serve, such as borage, chives, garlic chives or wild garlic, pea shoots and flowers, roses, sweet cicely, thyme . . .
- Cold-pressed oil, to serve

Once these tangy and fresh yogurt cheeses are made, they can be stored in an airtight container, submerged in good olive oil. Covered and chilled, they will keep for up to three weeks. Save the drained, slightly acidic whey from the first straining step to make Dill-Pickled Green Beans (page 241). Serve them with a selection of antipasti or good bread.

1 Line a very large sieve or colander with a square of muslin or cheesecloth. Spoon in the yogurt, set over a large bowl and chill for about 16 hours. Gather the cloth up every now and then and give the bag a squeeze to encourage it to drain. The yogurt should reduce in volume drastically.

2 Transfer the strained yogurt into a large mixing bowl and fold in the garlic, lemon zest, if using, and chopped herbs. Add a generous pinch of salt and taste, adding more seasoning if you wish, though remember the yogurt will lose more volume and all the flavors will concentrate as it does so.

3 Line six 5-ounce (150 ml) ramekins or dessert molds with squares of muslin or cheesecloth. The fabric squares should be large enough to generously overhang the molds, ready to fold back over the tops of the cheeses with room to spare. Spoon the herb-flecked cheese into the lined molds. Fold the excess fabric over and weigh each mold down with a heavy object such as a potato or a jar. Set aside in a cool place for at least an hour or overnight to firm up as much as you would like. Turn the delicate cheeses out and unwrap the damp muslin or cheesecloth.

4 Serve the cheeses with herbs, leaves and edible flowers and cold-pressed oil.

Grated Brassica and Date Salad

Serves 4

- 1 largish cauliflower
- 1 small head broccoli
- 4 ounces (120 g) kale (about 6 or 7 leaves), coarse stalks removed
- ½ cup (90 g) pitted Medjool dates
- ⅓ cup (60 g) sesame seeds
- 3 tablespoons mild canola oil
- 1 tablespoon light soy sauce
- 1 tablespoon toasted sesame oil
- Juice of 2 limes
- Sea salt and freshly ground black pepper
- 4 scallions, trimmed and sliced
- 1 red chile, deseeded and chopped
- ½ pomegranate, seeds only

t's no secret that the plants of the brassica family are all incredibly good for you, but to make them easy to eat raw, a bit of care is needed at the cutting stage, as I detail below. I know it's hard to imagine greatness from a glance at the ingredients list, but this is a beautiful, simple recipe, well worth making. It goes well with salty fried or grated halloumi or salted ricotta, if you need an extra element.

1 Use a box grater to grate the outer parts of the cauliflower and broccoli florets, shaving the crowns down a bit in the process. Now go in with a sharp knife or a mandoline, if you have one, taking your time to finely slice the remaining florets and any tender stalks.

2 Stack a couple of kale leaves up and roll into a cigar. Slice very finely, avoiding any remaining stalk, to create thin shreds. Repeat with the rest of the kale. Put all the prepared vegetables in a large serving bowl.

3 Chop the dates.

4 To make the dressing, put half the chopped dates in a powerful blender or mini food processor with 1 tablespoon of the sesame seeds, the canola oil, soy sauce, toasted sesame oil and lime juice. Give it a good blend to make a smoothish paste, then add 3 tablespoons of water and blend again. You should have a dressing with the texture of heavy cream. Season lightly with salt and pepper.

5 Toss the dressing through the bowl of brassicas; the easiest way to do this properly is with clean hands. Don't be too dainty about it; you can afford to bruise the kale a bit. Add the remaining dates, remaining sesame seeds, the scallions, chile and pomegranate seeds. Toss through to finish.

Raw Salad of Jerusalem Artichokes with Walnuts

Serves 3 to 4

- 1 lemon, halved
- 6 large Jerusalem artichokes (sunchokes)
- 8 ounces (225 g) pole or runner beans
- 2 yellow zucchini
- Sea salt and freshly ground black pepper
- 2 tablespoons red wine vinegar
- 1 teaspoon Dijon mustard
- 1 teaspoon mild honey
- 2 tablespoons chopped chives
- 1 garlic clove, crushed
- 2 tablespoons mild canola oil
- 2 tablespoons walnut oil
- 1 cup (100 g) sprouts, such as alfalfa, lentil or chickpea
- ⅓ cup (50 g) walnut halves, crushed

t's far more common to see Jerusalem artichokes—or sunchokes—in cooked form, but they make an elegant salad, especially with this gentle walnut dressing. Be sure to slice them very finely and immediately soak in a lemon-water bath to crisp up. A mandoline will do you great service here, but you can get the same effect with a sharp knife and nifty skills.

1 Fill a bowl with cold water and squeeze the lemon juice in, then drop in the empty lemon halves.

2 Peel the Jerusalem artichokes with a vegetable peeler. Using a mandoline if you have one, or a very sharp knife and some patience if you don't, slice them paper-thin. Put them in the lemon water as you slice to firm them up and keep them from oxidizing.

3 Trim the pole beans, removing any strings from their edges, and cut them in half across their middles. Cut as thinly as you can from top to bottom to make shred-like slices.

4 If you have a shredder tool, use it to shred the zucchini. Otherwise, use a grater. Scatter lightly with salt and set aside for 5 minutes, then squeeze the shreds or gratings out in a kitchen towel to remove excess water.

5 To make the dressing, mix the vinegar, mustard, honey, chives and garlic in a bowl. Whisk in the oils with 1 tablespoon of water until well combined. Season generously with salt and pepper.

6 Drain the artichokes and combine with the pole beans, zucchini and sprouts in a large bowl. Toss the dressing through the salad with the crushed walnuts and serve immediately.

SPROUTING AND HOW TO DO IT

Diminutive and delicate they may be, but sprouts contain huge quantities of essential nutrients, including vitamin C, magnesium and chlorophyll, which promotes calcium absorption. They are also rich in the nourishing enzymes we rely on to metabolize food and assimilate energy. In short, they are one of the most nutritious and complete foods . . . and incredibly easy to grow.

There are other benefits besides: For the cook, there is no greater boon than natural flavor, and sprouts deliver that in spades, from soft and fragrant to spicy and peppery. The nature of a seed or a full-grown plant is a good clue to the taste of its sprout. For example, in sprouted form, peppery radish or curried fenugreek taste as you might imagine, but fresher, greener and more concentrated. Perfect for scattering over salads and dips, as you might herbs; you won't get a shorter harvest-to-plate time.

There is no need for any equipment, space, soil, or fuss and the results are swift; all sprouts need to grow is a few minutes of daily attention.

WHAT, AND HOW MUCH, TO SOAK IN EACH BATCH

SMALL SEEDS: Soak for 8 hours, sprout for 1 to 2 days. Use 2 to 3 tablespoons of alfalfa, broccoli, fenugreek, mustard, radish, sesame, watercress and so on.

GRAINS AND SMALL PULSES: Soak for 12 hours, sprout for 2 to 3 days. Use ⅓ cup (75 g) whole lentils, mung beans, oat groats, quinoa, wheat grains and so on.

LARGE LEGUMES AND NUTS: Soak for 24 hours, sprout for 2 to 5 days. Use 1½ cups (200 g) almonds, chickpeas, dried beans, peas, peanuts and so on.

SUNFLOWER SEEDS (PROLIFIC AND EASY): Soak for 8 hours, sprout for 1 to 3 days. Use 3 cups (400 g).

HOW TO DO IT

1 Put your chosen seeds in a large wide-mouthed glass jar (2 if you are sprouting lots of sunflower seeds) and cover with plenty of cold water.

2 After the soaking time, firmly secure a piece of muslin, cheesecloth or gauze, or a cut-up pair of tights, over the top of the jar with a rubber band. The material must be

loosely woven to allow the air to circulate freely, otherwise you risk the dreaded mold.

3 Invert the jar and drain the water away.

4 Prop the jar up at a 45-degree angle, opening-end down and with a tray underneath to catch any drips. Leave in a cool place, out of direct sunlight. The seeds should now be evenly spread out down one side of the jar.

5 Twice a day, rinse the jar out with clean, cool water and return it to its angled position with the material or tights resecured over its mouth. This rinsing will keep the sprouts fresh.

6 Depending on your seeds, shoots can start to grow in as little as one day. Do keep rinsing and swirling them with cool water twice every day to keep them fresh as they grow.

7 Refrigerate the finished sprouts whenever you like the look and taste of them (too long at the growing stage can make them bitter, so be aware) and enjoy over the next couple of days on soups, salads and dips, or in sandwiches, or juices.

Shaved Beets with Sprouts, Kefir and Dukkah

Serves 4 as a starte

For the salad
- 16 small, mixed-colored beets, scrubbed, leaves trimmed off (any tender young leaves reserved)
- 1 garlic clove, skin on
- 3 sprigs of thyme
- Handful of sprouts or microherbs
- Handful of young beet or chard leaves

For the dukkah
- 2 tablespoons sesame seeds (I used black and white)
- 1½ tablespoons coriander seeds
- 1½ tablespoons cumin seeds
- 1 tablespoon blanched hazelnuts
- 1 tablespoon mixed seeds (flax, pumpkin, sesame, sunflower seeds . . .)
- Pinch of dried thyme
- Sea salt and freshly ground black pepper

For the dressing
- ¼ cup (60 ml) kefir
- 2 tablespoons extra virgin olive oil
- 1 tablespoon lemon juice
- 1 teaspoon blossom honey

Raw beet, so mesmerizingly beautiful when in candy-striped form, is, I think, most enjoyable when sliced wafer-thin or grated. This elegant salad combines delicate, uncooked shavings with sweetly roasted beets, seeded dukkah and a mild kefir dressing. Substitute buttermilk or even thin yogurt for the kefir, if you prefer.

1 Preheat the oven to 375°F (190°C). Put 8 of the freshly washed beets in the center of a large square of foil. Add the garlic and thyme and bring the foil up, scrunching the edges together to form a loose, tightly-sealed package. Place on a baking sheet and cook for 40 minutes, until the beets are tender to the point of a knife. Leave to cool slightly before peeling them—the skin will just rub off—and cutting them in halves or quarters, depending on size (reserve the garlic clove). It's nice to chop the odd beet here, too, to add more interest and texture to the finished salad.

2 To make the dukkah, toast the sesame seeds, coriander seeds, cumin seeds, and hazelnuts in a dry frying pan over medium heat, until fragrant, then let cool. Either roughly pound with a mortar and pestle, or pulse very briefly in a food processor, to make a coarsely ground mix. Toast the mixed seeds separately, until fragrant, then stir into the mix with the dried thyme and a pinch of salt.

3 Slice the remaining beets into very thin rounds of ¹⁄₁₆-inch (1 to 2 mm) thickness. The best way to do this is with a mandoline, but a very sharp knife or the slicing attachment of a food processor will also work well.

4 Mash the roasted garlic in a small bowl and whisk in the remaining dressing ingredients. Season well. Kefirs vary in consistency, so add 1 tablespoon of water to the dressing to loosen it, if yours was on the thicker side.

5 Toss the cooked and raw beets together with the sprouts and beet leaves. Arrange on serving plates, spoon the dressing over and finish with a scattering of dukkah.

FERMENTING

In simple terms, fermentation describes the conversion of carbohydrates—namely sugars—into alcohol and acid. For many Westerners, a certain squeamishness persists toward the bacteria facilitating this conversion, and no wonder when the wrong sort can do us great harm. So-called "good" strains of bacteria are essential to our health, however, even if we are not aware of them. If we drink wine, eat yogurt or olives, soy sauce, tempeh or kimchi, to name a few examples, we will be ingesting *Lactobacillus acidophilus*, the good bacteria needed to enable our bodies to minimize inflammation, produce vitamin K2 (essential for cardiovascular health) and assimilate energy, among other things.

Kimchi, the fiery-sour, pungent Korean pickle, is a perfect introduction to fermenting at home, because it's almost impossible to get wrong. It's an example of lactic fermentation, where bacteria convert the sugar in vegetables into lactic acid, which acts as a preservative. And the results are delicious. Start with my Ruby Red Kimchi (page 240). If you are timid, keep the fermentation levels low by refrigerating your jar and eat the kimchi as a pickle. It will still be terrific. Once you get into the swing of it, you can experiment with other vegetables and a slower fermentation to develop complex flavors. Kombucha, a fermented, flavored tea, is a slightly more advanced project, but not hard; it just needs more attention to create the ideal environment for the culture to flourish (page 242).

Aside from all the health benefits, the range of fermented foods available to us either to buy or make will add untold interest to your cooking. Most are complex in flavor, adding depth to the simplest dishes. Miso, for example, the rich and salty paste made from fermented soybeans, can be found in myriad incarnations, from sweet and mellow white through to deep, sharp rusty red. It is an excellent vegan source of umami in soups, sauces and relishes; a mere spoonful adds a barely perceptible accent.

A note or two on fermenting at home: Sterilization and cleanliness are essential to prevent unwanted strains of bacteria multiplying, so make sure all (heatproof) containers and lids are put through the hot wash of a dishwasher, or washed in hot, soapy water and dried out in a low oven. Secondly, if a recipe calls for water, use bottled mineral or filtered water, as the chlorine in tap water will inhibit fermentation. Fermentation will be more successful and resonant if it happens slowly, at cool room temperatures, so don't be tempted to rush things along in a hot room. This is slow food from a forgotten time, after all. Beyond these simple pointers, the possibilities are endless, so go forth and multiply. . . .

Raw Summer Rolls with Tempeh

Makes 12

For the tempeh and dipping sauce

- ⅓ cup (60 g) unsalted peanuts
- 7 ounces (200 g) tempeh
- 1- to 1½-inch (2.5 to 4 cm) piece fresh ginger root
- 1 large red chile
- ¼ cup (60 ml) tamari or light soy sauce, or to taste
- 2 teaspoons palm sugar or light brown sugar, or to taste
- 1 tablespoon peanut oil
- Juice of 2 small limes
- 2 tablespoons toasted sesame oil

To assemble

- 1 avocado, halved, pitted and peeled
- 4 scallions
- 12 large round rice paper wrappers
- Handful of bean sprouts
- Handful of shiso leaves
- Handful each of Thai basil and cilantro leaves
- Handful of sprouts or microherbs, such as alfalfa or cilantro
- 1 small container of mustard cress, snipped

When tempeh is perked up with a simple marinade, a rainbow of fragrant accompaniments and buttery avocado, its pleasingly sour flavor comes into its own. You could, of course, substitute its marinated or smoked cousin, tofu, if you want. Shiso, a heart-shaped, frilly-edged leaf often served with sushi, is a revelation: peppery and perfumed. The world won't end if you can't find it; just increase the other herbs.

1 Preheat the oven to 375°F (190°C). Spread the peanuts out on a baking sheet and roast for 6 to 8 minutes, until golden brown. Cool slightly, then crush or chop quite finely.

2 Slice the tempeh into chubby matchsticks. Peel and finely grate the ginger and finely chop the chile, deseeding it first, if you like.

3 Combine the tempeh in a bowl with half the ginger, half the chile, half the tamari and a pinch of the sugar, mixing to evenly blend it with the flavorings. If time allows, leave to marinate for at least 30 minutes or—covered and in the fridge—for up to 2 days.

4 Heat the peanut oil in a large frying pan over high heat. Sear the tempeh pieces on all sides, turning with tongs, until golden all around. Set aside.

5 Combine the remaining ginger, chile, tamari and sugar with all but 1 teaspoon of the lime juice, the sesame oil and a splash of water to make a dipping sauce. Taste and adjust the sugar, lime or soy sauce, if needed.

6 Slice the avocado into chubby matchsticks and toss with the reserved 1 teaspoon of lime juice to prevent browning. Trim the scallions and slice them finely lengthwise.

7 Fill a large bowl with lukewarm water, dip a rice paper round into the water, turning it until just soft enough to bend without cracking, then shaking off the excess. Lay the pliable rice paper flat on a clean, damp kitchen towel. If you can, work with 2 or even 3 dipped wrappers at a time to make the rolling process quicker. Either way, have all the filling ingredients prepared and close at hand.

recipe continues . . .

8 At the end of the rice paper round nearest to you, arrange a couple of avocado sticks, some sliced scallion, bean sprouts, shiso leaves and other soft herbs, sprouts and cress. Top with a couple of pieces of tempeh and a pinch of crushed peanuts. The total volume should be about 2 tablespoons or so; any more and you risk overfilling and splitting the rice paper.

9 Fold in the left and right vertical sides to cover the ends of the line of filling and roll the rice paper up from the base, taking the filling with it, to form a squat, tight, sealed cylinder. Set aside and cover loosely with a damp cloth to stop the finished rolls drying out. Repeat with the remaining ingredients.

10 Eat immediately or store in an airtight container in the fridge for up to 4 hours. Serve with the dipping sauce and the remaining peanuts, the idea being to dip into the sauce then into the crushed nuts before eating.

Ruby Red Kimchi

Makes 1 large jar

- ½ small head red cabbage
- ¼ head napa cabbage
- 2 tablespoons sea salt
- About 2 quarts (2 L) bottled mineral water (see note on page 236)
- 3 tablespoons tamari sauce
- 2 teaspoons Korean red pepper powder (gochugaru)
- 1-inch (2.5 cm) piece fresh ginger root, peeled and finely grated
- 2 garlic cloves, crushed
- 3 scallions, finely chopped
- ½ teaspoon kombu seaweed flakes, optional
- ½ apple, grated
- 1 small carrot, shredded

This is a full-flavored kimchi, with the addition of inauthentic apple instead of added sugar. I've given you two choices here for the fermentation, one for old hands and also a beginner's introduction. Buy the sweet, smoky, hot Korean red pepper powder from East Asian food shops or online. It is essential for kimchi, though you could try using chile flakes and a whisper of hot smoked paprika, I suppose.

1 It is extremely important to start with a sterilized jar. Either put a large (at least 1½ quart/1.5 L, preferably larger) jar and lid through the hot cycle of a dishwasher, or wash both in hot soapy water and dry out in a low oven.

2 Core and chop the red and napa cabbage into bite-size shreds. Toss with the salt in a large bowl, using clean or plastic-gloved hands to really work the salt into the leaves. Add ¾ cup (200 ml) of the bottled water and set aside for 20 minutes; it will become crisp. Drain in a colander and rinse well with bottled water. Drain again and pat dry with a kitchen towel.

3 Combine the tamari, gochugaru, ginger, garlic and scallions in a mixing bowl, including the kombu flakes if you want to increase the umami flavor. Add 1 tablespoon more of the bottled water and mix well, followed by the cabbage, apple and carrot, tossing and "massaging" to mix through. Leave for 5 minutes, mix again, then transfer to the sterilized jar; it should not come right to the top, to allow room for carbon dioxide to form. Cover with the lid—barely screwed on—and leave at room temperature for 1 to 2 days to allow to ferment slightly and develop in flavor.

4 You should see little bubbles at the top of the jar. Taste and see if it is to your liking; it should be pleasantly sour and smell very strong (but not repugnant). You can leave it to ferment for a further 2 to 3 days to increase that sour fermented flavor but, if this is your first time making it, I would screw the lid on tightly and chill the jar at this point to slow the fermentation. Ideally, chill the kimchi for 5 days to allow the flavors to develop, though you can use it immediately if you are impatient.

5 When you are happy with the flavor, keep the kimchi jar covered and chilled. It will last for several months and will mellow and settle, but if you develop a habit of adding it to any noodle bowl/rice/salad/sandwich/stir-fry/soup, a single jar is unlikely to last very long at all.

Dill-Pickled Green Beans

Makes one 24-ounce (600 ml) jar

- 6 ounces (175 g) very fresh green beans
- 1 banana shallot or large shallot, sliced
- 1 garlic clove, sliced
- 1 teaspoon black peppercorns
- 4 sprigs of dill
- 2 slices of bird's eye chile
- 1⅔ cups (400 ml) bottled mineral water (see note on page 236) or as needed
- ¼ cup (60 ml) whey (see recipe introduction)
- 1 tablespoon sea salt

Pickles don't have to be sugar-laden. This naturally fermented recipe uses the whey drained from yogurt after straining to make cheeses or ice creams. You can replace it with a scant tablespoon of salt and a little extra water, but the pickles might need a couple more days fermenting. These are good with fried eggs and polenta, or in a salad with feta, roasted squash and lima beans.

1 Slice off the hard ends of the beans, then cut them into roughly 2-inch (5 cm) lengths. Blanch them in boiling water for 2½ to 3 minutes, or until only just tender. Drain and refresh under cool water (to be really fussy, use bottled water to refresh rather than tap water, but this isn't strictly necessary here).

2 Put the beans in a sterilized 24-ounce (600 ml) lidded jar (see step 1 opposite), layering them up with the shallot and garlic slices, peppercorns and sprigs of dill. Tuck in the chile slices to finish.

3 Mix the bottled water, whey and sea salt in a large container, stirring well. Pour into the jar, stirring the container as you do so to make sure any undissolved salt is evenly distributed in the liquid. Make sure there is a gap of 1 to 1½ inches (3 cm) between the top of the liquid and the jar lid and that the vegetables are completely covered. Screw the lid on tightly and shake well.

4 Leave the jar in a very cool, dark place for 7 days, then unscrew the lid and reseal, to release any gases. Leave for a further 3 to 5 days before eating. At this point, the bean jar should be transferred to the fridge, where the pickles will continue to ferment at a much slower rate. Eat them up within a month.

Kombucha

Makes 1 large jar

- 6 best-quality green, black or white tea bags
- ¾ cup (175 g) granulated sugar (essential for the scoby to brew)
- 1 medium, fresh scoby (see recipe introduction)
- Assorted flavorings, optional (see recipe method)

The kombucha culture—known as a scoby—that you need to brew this flavored, naturally fermented tea is a bizarre-looking slimy disc. I bought mine online and followed the accompanying instructions pretty closely. They recommended starting with just one small glassful of the probiotic tea each day, until your body is used to it. Use nonmetallic utensils to handle kombucha, as metal can affect the brew.

1 Put the tea bags and sugar in a large, very clean (ideally sterilized, see note on page 236) jar or similar container (2¼-quart/2.2 L minimum capacity). Bring 7½ cups (1.8 L) of water to a boil and pour on to the tea. Stir, leave for 30 minutes, then remove the tea bags with a spatula. Leave until just cool. Add the scoby and place a square of muslin or kitchen towel over the jar opening to cover, tying it in place with a rubber band. Leave in a warm room out of direct sunlight—an airing pantry or warm kitchen at a constant 68 to 73°F (20 to 23°C) is ideal—for 6 to 10 days to brew. Mine took 6 days and I started tasting it after 4 days (removing a little with a plastic ladle), replacing the muslin or towel each time. The tea is slightly cloudy and tastes pleasantly fruity or fizzy.

2 Pour it into a large container and chill to all-but-halt fermentation, leaving enough behind after transferring to cover the scoby. I find it easier to put the scoby in a holding bay of a smaller container with about ¾ cup (200 ml) of his brew while I make another batch in the jar, re-adding him and his brew to the new, cooled tea to continue the cycle. You may even get kombucha babies growing after a few cycles; these can be used to start their own teas, so you can have various flavors going at any one time. If you don't want to brew again immediately, the scoby—in his brew-bath—can be covered for a couple of days without any harm, before you start again.

3 Your chilled, slightly fizzy tea can be bottled up (keep it chilled) and enjoyed plain, but I prefer to infuse it. My favorite flavorings are:

> 7 ounces (about 1¼ dry pints/200 g) fresh, ripe berries, slightly crushed
> 2 ripe peaches, chopped, with 1 split vanilla pod
> 1 cup (200 g) ripe chopped pineapple, with 2 bruised makrut lime leaves
> 1 ripe pear, chopped, with 2 tablespoons finely grated fresh ginger root

Add your chosen aromatics to the tea and chill for 2 to 3 days to infuse. Strain before drinking, bottle up if you like and keep chilled.

Miso Soup with Dulse and Winter Vegetables

Serves 2

- 2 leeks, trimmed
- 1 tablespoon unsalted butter
- 1 celery stalk, finely sliced
- 1-inch (2.5 cm) piece fresh ginger root, bruised
- 1 red chile, slit open
- 1 fresh bay leaf
- 1 parsnip, scrubbed
- 1 sweet potato, peeled
- 2½ cups (600 ml) weak vegetable stock
- ¼ sweetheart (pointed or hispi) cabbage, thickly sliced
- Small handful of shredded dulse seaweed
- 1 tablespoon yellow miso paste (a mellow one)
- 1 tablespoon mirin, or to taste

A very simple soup to reset your inner balance in cold weather, proving once again that comfort food doesn't have to be laden with bread and molten cheese, though it often helps. . . . Butter adds rich flavor but is easily swapped for a flavorless oil, or coconut oil if you like the taste.

1 Finely slice the white and light green parts of the leeks only. Rinse to remove any grit and drain well. Melt the butter in a medium saucepan set over low-ish heat and add the leeks, celery, bruised ginger, slit chile and bay leaf. Cook for a few minutes, stirring, then cover and leave to braise for 5 minutes or so.

2 Meanwhile, chop the parsnip and sweet potato into smallish cubes. Uncover the pan and stir them in with the stock. Bring to a boil, then reduce the heat to a gentle simmer and partially cover, adding the cabbage after 10 minutes. Cook for 5 minutes more, until the vegetables are soft.

3 Remove the bay, chile and ginger with a slotted spoon; they have done their job now. Stir in the seaweed and leave to soften for a few seconds, then add the miso to cloud the broth, seasoning with the mirin. Taste and add more mirin if it needs more sweetness to balance it (this will depend on the sharpness of your miso). Ladle into 2 large bowls and serve.

Spiced Turmeric Broth with Roasted Vegetables

Serves 4

- 6 small carrots, scrubbed and thickly sliced if on the larger side
- 2 parsnips, scrubbed and thickly sliced
- 1 small celery root, peeled and roughly chopped
- Sea salt and freshly ground black pepper
- 3 tablespoons coconut oil
- 1-inch (2.5 cm) piece fresh ginger root
- 1-inch (2.5 cm) piece fresh turmeric
- Small handful of cilantro with roots
- 2 shallots, finely sliced
- 1 teaspoon black mustard seeds
- 1 garlic clove, finely chopped
- 1 sprig of fresh curry leaves
- 3 green cardamom pods, lightly crushed
- 1 dried red chile
- ¾ cup (200 ml) coconut cream
- Juice of ½ lime
- 1 cup (200 g) cooked wild rice
- Red amaranth greens or other herbs to serve, optional

find this very special bowl, a fragrant curry of sorts, is the vegetarian equivalent of a chicken noodle soup, both for comfort and health benefits. Add more coconut cream or milk if you would like more of a soup-y feel; the recipe here provides more of a sauce at the base of the bowl. Curry leaves can be tricky to find fresh, but are transformative; try Asian food shops, large supermarkets and the Internet.

1 Preheat the oven to 400°F (200°C). Spread the root vegetables out in a large roasting pan, season well with salt and pepper and crumble 2 tablespoons of the coconut oil over them (or pour, if it is warm and liquid). Roast for 15 minutes, then use a spatula to toss the vegetables, distributing the melted oil evenly. Return to the oven for a further 15 minutes or so, until soft and caramelized.

2 Meanwhile, peel and finely chop the ginger and turmeric. Finely chop the cilantro roots and stalks. Set the cilantro leaves aside.

3 Put the remaining 1 tablespoon of coconut oil in a deep frying pan or medium saucepan and set it over medium-low heat. Add the shallots with a pinch of salt and fry gently for a few minutes, stirring now and then. Increase the heat and cook until they are beginning to catch at the edges, then add the mustard seeds and cook for a minute or two; they should pop and sizzle. Add the ginger, turmeric, cilantro roots and stalks, garlic, curry leaves, cardamom and dried chile, sautéing for 2 to 3 minutes. Stir in the coconut cream with ¾ cup (200 ml) water, bring to a boil, then reduce the heat and simmer gently for 10 minutes. Season with salt and pepper and add the lime juice to brighten the flavors.

4 Divide the roasted vegetables between serving bowls with the cooked wild rice. Ladle the broth over the top and finish with the cilantro leaves and any other Asian herbs you have, such as red amaranth or Thai basil.

Winter Rolls

Makes 10

- 12 ounces (350 g) sweet potato
- 2 tablespoons peanut oil
- Sea salt and freshly ground black pepper
- 2 tablespoons black or white sesame seeds
- 2 cups (150 g) sliced button mushrooms
- 1-inch (2.5 cm) piece fresh ginger root, peeled and grated
- 1 red chile, finely chopped
- 1 tablespoon tamari or light soy sauce
- 20 tender, palm-size kale leaves
- Handful of bean sprouts
- Handful of sprigs of cilantro
- 10 large round rice paper wrappers
- ½ batch Caramelized Peanut Sauce (page 305)

Colorful rolls filled with chile-ginger seared mushrooms, roasted sweet potato spears and raw kale. If you don't want to make the satay-style sauce, just mix a quick, cool dip from lime juice, tamari sauce and a touch of palm sugar or maple syrup to take the edge off. Stir in chopped chile or grated fresh ginger root. If you can find or grow them (see pages 232 to 233), sunflower sprouts are delicious in place of the bean sprouts.

1 Preheat the oven to 425°F (220°C). Peel the sweet potato and slice into chubby fries. Toss with half the oil, season with salt and pepper and lay out on a baking sheet. Roast for 15 minutes, then scatter with the sesame seeds and roast for 5 minutes more, until just tender. Set aside to cool.

2 Put the remaining oil in a large frying pan set over high heat. Add the mushrooms and cook, stirring, until any liquid evaporates and they start to sear. Add the ginger and chile and cook for a minute. Add the tamari, cook for a few seconds, then remove from the heat.

3 Trim the stalks from the kale and pile on a large baking sheet with the sweet potato, mushrooms, bean sprouts and cilantro, all laid out in piles.

4 Fill a large bowl with lukewarm water, dip a rice paper round into the water, turning it until just soft enough to bend without cracking, then shaking off the excess. Lay the pliable rice paper flat on a clean, damp kitchen towel. If you can, work with 2 or even 3 dipped wrappers at a time to make the rolling process quicker. Have the tray of fillings close at hand.

5 Lay 2 kale leaves on each soaked rice paper round and, concentrating on the end of the rice paper nearest to you, lay a few sweet potato sticks on top, followed by a spoonful of mushrooms, a few bean sprouts and a couple of sprigs of cilantro. The total volume should be about 2 tablespoons or so; any more and you risk overfilling and splitting the rice paper.

6 Fold in the left and right vertical sides to cover the ends of the line of filling and roll the rice paper up from the base, taking the filling with it, to form a squat, tight, sealed cylinder. Set aside and cover loosely with a damp cloth to keep the finished rolls from drying out. Repeat with the remaining ingredients. Eat immediately with the peanut sauce, or store in an airtight container in the fridge for up to 4 hours.

Almond-Stuffed Vine Leaves

Serves 4 / Makes 20 to 24

For the stuffed vine leaves
- 1¼ cups (150 g) whole almonds (skins on)
- About 24 large vine leaves, fresh or brined
- ¼ cup (30 g) pine nuts
- 4 cups (400 g) cauliflower florets
- 1 garlic clove, crushed
- Finely grated zest and juice of 1 unwaxed lemon
- ½ teaspoon ground cinnamon
- Small handful of dill fronds
- Small handful of mint leaves
- Sea salt and freshly ground black pepper
- 3 tablespoons extra virgin olive oil, or to taste
- ⅓ cup (50 g) golden raisins

For the salsa
- 10.5 ounces (300 g) ripe tomatoes
- ⅓ cup (50 g) pitted green olives
- 1 shallot, finely chopped
- Extra virgin olive oil

A grape vine rampages across the top of my garden, a happy inheritance from owners past, so I've a ready supply of grape leaves to stuff. Packs of preserved vine leaves will work just as well in this raw spin on dolmades, or you could use any soft lettuce leaf or tender cabbage or kale leaf instead. This is a lovely little recipe, set off by a simple tomato salsa to spoon over the vine leaf cigars as you eat.

1 Put the almonds in a heatproof bowl. Boil a kettle and pour enough hot water over the almonds to cover. Set aside for 20 minutes. (If you have time, soak the almonds in cool water for 6 hours instead.)

2 Rinse and drain the vine leaves. Put them in a saucepan and cover with just-boiled water. Simmer over low heat for 3 to 4 minutes, then drain and refresh under cool water.

3 Put the pine nuts in a small frying pan set over medium heat. Toast, stirring often, until pale golden all over. Let cool.

4 Drain the almonds thoroughly and put in a food processor with the cauliflower, garlic, lemon zest and half the juice, the cinnamon, dill and two thirds of the mint. Season well with salt and pepper and pour in about 3 tablespoons of olive oil. Blend until evenly and very finely chopped. Add the raisins and blend briefly again to chop slightly. Transfer into a bowl and stir in the toasted pine nuts.

5 Lay a drained vine leaf out on a chopping board, veiny side up (shiny side down) and cut out the coarse lower part of the stalk, leaving the leaf as intact as possible. Place a scant 1 tablespoon of filling on the base of the leaf, fold in both sides and roll away from you firmly to create a neatly plump cigar. It gets easier with practice. Repeat to make 20 to 24 rolls, transferring them to a platter as you work.

6 Chop the tomatoes and green olives quite finely (you can do this in a food processor, but it will inevitably make the salsa more watery) and scoop into a bowl. Finely chop the reserved mint leaves and stir into the tomatoes with the shallot, remaining lemon juice and a generous drizzle of olive oil. Serve alongside, or spooned over, the vine leaf cigars.

Summer Herb Broth with Cannellini and Pistou

Serves 4

A gentle, uncomplicated and nourishing soup to showcase the best summer herbs and vegetables. Cannellini, or haricot, beans give it body, and a lively vegan pistou spooned over when serving perks the broth up no end. Choose any soft summer herbs and leaves you like and can find easily. Basil, chervil, chives, dill, fennel, mint, parsley, sorrel, spinach and watercress would all be good options.

For the pistou

- ¼ cup (30 g) chopped almonds
- 1 garlic clove, chopped
- Sea salt and freshly ground black pepper
- Large handful of soft summer herbs, chopped (see recipe introduction)
- Extra virgin olive oil, as needed
- Lemon juice, to taste

For the soup

- 2 tablespoons olive oil
- 2 garlic cloves, finely chopped
- 2 shallots, finely chopped
- 2 celery stalks, finely chopped
- 1 fennel bulb, finely chopped
- 1 quart (950 ml) good vegetable stock
- One 15-ounce (400 g) can cannellini beans, drained and rinsed
- 2 cups (200 g) halved sugar snap peas
- 1¼ cups (200 g) sliced green beans
- Handful of soft summer herbs and leaves (see recipe introduction)

1 Start by making the pistou with a mortar and pestle or in a mini food processor. Pound or blend the almonds and garlic with a pinch of salt until crushed. Add the herbs and pound or blend to a rough purée, pouring in enough oil to loosen to a spoonable consistency. Season with salt and pepper to taste and spike with a few drops of lemon juice to lift the flavors.

2 For the soup, heat the oil in a large saucepan over low heat and soften the garlic, shallots, celery and fennel with a pinch of salt. In about 15 minutes they will become soft and sweet. Don't let them take on any real color.

3 Add the stock and cannellini beans and bring to a boil. Reduce the heat and simmer very gently for about 15 minutes.

4 Add the sugar snaps and green beans and cook (a little less gently) for 5 minutes more. Remove the pan from the heat, throw in the herbs and season to taste. A squeeze of lemon juice will, again, perk up the flavors.

5 Ladle into warm bowls and finish with spoonfuls of pistou.

Zen Vegetables with Soy and Sesame

Serves 2

- ½ cup (125 ml) Kombu Stock (page 305)
- ¼ cup (60 ml) tamari or light soy sauce
- 3 tablespoons rice wine vinegar
- 2 tablespoons mirin
- ½- to 1-inch (1.3 to 2.5 cm) piece fresh ginger root, peeled and finely grated
- 2 sweet potatoes, sliced
- 1 winter squash wedge (about 14 ounces/400 g), deseeded and thinly sliced
- 1 small eggplant, thickly sliced
- 4 baby leeks, trimmed
- Large handful of robust Asian greens
- 1 tablespoon sesame seeds, toasted

You steam a good quantity of vegetables here, so have a couple of bamboo or metal baskets to stack up over a simmering pan. Prepare the vegetables carefully; presentation is all when the recipe is this simple. Cut slower-cooking veggies, such as squash, into slim slices, so they cook in the same time as the greens (think bok choy, mustard greens, choy sum . . .) and don't remove the skins unless particularly thick. Offer steamed rice on the side to make this more filling, but no less Zen.

1 Put the stock in a small saucepan. Add the tamari, rice vinegar, and mirin. Warm through over medium heat, until the mixture is piping hot, but not boiling. Pour into a serving bowl and set aside to cool. Once the dressing has cooled, stir in the ginger.

2 Bring a saucepan of water to a boil and divide the vegetables between 2 steamer baskets: the sweet potatoes and squash in 1 basket; the eggplant, leeks and Asian greens in the other.

3 Steam the lidded sweet potato and squash basket for 6 to 7 minutes, then stack the second steamer basket on top and replace the lid, being careful of the steam as you do so. Continue to cook for a further 3 to 5 minutes, until all the vegetables are just tender or cooked to your liking. Serve straight from the steamer baskets, scattered with sesame seeds and with the dressing on hand to spoon over each serving at the table.

SEAWEED

Seaweed is finally entering the mainstream. It is coming to the attention of more cooks in the Western world, who are trying to catch up with the experts of the Far East. About time, too, especially for vegetarians, as seaweed is a rich and cheap source of the iodine that a plant-free diet can lack and is also a plentiful food, if sustainably harvested. Look for hand-harvested seaweeds to support sustainable practices, if you can.

As well as iodine, seaweeds boast intense umami flavor and high levels of B vitamins, namely thiamine and niacin, needed for healthy eyes, nails and skin. Despite their diminutive weight, dried seaweeds are very dense in minerals such as calcium and iron as well as amino acids and protein, though you'd have to eat an awful lot to greatly enhance protein intake.

You can gather your own fresh seaweeds from safe sources, and some specialty shops sell chilled varieties, but they are most commonly sold dried. These make a practical choice, as they store well in cool airtight containers and are simple and quick to rehydrate when needed. (Incidentally, if you grow herbs, they love being watered with mineral-rich seaweed soaking liquid.)

I would wager that nori is our best-known seaweed in the form of toasted sheets, usually wrapped around sushi rice. Toasted or not, it makes an excellent wrap for so many other foods—crunchy raw shredded veggies with avocado, crushed nuts and smoked tofu, for example—and children love its mild, grassy flavor. Scatter nori flakes or powder over roasted root veggies or soups, or use scissors to snip into shreds over rice or noodle bowls.

Kombu is an easy variety to use and a natural flavor enhancer. I often throw it into the water when simmering legumes, as it's said to soften their skins, making them more digestible and reducing any unwelcome effects. I give a simple kombu stock recipe (see page 305) elsewhere; to add more depth, throw in a few dried shiitakes, which combine well with all seaweeds.

It is worth mentioning agar agar, a virtually tasteless, clear seaweed with gelatine-like setting properties, useful for vegetarian jellies and mousses. Other varieties include purple-red and tangy dulse; wakame, a deep green and soft seaweed ideal for soups or sprinkled over my wholesome version of bibimbap (see page 203); and hijiki with its black strands and buds. (Food agencies in the US, Canada, and Britain have advised against eating hijiki, warning of high levels of inorganic arsenic. Always buy a variety that has been grown in uncontaminated waters and is safe for human consumption, and be careful not to consume more than 2 tablespoons of hijiki per week; you may also substitute with arame. For more information, visit edenfoods.com/hiziki.)

Rather than using seaweed as the central part of a dish, you could begin by using it as an accent or a seasoning, much as you would salt. There are plenty of ideas in this chapter and peppered throughout the book.

Smoky Kombu and Kale Chips

Serves 2 to 4 as a snack

- 1 large piece kombu seaweed (about 2×4 inches/5×10 cm)
- 5.5 ounces (150 g) kale (about 8 leaves), washed and dried
- 1½ tablespoons olive oil
- 1 teaspoon sweet smoked paprika
- 1 scant teaspoon sea salt
- 2 teaspoons sesame seeds

Easy to make and far cheaper than package versions. You can buy a kaleidoscope of ready-to-serve kale chips from supermarkets and health food shops, but here is something a little different: seaweed chips. I've used a smoky coating of paprika and sesame that suits both kale and kombu well, but you could use curry-style spices, grated vegetarian Parmesan-style cheese, or finely chopped rosemary instead.

1 Preheat the oven to 350°F (180°C). Line a large baking sheet with parchment paper.

2 Rinse the kombu and soak it in warm water for 10 minutes. Drain well and slice into bite-size pieces.

3 With a knife or kitchen scissors, cut the kale leaves from the thick stems and tear them into bite-size pieces.

4 Spread the kombu and kale out on the prepared baking sheet and drizzle with the olive oil, paprika and salt, tossing to coat evenly.

5 Bake for 5 minutes, then shake the pan well and scatter with the sesame seeds. Cook for 4 to 5 minutes more, until the kale edges brown slightly, but are not burned, and the kombu appears crisp.

Vegetable, Nut and Seaweed Fritters

Serves 4 / Makes about 16

- 2 tablespoons whole almonds
- 1 small zucchini, trimmed
- 7 ounces (200 g/about 1½ medium) sweet potatoes, peeled
- 3.5 ounces (100 g/about 2 small) carrots, scrubbed
- 7 ounces (200 g/about ½ small) celery root, peeled
- 1 small red onion, halved and finely sliced
- 2 tablespoons dried dulse seaweed flakes
- 1 heaping tablespoon chickpea (gram) flour
- 1 red chile, finely chopped
- Sea salt and freshly ground black pepper
- 3 eggs, lightly beaten
- Olive oil
- Salad leaves, to serve
- Lemon wedges, to serve

Dried dulse flakes, found in health food shops and online, add an umami oomph to these forgiving, gluten-free fritters. You could replace it with grated vegetarian Parmesan-style cheese or a teaspoon of miso. Cooking fritters is all in the technique: You want the middles to steam gently, binding with the eggs, so leave them be as they cook; turning them before they are ready will leave you with a hash.

1 If you have time, soak the almonds for a few hours before chopping. Chop them quite finely and set aside.

2 The easiest way to prepare the vegetables is with a food processor fitted with a shredding attachment, but you could as easily use a box grater to shred or grate them all. Put all the shredded or grated vegetables, the onion, dulse flakes, chickpea flour, chile and chopped almonds in a large bowl. Season with a little salt and plenty of black pepper, add the eggs and mix well to combine.

3 Pour enough oil into a heavy-based frying pan to lightly coat the base and set it over medium heat. Scoop heaping tablespoons of the fritter mixture into the pan, pressing them down with a spatula to flatten slightly. Working in batches, cook the fritters for 2 to 3 minutes undisturbed, until crispy and browned underneath, then carefully flip them and cook for 2 to 3 minutes more. Transfer to a plate and keep warm in the low oven while you cook the rest, adding more oil if needed.

4 Serve hot with handfuls of salad leaves and lemon wedges.

Seaweed, Shredded Roots and Avocado Salad

Serves 4

- 0.2 ounces (5 g; about a handful) dried hijiki seaweed
- Juice of 1 large lemon
- 1-inch (2.5 cm) piece fresh ginger root, peeled and finely grated
- 2 tablespoons poppy seeds
- 1 tablespoon honey or maple syrup
- 1 teaspoon mellow miso paste
- ¼ cup (60 ml) canola oil
- Sea salt and freshly ground black pepper
- 2 large carrots
- 2 parsnips
- 2 beets
- 1 pound (450 g) celery root
- Large handful of mint leaves, finely chopped
- 1 ripe avocado, finely chopped

A toothsome salad of roots you might not ordinarily eat raw, with a vibrant poppy seed dressing and ripe avocado. The seaweed of choice here is hijiki, which you can buy quite easily in black, dried form. A little goes a long way, as it swells right up after soaking, so don't be tempted to start with too much. (See page 252 for more about hijiki safety.)

1 Put the hijiki in a large bowl and cover it with warm water. Set aside for 30 minutes, until it has swollen up and softened. Pour the hijiki into a sieve held over the sink and rinse under running water. Drain thoroughly.

2 To make the dressing, combine the lemon juice, ginger, poppy seeds, honey and miso in a bowl. Gradually whisk in the oil with 1 tablespoon of water to make a dressing. Season with salt and pepper.

3 The easiest and quickest way to prepare the roots is with a food processor fitted with a shredding attachment. Otherwise, use a grater or a shredder tool to grate or shred the carrots, parsnips, beets and celery root. Combine all the vegetables in a bowl and toss with half the dressing to keep them from browning.

4 Now add the hijiki, mint and avocado to the bowl and toss through gently to mix. Serve with the remaining dressing.

Silken Tofu with Seaweed Dressing

Serves 2

- ½- to 1-inch (1.3 to 2.5 cm) piece fresh ginger root
- 2 tablespoons tamari or light soy sauce
- 1 tablespoon mirin
- 1 tablespoon rice wine vinegar
- 1 teaspoon toasted sesame oil
- 14 ounces (400 g) silken tofu, drained
- 2 tablespoons peanut oil
- Very small handful of dulse seaweed ribbons
- 1 scallion, finely sliced

This is a simple dish that relies on its contrasting textures and the very freshest ingredients, so do look out for chilled, silken tofu in Japanese food shops, Asian markets or similar. The silken tofu found in little boxes in most supermarkets will do in a pinch . . . but I wouldn't choose it if you have other options. If you can't find dulse, simply snip some toasted nori seaweed over to finish.

1 Peel the ginger and slice it into fine matchsticks. Combine the tamari, mirin, rice wine vinegar and sesame oil in a small bowl.

2 Put the tofu on a small plate that will fit into a steamer basket, being very careful not to damage the block in the process. Bring the pan of water for your steamer to a boil and sit the covered steamer basket on top. Leave the tofu to gently steam and heat through for 5 minutes.

3 Meanwhile, put a frying pan over high heat and add the peanut oil. Add the ginger and dulse to the pan and fry briskly, stirring often, until the ginger is beginning to brown lightly. Transfer onto paper towels to drain and crisp up.

4 Remove the tofu plate from the steamer, dabbing any moisture on the plate away with paper towels. Pour the dressing over the top and scatter with the scallion. Finish with the crisp ginger and dulse and eat immediately.

afters

To CLARIFY MY OPINION ON the subject of dessert: The wholesome nature of the recipes in this chapter should not imply that I take a hard-line stance against the odd, or regular, bit of flat-out indulgence, or that I don't have a deep love for ice cream and pretty much all things sweet. . . . Everything in moderation and so on. I, and many others besides, have written reams of immoderate sweet recipes for special occasions, and I hope to write more in the future, but, in order to provide a solution to modern-day culinary conundrums, I had to keep this chapter of last courses in line with the premise of the others.

The nature of my cooking revolves around whole foods, a plethora of vegetables and unprocessed ingredients, whether sweet or savory, so it would be pretty odd for me to present a chapter of white-sugar-laden and refined-flour-rich desserts in the latter part of the book, even if I do make my own exceptions to the rule every now and then. Cooking with unrefined sugars (they still count as sugars, mind you; more on that later . . .) and whole-grain flours doesn't just add trace minerals and fiber, it also brings character and flavor, both traits I value greatly in a recipe.

Allergies and sensitivities appear to be more widespread than ever, and everybody involved in the world of professional cooking has to take notice. Gone are the days, I hope, of dismissing restaurant customers as fussy if they volunteer an allergy, and home cooks have to follow suit when cooking for friends and family. Sufferers will be used to preparing and choosing their food accordingly, but, as with the rest of the recipes in this book, I want to give you choices and solve potential problems.

You might be cooking for a group where only one person is lactose intolerant. Instead of making an entirely separate dessert—creating more work for yourself and perhaps making that diner feel segregated—I have developed sweet recipes using familiar and wholesome ingredients (you'll find no fillers or gums here) and easy methods that are without common allergens such as dairy, gluten or wheat, but are no less delicious for that.

By focusing largely on cake and ice creams or frozen yogurts (who wouldn't want either for dessert?), I hope I have given you choices for vegan, wheat-free, gluten-free and dairy-free diets, as well as a few more general wholesome options. Where relevant, I have given hints on tweaking recipes to suit. For example, butter, a natural ingredient I love to cook with, can be swapped for coconut oil in soft-but-solid form. Choose unrefined or extra virgin versions if you like the coconut taste, or refined if you don't.

As I have mentioned elsewhere, spelt is a strain of wheat, and any flour made from it contains all the gluten that implies. However, compared to our overprocessed modern wheat flours, spelt is higher in protein and B vitamins and is widely thought to be better tolerated by modern humans than wheat is. I enjoy its soft, sweet flavor but concede that, for those who are skeptical about food sensitivities, the equivalent whole-grain wheat flour (by which I mean not stripped or mass-produced) will be comparable, so do directly substitute as you wish. Rye, though not a wheat flour, still contains gluten, but I love the way it combines with a judicious amount of sugar to add toasted flavor notes and a short, pleasingly sandy texture in baked goods. You could try using gluten-free buckwheat flour as a direct or partial replacement for rye. Nuts have proved useful in all forms in this chapter, often replacing flour completely, adding welcome fats, crunch or bolster in the process.

It has been in vogue for a while now to flag recipes as "refined-sugar-free" as a selling point, and I absolutely agree that honey, maple syrup, raw cane sugar, molasses, coconut sugar and the like have merits over white sugar, not least in their amazing range of flavors. They are also relatively unprocessed, depending on what you buy, and contain beneficial minerals such as calcium, magnesium and iron. In the case of agave nectar, honey and maple syrup, you will need about one third less by volume to attain the same sweetness levels as white sugar, and cooking with less sugar can only be a good thing. Add fiber to the mix, in the form of dried dates or other sweet dried fruits, for example, and you can be sure the body will break those sugars down more slowly than the refined equivalent.

But, and here's the rub: Unrefined sugar is still sugar. Or, to put it another way, *refined-sugar-free* does not mean sugar-free! I would suggest that using a little less sugar in your desserts where possible—and choosing unrefined and interesting whole ingredients to replace some of those empty calories from refined sugar with real and natural flavors—is a far more sensible approach. I have certainly done my best to keep sugar levels in these recipes as low as possible without compromising taste, hopefully giving those other flavors the space to shine through.

Beyond that, if you eat a colorful array of fresh and thoughtfully cooked vegetables and salads combined with whole grains, a treat here and there is to be enjoyed wholeheartedly, rather than agonized over and wrangled into something it isn't.

Roasted Pineapple, Coconut and Makrut Lime Sorbet

Serves 6 / Makes 1 quart (1 L)

- 1 large ripe pineapple
- ½ cup (120 g) palm sugar (the kind in a container, not a block)
- One 13.5-ounce (400 ml) can coconut milk
- 4 fresh or frozen makrut lime leaves, bruised
- Juice of 1 large lime
- Pinch of fine salt

Roasting the pineapple has a twofold effect: Firstly, it renders even mediocre pineapples fragrant and sweet, and secondly, the oven's heat stops the fruit's bromelain enzyme from causing a soapy taste when it is mixed with coconut milk. Serve this refreshing sorbet in scoops or, if you don't have a machine and can't face the regular whipping, freeze it in pop molds without churning.

1 Preheat the oven to 400°F (200°C). Snap the green top from the pineapple, place the fruit in a roasting pan and cook, skin and all, for 1 hour, until tender. Set aside to cool for at least 15 minutes.

2 Put the sugar in a saucepan with 3 tablespoons of water and 3 tablespoons of the coconut milk. Bring to a boil very slowly, stirring to dissolve the sugar. Once dissolved, simmer for 2 minutes. Add the bruised makrut lime leaves and remove from the heat. Let cool completely (this will take at least 20 minutes), remove the lime leaves, then stir in the lime juice and salt.

3 Meanwhile, cut the skin away from the roasted pineapple, removing any eyes in the process, and roughly chop the flesh, discarding the central core. Blend the chopped pineapple, with any of its juice, and remaining coconut milk in an upright blender (or with a hand version) until completely smooth. Add the lime syrup and blend again to combine. To make the sorbet really smooth, pass it through a fine sieve.

4 Churn in an ice cream machine according to the manufacturer's instructions, until the blade stops. Then transfer to a freezable container, cover and freeze for 4 hours, or overnight.

5 To make without a machine, pour the mixture into a shallow, wide freezable container and freeze for 1 hour, until the mixture freezes in a border around the edge. Break up the ice crystals with a whisk and return to the freezer. Repeat this whisking every 30 minutes, until evenly set and too thick to whip. This should take about 3 hours in total. Cover and freeze undisturbed for 4 hours, or overnight.

6 Soften in the fridge for 15 to 20 minutes before scooping and serving.

Toasted Marzipan Ice Cream

Serves 4 to 6
Makes 3⅓ cups (800 ml)

- 11 ounces (320 g) natural marzipan (store-bought or homemade, see recipe introduction)
- 3⅓ cups (800 ml) coconut milk
- Cherries (see below), to serve

A luxurious vegan ice cream made with only two ingredients, if you use store-bought, natural marzipan that is. If you want to make your own, blend 2½ cups (250 g) almond meal with ½ cup (75 g) Medjool dates and ½ teaspoon almond extract in a food processor to make a paste. Toast the homemade marzipan for a little longer, and strain the mixture after blending with the coconut milk to make a smoother base.

1 Preheat the oven to 375°F (190°C). Tear the marzipan into small pieces and spread out on a baking sheet lined with parchment paper. Bake for 5 to 10 minutes, until turning golden in places. Store-bought marzipan will brown in about 5 minutes and homemade takes about 12, so keep watch. Transfer into a blender with the coconut milk and blend until silky smooth. Chill for 2 hours.

2 Churn in an ice cream machine according to the manufacturer's instructions, until the blade stops. Then transfer to a freezable container, cover and freeze for 4 hours, or overnight.

3 To make without a machine, pour the mixture into a shallow, wide freezable container and freeze for 1 hour, until the mixture freezes in a border around the edge. Break up the ice crystals with a whisk and return to the freezer. Repeat this whisking every 30 minutes, until evenly set and too thick to whip. This should take about 3 hours in total. Cover and freeze undisturbed for 4 hours, or overnight.

4 Soften the ice cream in the fridge for 15 to 20 minutes before scooping. Serve with fresh cherries or, when they aren't in season, frozen or canned cherries simmered in a covered pan for 15 minutes with a splash of water and a little maple syrup, to taste.

Beet, Cardamom and Black Currant Frozen Yogurt

Serves 3 to 4
Makes 2 cups (500 ml)

- 1⅓ cups (300 g) full-fat Greek yogurt
- 4 green cardamom pods
- 5.5 ounces (150 g; about 3 small) purple beets
- 1¼ cups (150 g) black currants, fresh or frozen
- ⅓ cup (90 ml) maple syrup
- Pinch of fine salt
- Juice of ½ lemon

With its black currant tang, earthy beet background notes and cardamom fragrance, this is more of an exotic sorbet, really, than a frozen yogurt. It does need the silky heft of full-fat yogurt to make it smooth and scoopable. Low-fat versions just won't work here.

1 Line a sieve with a single layer of muslin or cheesecloth. Empty the yogurt into the sieve and leave to drain over a bowl or the sink for 30 minutes.

2 Give the cardamom pods a good smash with a jar or rolling pin and shake out the dark seeds. Scrub and coarsely grate the beets.

3 Put the grated beets, black currants, maple syrup, salt and cardamom seeds in a saucepan with ¼ cup (60 ml) water. Cook over low heat for 5 to 7 minutes, stirring often, until the currants begin to pop. Let cool, then transfer into a blender with the strained yogurt and lemon juice and blend until smooth (or blend everything in the saucepan with a hand blender). Pass through a sieve for a smoother result, pushing and scraping the purée with a spatula, or leave as is if you don't mind a little texture.

4 Churn in an ice cream machine according to the manufacturer's instructions, until the blade stops. Then transfer to a freezable container, cover and freeze for 4 hours, or overnight.

5 To make without a machine, pour the mixture into a shallow, wide freezable container and freeze for 1 hour, until the mixture freezes in a border around the edge. Break up the ice crystals with a whisk and return to the freezer. Repeat this whisking every 30 minutes, until evenly set and too thick to whip. This should take about 3 hours in total. Cover and freeze undisturbed for 4 hours, or overnight.

6 Soften in the fridge for 15 to 20 minutes before scooping.

Geranium Leaf Frozen Yogurt with Berry Ripple

Serves 4 to 5
Makes 2½ cups (600 ml)

- One 32-ounce (1 kg) container full-fat plain yogurt
- 6 lemon- or rose-scented geranium leaves
- ⅔ cup (190 g) acacia or other mild floral honey
- Juice of 1 large lemon
- Small pinch of fine salt
- 10.5 ounces (about 1 dry pint/300 g) blackberries or black mulberries

Blame it on romance or nostalgia, but I can't resist the lure of scented leaves or petals to fragrance syrups and custards. I have made this with geranium leaves and without; both versions are outstanding so don't worry if you can't get hold of any; they just add a hint of Turkish delight. The berry ripple is tart, to contrast with the soft and velveteen yogurt, but you may wish to up the honey by a tablespoon or two.

1 Line a large sieve with muslin or cheesecloth and set over a large bowl. Spoon in the yogurt and chill overnight, or for at least 8 hours. If you don't want to do this, simply use a 16-ounce (500 g) container of thick Greek yogurt and skip the straining step.

2 Holding them over a small saucepan, snip the geranium leaves into pieces with scissors. Add ½ cup (160 g) of the honey to the pan with all but 1 teaspoon of the lemon juice and the salt. Bring to a boil slowly, then reduce the heat and simmer gently until reduced by half. Cool for 10 minutes, then strain into a container through a sieve to remove the leaves. Cool completely.

3 To make the blackberry ripple, put the berries in a saucepan with the remaining honey. Heat through gently over medium-low heat, stirring occasionally, for 10 to 15 minutes, until the berries burst, look "saucy" and reduce down to thicken slightly. Stir in the reserved 1 teaspoon of lemon juice and set aside to cool. Chill until needed.

4 These three steps can all be done, or started in the case of the yogurt straining, the night before, or even a couple of days before freezing. When ready to churn, combine the strained yogurt and honey syrup thoroughly.

5 Churn in an ice cream machine according to the manufacturer's instructions, until the blade stops. Or, to make without a machine, pour the mixture into a shallow, wide freezable container and freeze for 1 hour, until the mixture freezes in a border around the edge. Break up the ice crystals with a whisk and return to the freezer. Repeat this whisking every 30 minutes, until evenly set and too thick to whip. This should take about 3 hours in total. Either way, at this stage, ripple in the chilled berry mixture, cover and freeze undisturbed for 4 hours, or overnight.

6 Soften in the fridge for 15 to 20 minutes before scooping.

Fig and Leaf Ice Cream with Fresh Figs

Serves 4 / Makes 2½ cups (600 ml)

- One 13.5-ounce (400 ml) can full-fat coconut milk
- 1 tablespoon arrowroot powder or cornstarch
- 4 large fig leaves
- 1 vanilla pod, split lengthwise
- ⅓ cup (100 g) blossom honey
- ¼ teaspoon fine salt
- 4 ripe figs, plus plenty more ripe figs, to serve
- 1 tablespoon lemon juice

Make this intriguing "ice cream"—strictly a misnomer as it contains none of the usual dairy or eggs—when trays of plump figs are selling cheap, and offer more fresh figs on the side. You should have a good chance of finding a few fig leaves then, too, but don't worry if they prove elusive. If you are curious, they impart a grown-up and intriguing taste, reminiscent of coconut, vanilla and roasted nuts.

1 In a small bowl, combine 3 tablespoons of the coconut milk with the arrowroot to make a paste.

2 Wash, dry and crumple the fig leaves to bruise slightly. Put them in a saucepan with the remaining coconut milk and split vanilla pod. Slowly bring to a boil, then remove from the heat and set aside to infuse for 20 minutes or up to a few hours for a stronger fragrance. Strain, pressing down on the leaves to extract all their flavor. Return the infused coconut milk to the pan, add the honey and salt and heat through gently. Stir in the arrowroot paste and bring to a boil, stirring constantly. Reduce the heat and simmer gently for 1 minute until slightly thickened, then remove from the heat, cover the surface with plastic wrap and allow to cool. Chill overnight if you have time.

3 Chop the 4 figs and blend them with the chilled custard and the lemon juice in a blender. The mixture will turn a pale purplish pink.

4 Pour into an ice cream maker and churn according to the manufacturer's instructions, until the blade stops.

5 To make without a machine, pour the mixture into a shallow, wide freezable container and freeze for 1 hour, until the mixture freezes in a border around the edge. Break up the ice crystals with a whisk and return to the freezer. Repeat this whisking every 30 minutes, until evenly set and too thick to whip. This should take about 3 hours in total.

6 Either way, spoon the soft ice cream into an airtight freezable container and freeze for at least 4 hours or overnight, until firm. Let soften in the fridge for about 15 minutes before serving with torn ripe figs.

Macaroon and Passion Fruit Curd Tart

Serves 8

For the macaroon tart crust
- Coconut oil, for the pan
- 1 egg white
- ¼ teaspoon cream of tartar
- 3 tablespoons raw cane sugar
- 1 tablespoon almond meal
- ½ teaspoon vanilla extract
- ¼ teaspoon fine salt
- 1½ cups (120 g) unsweetened desiccated coconut
- Finely grated zest of 1 lime

For the curd
- 2 large, ripe passion fruits, plus more if needed
- Juice of 1 lime, plus more if needed
- 2 eggs, plus 1 egg yolk
- ¼ cup (50 g) raw cane sugar
- 5 tablespoons unsalted butter, softened
- Ripe tropical fruit (pineapple, mango, papaya . . .), to serve

happened upon a good method when saving a curd I'd cooked too quickly: Blending it on a high speed introduces air, changing the consistency from dense and buttery to mousse-y and light. This tart sets and cuts like a dream in its macaroon shell. Do choose shriveled passion fruits; the taut, unripe fruits will be sharp, since they haven't had time to develop their soft, muscat fragrance as they wrinkle up.

1 To make the macaroon tart crust, preheat the oven to 340°F (170°C). Lightly oil an 8-inch (20 cm) tart pan with a removable base.

2 With a balloon whisk, whip the egg white and cream of tartar in a large, clean mixing bowl until the mixture forms soft peaks. Add the sugar and continue to whisk until stiff and shiny. Fold in the remaining macaroon ingredients to make a sticky mixture. Being very firm, press the mixture evenly over the base and sides of the pan to make a tart crust. Wet your hands if it sticks and do use quite a bit of pressure when spreading it out.

3 Bake for 12 to 15 minutes, until pale golden, but do keep an eye if your oven runs hot because coconut catches easily. Let cool.

4 To make the curd, halve and scoop the filling from the passion fruits with a spoon and add to a container with the lime juice. There should be ½ cup (100 ml) in total; if not, add more passion fruit or lime juice. Add the eggs, egg yolk and sugar and transfer to a heatproof bowl. Don't be alarmed by the caramel color! It will change. . . .

5 Set the bowl over a saucepan of simmering water and stir continuously with a wooden spoon for 8 minutes, until thick, then remove from the heat and pour straight into a blender. Add the butter and blend at high speed until pale and thick with flecks of black throughout. Pour into the tart crust and chill for at least 2 hours to set the curd. Carefully remove the tart from its pan and serve in slices with lots of ripe tropical fruit.

Cinnamon, Apple and Walnut Cake

Serves 8 to 10

- ¾ cup (190 ml) mild canola oil, plus more for the pan
- 1⅔ cups (200 g) whole-grain spelt flour, plus more for the pan
- 4 eating apples, such as Braeburn, Gala, Jonagold or Granny Smith
- 1 cup plus 2 tablespoons (225 g) raw cane sugar
- 2 teaspoons ground cinnamon
- ⅓ cup (50 g) rye flour
- 2¼ teaspoons baking powder
- ¾ teaspoon fine salt
- 3 eggs, lightly beaten
- Juice of ½ lemon
- 2 teaspoons vanilla extract
- ⅔ cup (100 g) walnut pieces

A little rye flour combines so well with whole-grain spelt flour or plain flour, the former adding nutty flavor in the absence of any dairy, the latter keeping the structure solid and the crumb tender. A bundt or tube-shaped cake pan is pretty much essential here; as the apples are plentiful and juice-filled, they make it hard for a standard round cake to bake through properly without drying out at the edges.

1 Preheat the oven to 340°F (170°C). Oil a 9-inch (23 cm) bundt or tube-shaped cake pan with a little canola oil and dust very lightly with spelt flour, tapping the excess away.

2 Slice the cheeks off each apple around the core and lay the cheeks down on a chopping board, flat sides down. Slice thinly, skin and all, to make a pile of flattened half-moon shapes. Transfer to a bowl and toss with 3 tablespoons of the sugar and the ground cinnamon.

3 In a separate large mixing bowl, combine the 1⅔ cups spelt flour, rye flour, baking powder and salt together using a balloon whisk to aerate the ingredients. Measure the oil into a container and stir in the remaining sugar, the eggs, lemon juice and vanilla extract. Add the wet ingredients to the dry, along with the walnuts, and mix well. Spoon half this batter into the prepared pan and top with half the apple slices. Repeat the layers once more, finishing with the last of the apples and arranging them neatly.

4 Bake for 1 hour 15 minutes, or until risen, firm and pulling away from the sides of the pan. Check after 40 minutes and, if the cake looks to be browning too quickly, lay a square of foil over it to protect the top. A skewer inserted into the thickest part should come out with no trace of wet batter on it.

5 Let cool in the pan before turning out and slicing.

Blood Orange and Olive Oil Cake with Almonds

Serves 6 to 8

- 2 medium or 3 small unwaxed blood oranges, plus more sliced blood oranges to serve
- ½ cup (100 ml) fruity extra virgin olive oil, plus more for the pan
- ¾ cup (175 g) raw cane sugar
- 4 eggs, lightly beaten
- 1⅔ cups (175 g) almond meal
- 2 teaspoons baking powder (gluten-free if needed)

This is definitely a pudding cake, mousse-like and free of both dairy and gluten. Don't be put off if you're not a marmalade fan, for the citrus here is full-bodied rather than bitter, and also tempered by grassy olive oil. Later in the year, use regular oranges, add a tablespoon of finely chopped rosemary leaves and serve the cake with raspberries.

1 Wash the oranges and put them in a saucepan. Cover with water, bring to a boil and simmer for 30 minutes or so, until completely soft. Remove the oranges from the water with a slotted spoon and leave to cool.

2 Cut the oranges in half through their middles, discard any seeds and put the peel and pulp in a food processor. Blend to a purée and set aside.

3 Preheat the oven to 350°F (180°C). Lightly oil an 8-inch (20 cm) springform cake pan and line it with parchment paper. Whisk the ½ cup (100 ml) olive oil, the sugar and eggs together for 3 to 4 minutes, using electric beaters, until light and fluffy. Fold in the almond meal and baking powder with a large metal spoon. Fold through the puréed oranges until thoroughly mixed.

4 Spoon the batter into the prepared pan and bake for 50 minutes to 1 hour, until golden, well risen and no longer wobbly when the pan is jiggled.

5 Leave to cool in the pan until completely cold. Turn out and serve slices with more blood orange slices or segments.

Carrot and Lemon Polenta Drizzle Cake

Serves 8 to 10

- ⅔ cup (150 ml) fruity olive oil, plus more for the pan
- 2 cups (200 g) almond meal
- ⅔ cup (100 g) fine cornmeal or polenta
- 1½ teaspoons gluten-free baking powder
- ½ teaspoon fine salt
- ¾ cup (150 g) raw cane sugar
- ½ cup (60 g) pitted and chopped dates
- 3 eggs
- ½ cup (100 g) finely grated carrots
- Finely grated zest and juice of 2 small unwaxed lemons
- ¾ cups (100 g) unrefined powdered sugar

A handsome dairy- and gluten-free cake, though you'd never think it without being told. I've called it a drizzle, but to be honest the texture has little in common with a delicate lemon cake; it is robust, yet not heavy, and brimming with caramel flavor from the dates and cane sugar. This is excellent with sweet dessert wine, or as a tea cake.

1 Preheat the oven to 350°F (180°C). Oil an 8-inch (20 cm) springform cake pan and line it with parchment paper.

2 Using a balloon whisk to introduce a bit of air, thoroughly combine the almond meal, cornmeal, baking powder and salt in a mixing bowl.

3 In a second bowl, vigorously whisk the olive oil and sugar together until lighter in texture and paler in color. Add the dates to the bowl, then go back in with the whisk, whipping in each egg individually and breaking the dates down a little in the process. Fold in the almond mixture, followed by the grated carrots and lemon zest.

4 Pour into the pan. Bake the cake for about 40 minutes, until golden, risen and firm. You want it to be well cooked (any dates on the base of the pan will caramelize beautifully), so cover the top with a loose square of foil if it appears to be turning too dark too quickly.

5 Meanwhile, mix the lemon juice with the powdered sugar. Pierce the surface of the just-cooked cake repeatedly with a skewer and pour the icing over. Leave to cool in the pan, then turn out, icing side up, to serve.

Date, Cocoa and Pecan Cookies

Makes 24

- 2¼ cups (225 g) pecans
- 1½ cups (190 g) rye flour, plus more to dust
- 1 tablespoon cocoa powder
- 1 scant teaspoon baking powder
- ¼ teaspoon fine salt
- 1½ sticks (190 g) unsalted butter, at room temperature
- ¼ cup (60 g) raw cane sugar
- 3 tablespoons maple syrup
- ⅔ cup (100 g) pitted and chopped dates
- 3.5 ounces (100 g) milk or dark chocolate, finely chopped

These wheat-free (but not gluten-free) rye flour cookies are reminiscent of the muscovado and pecan freezer cookies my grandmother used to make . . . crossed with a shortbread of sorts. They're a little of this and a little of that, and not too sweet. Swap in solid coconut oil and use dark vegan chocolate to make them vegan-friendly. The well-wrapped cylinder of dough freezes well for up to three months.

1 Roughly chop ½ cup (50 g) of the pecans and set aside. Put the remaining pecans in a food processor and blend until finely ground (keep an eye; you don't want them to turn to an oily paste).

2 Beat together the ground pecans, rye flour, cocoa, baking powder, salt, butter, sugar and maple syrup in a bowl. Fold in the dates and the chopped pecans. Form into a fat (2-inch/5 to 6 cm diameter) log with rye-floured hands. Roll up in parchment paper, twist the ends and chill for at least 2 hours or up to 1 week.

3 Preheat the oven to 340°F (170°C) and line 2 baking sheets with parchment paper.

4 Slice ⅜-inch (1 cm) thick cookies from the cylinder and space out on the baking sheets. Bake for about 15 minutes, until slightly risen and dry looking. Let cool on the baking sheets for 5 minutes, then carefully transfer to a wire rack with a spatula or palette knife to cool completely.

5 Lay a sheet of parchment paper underneath the wire rack. Melt the chocolate in a bowl set over simmering water (the bowl should not touch the water), then transfer to a plastic bag. Snip a small corner off and drizzle the chocolate back and forth over the cookies in a fine stream. Let cool for at least 20 minutes in a cool place to set the chocolate, then keep in an airtight container for up to a week.

Chocolate-Muscovado Layer Cake

Serves 12 to 16

- ¾ cup (200 ml) sunflower oil, plus more for the pans
- 28 ounces (800 g) vegan vanilla yogurt
- 2¼ cups (455 g) dark muscovado sugar
- 3 tablespoons chia seeds
- 2 tablespoons strong espresso coffee
- 2 tablespoons white wine vinegar
- 1 tablespoon vanilla extract
- 3½ cups (450 g) white spelt flour
- ¼ cup plus 2 tablespoons (35 g) cocoa powder
- 2 teaspoons baking soda
- ½ teaspoon fine salt
- 7 ounces (about ½ a dry pint/200 g) halved cherries or sliced strawberries, plus more to decorate, optional
- 1 tablespoon unrefined powdered sugar, to dust
- Edible flowers or foliage, to decorate, optional

A vegan chocolate cake fit for a celebration. I've found vegan cakes tricky and liable to sink when baked in large pans, so have opted for a triple layer extravaganza, made in smaller pans. Admittedly, some companies specializing in vegan products make expensive cake fillings, but a vegan filling is easy to make, practical and a perfect foil for the rich sponge. If dairy is an option and you'd rather spend less, go for whipped cream, slightly sweetened and spiked with vanilla.

1 Preheat the oven to 350°F (180°C). Lightly oil three 6-inch (15 cm) cake pans with removable bases or springform pans. Line the bases with parchment paper.

2 Start with the filling. Empty the yogurt into a sieve lined with a layer of muslin or cheesecloth and set over a bowl. Set aside in a cool place to strain, stirring now and then. It should take 1 to 2 hours to thicken enough to hold its shape when stirred. Remember the cakes are heavy and it will need to stand up to their weight! Stir in 1 teaspoon of the muscovado and chill.

3 Combine the oil, chia seeds, coffee, vinegar, vanilla and 2 cups (450 ml) water in a large bowl. Set aside for 10 minutes to allow the chia seeds to swell. Spoon the mixture into a blender and blend on a high speed until smooth.

4 Combine the flour, remaining muscovado sugar, cocoa, baking soda and salt in a large bowl. Beat in the oil mixture to make a smooth batter, then divide between the prepared pans.

5 Bake for 20 to 25 minutes, until well risen. Do not overbake. They should be firm, and a skewer inserted in the middles should come out clean. Let cool for 10 minutes, then turn out onto wire racks to cool completely.

6 Choose the prettiest and most evenly domed sponge to be the top. Place one of the other cakes upside down on a cake stand, serving plate or platter. Spread with half the filling, leaving a ⅜-inch (1 cm) border at the edges to allow for spreading. Scatter with half the cherries or strawberries, if using. Top with a second upside-down cake and repeat the yogurt layer and optional fruit. Sit the favorite cake on top, the right way up. Press down a little so the filling layers bulge out slightly. Take a palette knife and, holding it as close to vertical as possible, swoosh around the outside, flush with the cake, spreading the filling to fill any gaps. Finish with a dusting of powdered sugar and leave plain, or decorate with fresh, edible flowers, such as honeysuckle, or extra cherries or strawberries, if you like.

Kumquat, Cardamom and Pistachio Syrup Cake

Serves 8

- ½ cup (175 g) blossom honey
- 9 ounces (250 g) kumquats
- 2 pinches of fine salt
- Finely grated zest and juice of 1 unwaxed lemon
- ⅔ cup (100 g) almonds (skins on)
- 5 green cardamom pods
- Flavorless oil, for the pan
- ¾ cup (100 g) unsalted and shelled pistachios
- ⅔ cup (125 g) raw cane sugar
- 1 teaspoon vanilla bean paste or extract
- 1 tablespoon rice flour
- 1 teaspoon gluten-free baking powder
- 4 eggs, separated

A gluten-, flour- and dairy-free gateau with a fallen mousse texture and a mere whisper of cardamom. Expect some slumping as it cools; this is entirely normal and you won't see it anyway, as a layer of jeweled kumquat slices hides any wrinkles. If they aren't in season, or are ridiculously priced, douse the cake with honey and lemon juice instead and pile it high with sweet, ripe berries. Serve it as is, or with cream or coconut yogurt.

1. Put the honey in a saucepan with the kumquats, a pinch of salt and ⅓ cup (75 ml) water. Heat gently and bring to a simmer. Cook, stirring often, for 10 minutes, until the liquid reduces to a syrup and the kumquats turn translucent. Stir in the lemon juice and remove from the heat. Let cool.

2. Put the almonds in a bowl and cover with just-boiled water. Set aside for 20 minutes, then drain thoroughly and dry gently in a kitchen towel.

3. Bruise the cardamom pods hard enough to split them and shake their black seeds into a mortar and crush to a rough powder with the pestle.

4. Preheat the oven to 340°F (170°C). Oil an 8-inch (20 cm) square or 9-inch (23 cm) round cake pan. Line the base and sides with parchment paper.

5. Put the drained almonds in a food processor and blend until they resemble fine bread crumbs. Add the lemon zest, crushed cardamom, pistachios, sugar, vanilla and second pinch of salt. Blend until the mixture looks like sand. Transfer into a mixing bowl and stir in the rice flour, baking powder and egg yolks, mixing well with a spatula to make a stiff paste.

6. Whisk the egg whites in a separate, clean mixing bowl until they form stiff peaks. Fold a spoonful of egg whites into the cake batter to loosen it, then fold in the remaining whites in 2 batches, retaining as much air in them as possible. Spoon into the prepared pan and bake for 35 to 40 minutes, until the cake is golden and risen. A skewer inserted into the center should come out clean. Check after 25 minutes and loosely cover the top with foil if it appears to be browning too quickly.

7. Spoon the kumquats and syrup over the hot cake in the pan and let cool. Cut into pieces and serve.

Chocolate-Beet Spelt Loaf

Serves 10

- 2 sticks (225 g) unsalted butter, very soft, plus more for the pan
- 3.5 ounces (100 g) dark chocolate with 70 percent cocoa solids, chopped
- 1⅔ cups (190 g) whole-grain spelt flour
- 2 tablespoons cocoa powder
- 1 teaspoon baking soda
- ½ teaspoon fine salt
- 1¼ cups (250 g) raw cane sugar
- 2 eggs
- 2 teaspoons vanilla bean paste or extract
- 1 cup (160 g) raw grated beet
- ⅔ cup (150 ml) hot black coffee or hot water

This intensely chocolaty, slightly slumped cake is loosely based on Nigella Lawson's Dense Chocolate Loaf Cake. My version is rich with beet—and you can really taste it, so this isn't a cake for beet naysayers—and a little more frugal in sugar, and enjoys a hit of coffee to set the flavors off. It is best, I think, a day or two after baking, served with raspberries and cream or yogurt.

1 Preheat the oven to 375°F (190°C). Line the base and sides of a 9 × 5-inch (23 × 12 cm) loaf pan with parchment paper, using a little butter to keep it in place, as needed.

2 Melt the chocolate in a bowl set over simmering water (do not allow the bowl to touch the water), stir and set aside to cool (but not reset).

3 Whisk the flour, cocoa, baking soda and salt in a bowl to aerate.

4 In a second bowl, or the bowl of a stand mixer, beat the butter and sugar together for several minutes, until very light and fluffy. It will be hard work at first. Beat in the eggs individually, followed by the cooled chocolate and the vanilla. Fold in the grated beet.

5 Fold in one third of the flour mixture, followed by a good pour of coffee. Keep adding the flour and coffee alternately, folding them in to make a loose batter.

6 Pour into the loaf pan and bake for 25 minutes, then reduce the oven temperature to 340°F (170°C) and bake for 20 minutes more. Leave to cool completely in the pan, whereupon it will sink slightly, before serving. It will keep well in an airtight container for a few days.

Coconut-Raspberry Cakes

Makes 8

- One 13.5-ounce (400 ml) can coconut milk
- ½ cup (60 g) coconut flour
- 1½ sticks (190 g) unsalted butter, soft, plus more for the pan
- ⅔ cup (125 g) coconut sugar or raw cane sugar
- 4 eggs
- 3 tablespoons desiccated coconut
- 2 teaspoons vanilla extract
- Finely grated zest of 1 unwaxed lemon
- Large pinch of fine salt
- 1⅔ cups (175 g) almond meal
- 2 teaspoons gluten-free baking powder
- 5.5 ounces (about ½ a dry pint/150 g) raspberries
- 3 tablespoons unrefined powdered sugar
- ⅓ cup (25 g) toasted coconut flakes

found this buttery gluten-free sponge for coconut lovers easier to make as individual cakes. They often bake with craggy, flat tops, so turning them upside down, then coating the domed sponge with a quick coconut frosting and a hat of toasted coconut flakes solves any aesthetic failings. Substitute firm coconut oil for the dairy butter, if you wish.

1 At least 2 hours before you want to make the cakes, chill the coconut milk can thoroughly, being careful not to disturb it too much. Open carefully and spoon out the set, thick coconut cream on top, leaving the thin milk behind. Chill the cream and measure out ⅔ cup (150 ml) of the milk (you won't need the rest here; pour it into a bowl and save it to add to a curry). Combine the ⅔ cup (150 ml) coconut milk with the coconut flour and set aside for 5 minutes; the flour will swell right up to form a spongy paste.

2 Preheat the oven to 350°F (180°C). Butter 8 holes of a large, 12-hole muffin pan. (If your muffin pan has slightly smaller holes, this recipe will make 10 or even 12 cakes.)

3 Beat the butter and sugar together until soft and fluffy. Add the eggs individually, as you continue to beat. Beat in the desiccated coconut, vanilla, lemon zest and salt. Stir in the coconut-milk-and-flour mixture, almond meal and baking powder to make a thick batter. Fold in the raspberries and divide between the muffin holes. Bake for 25 minutes or so, until risen, firm and golden brown. Let cool in the pan for 10 minutes before turning out and cooling on a wire rack.

4 Whisk the solidified coconut cream in a mixing bowl with the powdered sugar until light and fluffy. Put the toasted coconut flakes in a shallow bowl. Smoosh a generous dab of the coconut cream over the curved base of each cake (which will now become the top) and dip straight into the coconut flakes to coat.

Pear and Rosemary Tarts

Makes 8

- 1 batch Whole-Grain Flaky Puff (see page 307)
- A little flour of your choice, to dust
- 5 tablespoons salted butter, very soft
- ⅓ cup (75 g) raw sugar
- 1 egg
- ¾ cup (75 g) almond meal
- 1 teaspoon finely chopped rosemary, plus 8 small sprigs of rosemary
- 4 small, ripe pears
- 8 teaspoons honey

Honeyed baked pears combine so well with both rosemary and almonds in these quick tarts. If speed is a priority, use store-bought all-butter puff pastry, rolled out thinly. Or, to make the tarts gluten-free, use Gluten-Free Pastry (page 306). The frangipane, which can be made up to 3 days ahead of time if covered and chilled, keeps its shape pretty well when baking so won't spread, even without the slight puff from the outer edges of the flaky pastry to hold it in place.

1 Roll the pastry out between 2 sheets of parchment paper, until it is about ⅛ inch (3 to 4 mm) thick. Peel off the top paper layer. Stamp or cut eight 3 × 5-inch (8 × 12 cm) rounds out (dipping the knife or cutter into a little flour will stop it sticking) and space out on a large baking sheet, lined with the top sheet of paper from the pastry rolling. Chill for at least 30 minutes or up to 24 hours, until needed.

2 To make the frangipane, beat the soft butter with the sugar in a mixing bowl until very light and fluffy. Beat in the egg, followed by the almond meal and chopped rosemary. This can also be done ahead of time: Cover and chill the frangipane for up to 3 days, until needed.

3 When ready to cook, preheat the oven to 375°F (190°C). Halve the pears, scooping out their cores with a teaspoon or melon baller. Holding each pear by the stalk end, make 4 or 5 cuts from near the stalk right down through the base, so that you can fan it out into slices from the base, but keep the slices together at the top.

4 Spread one eighth of the frangipane out over each tart with a palette knife, keeping a ¾-inch (2 cm) border clear. Fan a pear half out on each tart and brush lightly with a teaspoon of the honey. Bake for 20 minutes, then top each pear half with a rosemary sprig and return to the oven for 5 minutes more, until the pears are tender and the pastry and frangipane are burnished and golden.

Pears
in Black
Mulberry
and Red
Wine Sauce

Serves 4 generously

- 1 vanilla pod, split lengthwise, seeds scraped out
- 1 bottle of good, fruity red wine
- ⅔ cup (120 g) light muscovado sugar
- 14 ounces (about 1¼ dry pints/400 g) black mulberries or blackberries, fresh or frozen
- 6 firm pears, peeled but kept whole

include this not because it contains any vegan pyrotechnics or mastery, but because a perfectly poached pear, cloaked in red wine and mulberry juice, is a marvelous thing and really needs no other accompaniment, though you can offer cream or ice cream if you like.

1 Put the vanilla pod and seeds in a large saucepan with the wine, sugar and mulberries.

2 Cut a sliver from the base of each pear so that they sit upright. Poach the pears by gently simmering, covered, for 20 to 30 minutes, turning every now and then to make sure they are covered in the wine. They should be tender to the point of a knife, but not on the point of collapse.

3 Take the pears from the pan with a slotted spoon, setting them aside in a shallow bowl. Simmer the liquid in the pan to reduce it by half, rendering it syrupy and rich. Pass the sauce through a fine sieve, pressing to release all the juice from the berries. Serve each pear cloaked in the sauce.

Vegan Chocolate Mousse with Walnut-Sesame Brittle

Serves 4

- 7 ounces (200 g) dark chocolate, chopped
- Pinch of sea salt
- 2 tablespoons maple or date syrup
- 1 vanilla pod, split lengthwise, seeds scraped out, or 2 teaspoons vanilla bean paste
- ½ batch Walnut-Sesame Crunch (see page 298)

This is based on Hervé This' ingenious method of making a chocolate mousse with little more than chocolate and water. When you take dairy and eggs out of a mousse, you are left with an incredible, uncluttered flavor. I have added maple syrup to sweeten it slightly and vanilla because it pairs so well, but you could use date or rice syrup and a little espresso, chile or cardamom instead.

1 Put the chocolate, salt and maple syrup in a saucepan with ¾ cup (175 ml) water. Set over low heat and warm the mixture through, stirring occasionally, until the chocolate has just melted.

2 Remove from the heat and stir in the vanilla seeds. Pour into a bowl, using a spatula to scrape every last drop out of the pan, and start to whip with a balloon whisk. Keep whisking and whisking until the chocolate just thickens and looks shiny, like a ganache. Stop before you think it looks like a mousse, as it will continue to set, but if you take it too far it isn't a disaster: A dry and thick mousse is rather delicious and, in any case, you can remelt it over gentle heat with 1 teaspoon of water and start all over again with the whisking. Divide between 4 smallish serving glasses or cups.

3 Using a mortar and pestle or a food processor, smash the Walnut-Sesame Crunch down to make a rough mixture. Scatter a little over each mousse to add texture.

Cashew, Date and Vanilla Freezer Cakes

Makes 10

- 1⅔ cups (225 g) cashews
- 1¼ cups (150 g) whole almonds
- ½ cup (60 g) pitted Medjool dates
- 2 pinches of sea salt
- 1 vanilla pod, split lengthwise
- ½ cup (100 ml) coconut milk
- ½ cup (100 ml) maple syrup
- ⅓ cup (75 ml) melted coconut oil
- Juice of 1 large lemon
- ¼ cup (75 g) almond butter
- 1 pound (about 1½ dry pints/450 g) blueberries

Similar creations are often called "cheesecakes" but, given their vegan status, these rich gluten-free creations are better thought of as chilled nut-butter cups. Add a good puddle of blueberry compote as I have suggested, or pitted cherries with melted dark chocolate, if you prefer.

1 Cover the cashews with plenty of cool water and leave for 4 to 6 hours, or, if you are short of time, cover with just-boiled water and leave for 1 hour.

2 To make the bases, blend the whole almonds and dates in a food processor with a pinch of salt. Cut 10 strips of nonstick parchment paper and sit them across 10 holes of a large muffin pan, or similar-size cups or molds if a muffin pan won't fit in your freezer. They will act as tabs, enabling you to pick the set cakes up. Divide the date mixture between the muffin pan cups or molds, pressing it down firmly to form the bases.

3 Drain the cashews thoroughly and put in a blender. Scrape in the seeds from the vanilla pod (keep the pod) and add the coconut milk, ⅓ cup (70 ml) of the maple syrup, the melted coconut oil, lemon juice, almond butter and the remaining pinch of salt. Blend on a high speed until completely and utterly smooth, stopping now and then to scrape the mixture down the sides as needed. Divide between the lined muffin pan holes and smooth the tops with a spatula. Make sure the paper tabs are standing up. Freeze for a minimum of 3 hours to set completely.

4 Put the blueberries in a saucepan with the empty vanilla pod, remaining maple syrup and a splash of water. Bring to a boil, reduce the heat and simmer gently, stirring often, until the berries burst and begin to turn jammy. Set aside to cool, then remove the vanilla pod.

5 Pull the set cakes out of their molds using the paper tabs and let sit in the fridge for 10 minutes or so. Serve with the blueberry compote spooned over generously.

Salted Chocolate and Almond Truffles

Makes about 36

For the truffles
- ¼ cup (50 g) coconut oil
- 1 tablespoon coconut sugar or maple sugar
- ¾ cup (200 g) white almond butter
- 7 ounces (200 g) dark chocolate with 70 percent cocoa solids, chopped into small pieces
- 2 large pinches of sea salt flakes, scrunched up in your fingers
- 1 vanilla pod, split lengthwise, seeds scraped out, or 1 teaspoon vanilla bean paste

For the coating
- Cocoa powder
- Unsweetened desiccated coconut
- Shelled and unsalted almonds, hazelnuts, pecans, pistachios and so on, finely chopped

This (incidentally) vegan mixture makes a rich and intense truffle, balanced with a good kick of salt.

1 Heat the coconut oil and sugar together in a saucepan set over low heat, stirring with a wooden spoon until the oil has melted and the sugar has dissolved. Add the almond butter, chocolate, a pinch of scrunched sea salt and all the vanilla seeds. Continue to stir gently until the chocolate is two-thirds melted. Remove from the heat and continue to stir intermittently until smooth and shiny.

2 To make square truffles, pour the mixture into an 8-inch (20 cm) square brownie pan lined with parchment paper. To make scoopable truffles, you can use a pan as above or a shallow bowl, about 8 inches (20 cm) in diameter. Either way, set the truffle mix aside to cool, then scatter with the remaining scrunched sea salt. Chill for 2 hours, until set solid.

3 Transfer the coating ingredients you want to use into shallow bowls; the amount you'll need will depend on how many different coatings you use in a batch, but make sure the bases of the bowls are covered generously to get an even covering.

4 To make square truffles, turn the mixture out onto a cool work surface and slice into small squares (the mixture is rich) then roll each gently in a coating. To scoop out curls, leave the mixture at room temperature for 15 minutes or so (this is a bit trial and error as weather and kitchen temperature vary so much), then scrape the surface with a teaspoon to scoop into curls and rough spirals. Roll each gently in a coating and keep cool or, if they feel soft, return them to the fridge to set the mixture up.

5 The coated truffles will last for 2 weeks or so if they are kept chilled in a sealed container. Or freeze them for a good month, defrosting in the fridge overnight when you need them.

chapter nine

pantry

WAS INITIALLY HESITANT ABOUT referring you, the reader, to additional, component recipes throughout the book, feeling it somehow disingenuous to put you to the trouble . . . but the same staples feature again and again, woven through the pages, and they warranted a separate home. Here you will find a mixture of core tools and spirited extras to thread into your cooking. My vegan alternative to fish sauce, for example, is used repeatedly, wherever that hit of umami-funk is required (page 300). Of course, you can substitute a 50/50 mix of soy sauce and water to thinner, yet comparable effect, or even use the original if you eat fish, but with so many East Asian recipes in the book a laudable alternative was essential.

Nowadays, I find myself turning to pastry less frequently, but it still features regularly enough to be a staple. So a handful of steadfast dough recipes, suited to most uses and dietary requirements, find their home here, to be used as the basis for sweet and savory tarts and pies (see pages 306 to 307).

And beyond these fundamentals there are optional extras in the form of quick relishes and condiments. These are the key to quirky cooking, adding characterful flourish and dash. You could use store-bought alternatives in most cases, but homemade is invariably better if you have the time, and, besides, there is nothing complicated here. True preserving is an art, using carefully sterilized vessels and ingredients in bulk . . . but I wanted something more immediate and, arguably, more vibrant than jars of long-simmered chutneys that can sit in your pantry for all eternity. Hence, the emphasis here is on bold flavor and quick results in small batches, often with a healthy dose of chile heat. Freedom from the tyranny of long-term preserving means adding far less sugar, compensating with intense flavor from the produce itself. The same principles apply as in general vegetarian cooking: Roasting, griddling and occasionally charring the ripest produce will drive off water, exaggerating natural sugars and concentrating precious flavors, to give a fierce and true result. Tomatoes and both sweet and hot peppers, full of the flavors of summer, make the ideal candidates for naturally sweet jams and relishes, and I have used them with abandon.

Most of these recipes are incredibly versatile, the idea being that if you make, say, a tomato and preserved lemon relish (see page 294) to go with falafel, you can enjoy it with vegetable fritters or flash-fried halloumi over the following days. Pickled Sour Cherries (page 299) are adaptable enough to go from cheese board to salad or bruschetta or, as I've suggested in the Grazing chapter, to scatter on slightly bitter tahini and sweet, nutty kibbeh. Here lies the ingenious contrast and balance in a well-considered dish and the value of a relish. Some others, as with the Sriracha Mayonnaise with Scallions (page 300), feature to provide a quick fix when inspiration is low or a straightforward supper needs extra pep.

A note on stock: It is a staple used throughout the book, adding subtle and satisfying layers of flavor. It would be impressive if you made your own every time. I keep a large container of Marigold Swiss vegetable bouillon (you can find it on Amazon) and use it often, favoring the light, powdered mix over greasy stock cubes. Having said that, a homemade broth can make an enormous difference to a dish. If you have the freezer space and the occasional time to spare, making a concentrated master stock is a nourishing way to use up leftover or tired vegetables, trimmings, peelings and herb stalks and is so simple it hardly warrants a recipe. Working on a simple ratio of 2¼ pounds (1 kg) of aromatic vegetables—always including celery and onion—to 2 quarts (2 L) of water, simmer gently for thirty to sixty minutes, then strain through a fine sieve. Use as is, or reduce down by half to freeze and dilute later. It will keep for a week in the fridge or for a three-month stint in the freezer. Customize your broth as you wish. For example, mushrooms add umami flavor; whole spices enhance when used judiciously; root vegetables and tomato paste bring sweet depth; while the peelings from aromatic ginger and lemongrass lend an East Asian flavor profile, perfect for noodle soups. Add classic French flavor with a bouquet garni, made by tying bay leaves, thyme, parsley and a few black peppercorns up in a piece of leek leaf. If you need a robust, characterful stock, as I did in my pho recipe (see page 129), roast or sauté larger vegetable pieces in a little oil to caramelize and concentrate their flavors before simmering, and be generous with the mushrooms. Only avoid members of the cabbage family, zucchini, green beans and potatoes in stocks: The last is too starchy and the others too pungent.

Interestingly, food writer Heidi Swanson brought my attention to a homemade bouillon, garnered in turn from Pam Corbin's *Preserves: River Cottage Handbook No 2*. It uses a food processor to blend a scant 2¼ pounds (1 kg) of chopped, stock-friendly vegetables (leeks, fennel, celery, onions, celery root, carrots) with a couple of tablespoons of chopped, sun-dried tomatoes for depth, a few garlic cloves, a handful of soft herbs and ¾ cup (250 g) of salt to a paste. The high salt content prevents this from freezing solid, so keep it in the freezer, ready to add to simmering water whenever light stock is needed. Just keep an eye on the salt used in the rest of the recipe, to prevent overseasoning.

Roasted Tomato and Pickled Lemon Relish

Makes 1 medium jar

- 1 pound 5 ounces (600 g) plum tomatoes, deseeded and coarsely chopped
- 2 preserved lemons, rind only, thinly sliced
- 3 garlic cloves, finely chopped
- 2 tablespoons sun-dried tomato paste
- 1 tablespoon sherry vinegar
- 1 teaspoon cumin seeds, roughly crushed
- Pinch of chile flakes
- Sea salt and freshly ground black pepper
- Handful of cilantro leaves, chopped, optional

This fresh, sour and salty relish contains no added sugar, so it won't keep for very long. It is fantastic with halloumi or baked feta (see page 89), or anything from the fritter/kofta family. Shades of the Middle East in the spicing lend it well to other foods from that part of the world, though it is approachable enough to lift most savory dishes.

❶ Preheat the oven to 350°F (180°C). Combine all the ingredients except the cilantro in a small roasting pan.

❷ Bake, uncovered, for about 45 minutes, until the tomatoes are soft, reduced and beginning to brown. Stir halfway through the cooking time to redistribute. Stir with a fork to break the relish down and season to taste with salt and pepper.

❸ Cool to room temperature and leave as is, or blend until smooth if you prefer. Stir in the cilantro, if using. Transfer to a clean jar and let cool. Cover with a lid, chill and use within 1 week.

Sweet Pepper and Chile Jam

Makes 1 medium jar

- 6 sweet red peppers (ideally the sweet, thin-skinned Romano or bull's horn if you can find them), halved, cored and deseeded
- 2 mild red chiles, halved and deseeded
- 1 pound 4 ounces (550 g; about 7 medium) fragrant, vine-ripened tomatoes, halved through their middles, seeds scooped out
- 1-inch (2.5 cm) piece fresh ginger root, peeled and finely grated (including the juice)
- 3 tablespoons rice wine vinegar or white wine vinegar
- 1 tablespoon palm sugar or unrefined brown sugar

Considering the punch this little jam packs, the amount of sugar added is minimal. You can leave it out, but remember the jam may need a little less acid for balance and will only keep in the fridge for a few days without the sugar's preserving qualities. Use in sandwiches and wraps, to go with quiches, tarts, omelets or fritattas . . . or, indeed, anything egg-based and savory.

1 Preheat the oven to 400°F (200°C). Lay the pepper halves and chiles, skin sides up, in a single layer in 1 roasting pan, and the tomatoes, skin sides up, in a second pan (they can be muddled together a little more than the peppers).

2 Roast both pans for 30 minutes or so, making sure the pepper tray is at the top of the oven, until the skins are shriveled and the peppers are blackened. All should be soft, so, if your peppers were particularly hefty, give them another 10 minutes in the oven. Cover the peppers with a baking sheet so they steam and set both pans aside to cool.

3 Peel off the tomato and pepper skins, not worrying too much about stubborn shreds and pieces of peel here and there—the odd black smoky piece is in fact a flavor advantage—and leaving the chiles unpeeled. Put all the flesh in a saucepan over high heat with the ginger, vinegar and sugar and heat through, stirring constantly to break the peppers down. Simmer down over medium-high heat, stirring often, until jammy and thick (this should take about 10 minutes). Transfer to a clean jar and let cool. Cover with a lid, chill and use within 3 weeks.

Spiced Mustard

Makes 1 small jar

- ⅓ cup (100 g) yellow mustard seeds, or a mixture of yellow and brown
- ½ cup (120 ml) white wine vinegar
- ½ cup (120 ml) dry white wine
- 2 tablespoons honey
- ½-inch (1.5 cm) piece fresh turmeric, peeled and finely chopped, or ½ teaspoon ground turmeric
- ½ teaspoon sea salt
- 1 teaspoon finely grated horseradish

Homemade mustards are usually hot and sharp compared to store-bought, and this is no exception. The finished mustard won't be completely smooth unless you own an incredible blender, but that is part of its charm. This is also good with chopped dill stirred through it, in which case increase the honey quantity to make a version of a Swedish mustard sauce.

1 Combine all the ingredients, except the horseradish, in a nonmetallic bowl. Cover and leave in a cool place (not the fridge) for 2 to 3 days, so that the mustard seeds can swell and soften.

2 Blend until smooth in a powerful (small) blender. You may need to add a splash of hot water to get the blades moving. Add the grated horseradish and blend again, but don't expect the mixture to be completely smooth, as most blenders won't be able to achieve that. It will thicken on standing. Use immediately or cover, chill and try to use within 1 month (it will keep happily for 3 months, but the flavor fades).

Walnut-Sesame Crunch

Makes about 4 ounces (120 g)

- ⅔ cup (100 g) walnut pieces
- 2 tablespoons sesame seeds
- 3 tablespoons brown rice syrup
- Small pinch of sea salt

Scatter these sweet-salty caramelized nuts over salads, grain bowls, or cakes and desserts.

Have a baking sheet lined with parchment or wax paper ready. Put the walnuts in a large frying pan and toast over low heat, stirring often, until just beginning to turn golden. Add the sesame seeds to the pan and continue to toast until the seeds are lightly browned. Increase the heat, add the rice syrup and toss through to coat. Scrunch the salt over and continue to cook until the nuts are evenly glazed. Pour onto the parchment or wax paper in an even layer and set aside to cool. Once completely cool, roughly or finely chop as needed. Keep in an airtight container in a cool place for up to 4 days.

Warm Tahini Dressing

Makes 1 small jar

- Juice of 1 lemon
- 1 garlic clove, crushed
- 3 tablespoons extra virgin olive oil
- 3 tablespoons light tahini
- Sea salt and freshly ground black pepper

A pot of magic to keep on hand, ready to spoon over fritters or falafel, or to spread over warm flatbreads to keep salad leaves in place before rolling. The taste of the finished sauce will depend entirely on the tahini you use, so make sure it is as fresh as possible and not too bitter, and stir the jar well before using.

❶ Combine the lemon juice, garlic, olive oil and tahini in a small saucepan, gradually stirring in ½ cup (100 ml) just-boiled water to thicken the sauce to the consistency of heavy cream. Season generously with salt and pepper and heat through very gently over low heat. Add a little more water to make a thinner dressing, if needed.

❷ Keep chilled for up to 2 weeks, letting down with a little hot water and rewarming gently in a saucepan before using.

Pickled Sour Cherries

Makes 1 medium jar

- 1¾ cups (300 g) dried sour cherries
- ½ cup (120 ml) red wine vinegar or sherry vinegar
- 3 tablespoons maple syrup
- 4 fresh bay leaves
- 1 tablespoon coriander seeds
- 1 teaspoon sea salt
- Pinch of chile flakes

As with most pickles and relishes in this chapter, these fragrant and spicy cherries have myriad uses, but you might want to start by adding them to a cheese board, or a salad of peppery leaves, blue cheese and pecans.

Put all the ingredients in a small saucepan with 3 tablespoons water and bring to a boil over medium-low heat, stirring often. Once bubbling, remove from the heat, pour into a clean jar and cover. Set aside to cool completely. Chill and use within 1 month.

Sesame Seed Za'atar

Makes about 3.5 ounces (100 g)

- ⅓ cup (50 g) black or white sesame seeds
- 1 tablespoon plus 1 teaspoon cumin seeds
- 1 tablespoon plus 1 teaspoon dried oregano
- 1 tablespoon plus 1 teaspoon ground sumac
- 1 teaspoon sea salt flakes
- ½ teaspoon freshly ground black pepper

This North African spice mix is wonderful sprinkled over soft-boiled eggs or split, baked sweet potatoes. Stir in a pinch of finely chopped fresh oregano leaves before using, if you like. Try za'atar blended with roasted almonds and spiked with extra herbs as a seasoning for polenta fries (see page 159), or add dried chile, lemon juice, oregano leaves and olive oil to make a dressing for roasted vegetables, feta or salad.

Put the sesame and cumin seeds in a large frying pan and toast over medium heat, tossing the pan for a minute or so, until the seeds are fragrant and a shade darker (hard to judge if you use black sesame seeds! Go with your nose). Transfer into a mini food processor, spice grinder or mortar and pestle and add the dried oregano, sumac, salt and pepper. Blend or grind as finely as you wish. Keep in a cool, dark place in an airtight jar for up to 1 month.

Vegetarian "Fish" Sauce

Makes about ¾ cup (200 ml)

- ¼ cup (5 g) dried mushrooms, preferably cloud ear or shiitake
- 2 tablespoons salted, fermented black beans
- 2 umeboshi plums (or you can substitute 2 tablespoons rice wine vinegar)
- 1 teaspoon miso paste, ideally a mild yellow or white
- ⅓ cup (75 ml) light soy sauce

The obvious trouble with being puritanical about using only fish sauce in Southeast Asian recipes is that it excludes non-fish eaters. (How many times in other recipes have I read, "Don't even think about substituting soy sauce?" All very laudable, but so tiresome for vegetarians and vegans.) This method gives you a complex, umami-rich, vegan substitute.

1 Cover the mushrooms, beans, plums and miso paste with ¾ cup (200 ml) just-boiled water and mash roughly with the back of a spoon. Set aside to soak for 10 minutes. Strain the soaking water through a fine sieve, pressing down firmly, and stir in the soy sauce.

2 Transfer to a clean jar and cover. Chill and it will last for a few weeks.

Sriracha Mayonnaise with Scallions

Serves 4 as a dip or accompaniment

- ¼ cup (60 g) mayonnaise
- 2 tablespoons sour cream or mild plain yogurt
- 1 or 2 tablespoons Sriracha sauce, to taste
- Squeeze of lime juice
- 3 scallions, finely chopped
- Sea salt and freshly ground black pepper

Admittedly, this is a little bit trashy, but it's excellent as a dip for baked potato skins, hot vegetable fritters or crunchy lettuce leaves. Japanese Kewpie mayonnaise is the ideal choice if you can track down a squishy package; it is made with rice wine vinegar and has a mild, sweet flavor.

Combine all the ingredients in a bowl (add the second tablespoon of Sriracha for a stronger kick) and season to taste. Keep, chilled and covered, for up to 4 days.

Sweet Miso and Seaweed Relish

Makes 1 small jar

- 1 square of toasted nori seaweed
- ¼ cup (60 ml) maple syrup or brown rice syrup
- 2 tablespoons mellow brown or yellow miso
- 2 tablespoons rice wine vinegar
- 1 tablespoon peeled and finely grated fresh ginger root

Tuck a spoonful of this umami-rich relish with its slight mineral tang into grain, noodle or salad bowls, stirring through as you eat.

Snip the nori into fine little shreds with scissors. Stir through the remaining ingredients, cover and chill for up to 2 weeks.

Vegetarian Nuoc Cham

Makes about 1 cup (240 ml)

- 2 tablespoons unrefined superfine sugar, or to taste
- ¼ cup (60 ml) rice wine vinegar
- ¼ cup (60 ml) Vegetarian "Fish" Sauce (page 300, or see recipe introduction), or to taste
- 1 bird's eye chile, finely sliced, or to taste
- 1 garlic clove, finely chopped
- Juice of 1 lime, or to taste

Use this as a dipping sauce for summer rolls or fritters, as a salad dressing, or to pour over noodles and rice. If you haven't made any of the Vegetarian "Fish" Sauce and can't track down a comparable store-bought version, substitute light soy sauce mixed with an equal amount of water.

Pour ½ cup (100 ml) water into a small saucepan and add the sugar. Warm through over low heat, stirring often to dissolve the sugar. Remove from the heat, add the vinegar and "fish" sauce, stir well and set aside to cool. Once cool, stir in the chile, garlic and lime juice. Taste to check you like the balance of sweet, hot, salty and sour, adjusting as necessary. Use immediately or keep chilled and covered for up to 5 days.

Sambal Oelek (Chile Paste)

Makes 1 tiny jar

- 1 lemongrass stalk, well trimmed
- 8 large red chiles, halved, deseeded and roughly chopped
- 1 teaspoon sea salt, or to taste
- 3 tablespoons lime juice or rice wine vinegar

This is a relatively primitive version of the Indonesian chile paste, with only a subtle hint of lemongrass. You can make the paste more complicated with garlic, ginger, sugar and lime zest, and you can also simmer the liquid to reduce. A robust mortar and pestle is essential to crush and break the chiles down.

Remove the outer layers from the lemongrass to reveal the soft core. Chop this roughly. Put half the chiles and lemongrass in a mortar and pestle and add half the salt. Pound to a rough purée. Scrape into a bowl and repeat. Stir in the lime juice or vinegar and taste. It should be extremely fiery and sharp, but a little bit sweet from the chiles. Add a little more salt if you like. Cover and keep chilled for up to 2 weeks.

Quick Vietnamese Pickles

Makes 1 medium bowlful

- ½ cup (90 g) unrefined superfine sugar
- ½ teaspoon sea salt
- ¾ cup (180 ml) rice wine vinegar
- 1¾ cups (200 g) peeled and shredded (or sliced, in the case of small) daikon and/or small regular radishes
- 1⅔ cups (200 g) peeled and shredded carrots

Keep a bowlful of these on hand for any Vietnamese salad, summer roll or noodle bowl.

Combine the sugar, salt and vinegar with ½ cup (100 ml) water in a bowl, stirring until the sugar dissolves. Add the vegetables and set aside for 2 hours. The pickles can be drained and eaten at this stage (rinse them for an even milder flavor), or chill them for 2 to 3 weeks. Their flavor will become more intense as the days go on.

Kombu Stock (or "Dashi, No Tuna")

Makes 1 quart (1 L)

- 1 piece dried kombu seaweed (about 2 × 4 inches/5 × 10 cm)

Use this mild but savory stock as a base for gentle Japanese-inspired noodle soups or mellow brothy rice bowls.

Snip the kombu with scissors to make a few cuts in it, releasing the flavor. Put the kombu in a saucepan and cover with 1 quart (1 L) water. To deepen the flavor, set aside to soak for anything from 2 hours to a day. Place over low heat and very slowly bring to a boil. As soon as the liquid begins to bubble, remove the soft kombu with tongs. Strain the broth through a muslin- or cheesecloth-lined sieve and let cool. Cover and chill if not using right away and keep for up to 2 days.

Caramelized Peanut Sauce

Makes about 2 cups (500 ml)

- 2 shallots, finely chopped
- 1-inch (2.5 cm) piece fresh ginger root, peeled and finely grated
- 2 red chiles, finely chopped
- 1 tablespoon peanut oil
- 1 garlic clove, crushed
- 1½ tablespoons palm or brown sugar, or to taste
- 1 cup (150 g) roughly chopped unsalted peanuts
- One 13.5-ounce (400 ml) can coconut milk
- 2 tablespoons light soy sauce, or to taste
- 2 tablespoons tamarind paste, or to taste

Or satay by another name; this is an addictive and versatile sauce, so I always make it in generous quantity. Serve it with Asian-style omelets, crisp tofu or fried rice, as a dressing for noodles or a dip for crunchy vegetables.

1 Gently fry the shallots, ginger and red chiles in the oil for 5 minutes, until soft but not colored. Now add the garlic, sugar and peanuts and cook for 5 minutes more, until the nuts are deeply golden and caramelized. Stir in the coconut milk, soy sauce and tamarind and simmer for a few minutes.

2 Purée as finely as you like with a hand blender, or in a food processor. Season with a little extra soy sauce if needed and/or up the tamarind or sugar. Return to the pan to heat through gently before serving. If making this in advance, it will thicken on cooling and will need a splash of water to thin it out when reheating.

3 It will keep, covered, in the refrigerator for 2 weeks.

FOUR ESSENTIAL PASTRY RECIPES

These should prove useful pastry variations in your day-to-day cooking. As a rough guide, 6 ounces (175 g) of pastry will line an 8-inch (20 cm) tart pan. To cover the top, too (to make a pie), you will need 8 ounces (225 g). About 15 ounces (420 g) of pastry will generously line (or make a lid for) a 10-inch (26 cm) tart pan or ovenproof dish, while the whole batch of gluten-free pastry here—about 18 ounces (520 g)—lines an 11- to 12-inch (28 to 30 cm) pan.

Spelt Pie Crust

Makes about 15 ounces (420 g)

- 2 cups (250 g) whole-grain spelt flour
- ½ teaspoon fine salt
- 1 stick (125 g) unsalted butter, chilled and chopped
- Ice water

 n excellent, everyday pastry. Not wheat- or gluten-free, but characterful and reliable.

Put the flour and salt in a food processor and pulse to aerate. Add the butter and pulse until the mixture resembles bread crumbs. (Or you can rub the butter in by hand, in a large mixing bowl.) Transfer into a bowl and add 2½ tablespoons of ice water, cutting it into the pastry with a table knife. Add a drop more water as needed to bring it together into a ball, leaving the bowl clean. Knead briefly to combine, form into a disc, wrap and set aside in a cool place to rest for 30 minutes before rolling out.

Gluten-Free Pastry

Makes about 18 ounces (520 g)

- 1 cup (120 g) arrowroot powder or tapioca flour
- 1 cup (120 g) brown rice flour
- ½ cup (60 g) glutinous rice flour
- ½ teaspoon fine salt
- 1½ sticks (200 g) unsalted butter, chilled and chopped
- Ice water

You will need to visit a health food or good East Asian shop for this. You can substitute coconut butter for the dairy kind, but it has a strong taste. If you can't get with that taste but want a dairy-free pastry, use the same amount of olive oil by weight and freeze for 1 to 2 hours in an empty yogurt container. Blend or rub into the flour, being careful not to overwork. This pastry will be slightly flaky, short and flavorful.

Combine the flours in the bowl of a food processor. Add the salt and pulse to mix. Add the butter and pulse until the mixture resembles bread crumbs with no visible pieces of butter. Transfer into a large mixing bowl and cut 3 tablespoons of ice water in with a table knife. You may need to add up to 2 tablespoons more to bring the dough together. Form into a disc, wrap in plastic wrap and chill for 30 to 60 minutes or up to 3 days, or freeze for a month, before rolling out between sheets of parchment paper.

Whole-Grain Flaky Puff

Makes about 15 ounces (420 g)

- 1¾ cups (220 g) whole-grain spelt or regular whole wheat flour
- ½ teaspoon fine salt
- 1 stick plus 2 tablespoons (150 g) unsalted butter, frozen solid
- Ice water

 buttery, delicate pastry with a nutty taste and none of the bother of making a classic puff.

Put the flour and salt in a bowl and stir with a balloon whisk to aerate. Wrap the end of the butter in foil so that you can hold it without it melting. Coarsely grate it straight into the flour, dipping the end of the butter block into the flour if it softens. Lightly toss it through the flour with a knife. Sprinkle 3 tablespoons of ice water over, cutting in with the knife. Add 3 to 5 tablespoons water to form a dough. With your hands, lightly bring the pastry into a ball that leaves the bowl clean. Divide into 2 and flatten each piece into a disc. Wrap and chill for 30 minutes before rolling out.

A Decent Vegan Pastry

Makes about 15 ounces (420 g)

- 2 cups (250 g) whole-grain spelt flour
- ½ teaspoon fine salt
- 1 tablespoon coconut sugar or unrefined brown sugar, optional (if making sweet pastry)
- ½ cup (125 g) extra virgin coconut butter, chilled and roughly chopped
- Ice water

White spelt, or regular all-purpose flour, is just as good here, but the water quantity may vary. The coconut flavor is noticeable (and delicious if you are a fan), so this "short" pastry is ideal for sweet recipes. For a subtler taste, use refined coconut butter.

Put the flour and salt in a food processor and pulse to aerate. If you want to add sugar, stir it in here. Add the coconut butter and continue to pulse until the mixture resembles bread crumbs. (Or you can rub the butter in by hand, in a large mixing bowl.) Transfer into a bowl and add 2½ tablespoons of ice water, cutting it into the pastry with a table knife. Add a drop more water as needed to bring it into a ball, leaving the bowl clean. Knead briefly to combine, form into a disc, wrap and set aside in a cool place to rest for 30 minutes before rolling out. If using this to line a tart pan, leave the sides overhanging and trim after baking, not before, to prevent shrinkage.

Sweet-Sour Tamarind Sauce

Makes 1 cup (225 ml)

- ⅔ cup (75 g) seedless tamarind pulp from a block
- ¼ cup (45 g) palm sugar, or to taste
- ¼ cup (60 ml) Vegetarian "Fish" Sauce (page 300, or use a store-bought version), or substitute 2 tablespoons light soy sauce mixed with 2 tablespoons water, or to taste
- Sea salt, as needed

A vital component of Son-in-Law Eggs with Green Mango (page 86) and excellent on plain fried eggs, too, or use this distinct and tangy sauce/dressing/chutney in any number of Asian-inspired recipes. Making tamarind purée from blocks of sour tamarind pulp takes barely two minutes and is completely worth it, both for the superior, intense flavor and the value for your money. I don't even consider the ready-to-serve purée in puny jars.

1 Put the tamarind pulp in a bowl and cover with ¾ cup (200 ml) boiling water. Stir and mash with a spoon to make a rough purée. Push this through a sieve into a small saucepan, scraping with the back of the spoon to force all the liquid through and leaving the seeds and fibers behind.

2 Add the sugar and "fish" sauce to the pan and warm through gently for a couple of minutes, stirring often to encourage the sugar to dissolve. Taste and adjust the salt and sugar as needed; the sauce should be thin in texture and should taste predominantly sour and sweet, with a salty background note. Cover and cool, then keep in the fridge for up to 2 weeks.

Spiced Bay Leaf Salt

Makes 1.75 ounces (50 g)

- 4 fresh bay leaves, roughly chopped
- ¼ cup (60 g) sea salt
- Leaves from 3 sprigs of thyme
- Finely grated zest of 1 unwaxed lemon
- 1 teaspoon chile flakes

Scatter this intense salt over vegetables before roasting, or combine it with butter and spoon into baked sweet potatoes.

Put the bay leaves in a mortar and pestle, or the small bowl of a food processor. Add a good pinch of the salt and pummel or blend until the salt turns green and the leaves are reduced to very small pieces. Add the thyme and lemon zest and blend or pummel again. Stir in the remaining salt and the chile flakes. Keep in a lidded jar in a cool place for a couple of months.

Thai-Style Roasted Chile Paste

Makes 1 jar

- 5.5 ounces (150 g) bird's eye chiles
- 1 cup (100 g) unpeeled and halved Thai shallots
- 6 fat garlic cloves, unpeeled
- Sea salt
- ⅓ cup (75 ml) peanut oil
- 2 tablespoons palm sugar or brown sugar
- 2 tablespoons tamarind purée (see page 308)
- 1 to 2 tablespoons light soy sauce

This makes an excellent and incredibly hot, oily paste. Not a bad thing, of course, but I'm just warning you about the heat levels. You could substitute a milder chile, if you prefer a less explosive mouthful. Add spoonfuls of this paste to stir-fries, soups, congee, grain bowls and salads, to add fire. Add more oil to the paste to make it into a roasted chile oil, if you think you will use that more often.

1 Set a large frying pan over high heat. Add the chiles and cook, stirring occasionally, until shiny, brittle and dry looking. Take your time; they will snap and crackle occasionally as they color and blister. Transfer out on to a plate.

2 Return the pan to the high heat and add the shallots and garlic cloves. Cook for a few minutes, turning now and then, until blackened in places and slightly shriveled. Transfer onto the chile plate.

3 Rubber gloves are an essential here: Slice the chiles in half, removing the stems and most of the seeds. Trim and peel the shallots and garlic. Either pound the chiles, shallots, and garlic to a paste with a mortar and pestle, in 2 or 3 batches with a pinch of salt to help things along, or blend in a mini food processor, stopping to scrape down the sides. Either way, you should have a slightly lumpy purée.

4 Put the oil in a wok or frying pan and set over medium heat. Add the chile paste and fry gently, stirring now and then, until darker and fragrant. This should take 4 to 6 minutes, so reduce the heat if it colors too quickly, as you don't want the paste to burn. Remove from the heat and let cool. Stir in the sugar, tamarind and 1 tablespoon of the soy sauce. Taste and add a little more soy sauce and salt if needed, depending on how much you used with the chiles. Spoon into a clean lidded jar.

5 Keep chilled and use within 1 month.

Resources

MEXGROCER
Mexican ingredients and cooking utensils.
mexgrocer.com

FRESH ORIGINS MICROGREENS
California farm growing edible flowers, shoots, microgreens, etc.
freshorigins.com

THE KOMBUCHA SHOP
Kombucha kits and supplies.
thekombuchashop.com

VITACOST
Healthy foods, including less common flours, oils and vinegars.
vitacost.com

FARMBOX DIRECT
Fresh, seasonal fruits and veggies delivered weekly right to your door.
farmboxdirect.com

NOM LIVING
Many of the photographed recipes in this book are set off by the handsome, earthy ceramics kindly lent by Nom Living.
nomliving.com

PENZEYS SPICES
Spices from around the world: curry blends, chili powders, etc.
penzeys.com

EFOODDEPOT
Foods organized by country.
efooddepot.com

YOUR LOCAL FARMERS MARKETS AND/OR CSA
Consider shopping at a local farmers market and/or joining a local CSA (Community Supported Agriculture).
ams.usda.gov/local-food-directories/farmersmarkets
localharvest.org/csa

YOUR LOCAL GROCERY STORE
Doesn't have to be fancy; buy what's colorful and seasonal and buy it cheap! Also, many grocery stores offer the option to shop online and pick up your purchased items in your local store.

Cook's Notes

BUTTER

Butter is unsalted unless stated otherwise. Do buy decent butter; all- (or predominantly) grass-fed, if you can.

DAIRY

The recipes have been tested using full-fat or whole dairy, unless stated otherwise.

EGGS

Eggs are large, unless stated otherwise, and always free-range for preference.

OVEN TEMPERATURE

Ovens run at varying temperatures and most have hot spots. A good, free-standing oven thermometer will do wonders for your cooking, helping you to understand your oven's habits. These recipes have been tested in both conventional and convection ovens, always using an oven thermometer for accuracy. Temperatures are in degrees Fahrenheit and Celsius, but please remember that convection ovens run hot, so temperatures will need to be adjusted down by about 25 to 30°F (20°C): in practice this means that a 350°F (180°C) temperature printed in this book means turning the dial on a convection oven to 320°F (160°C).

SEASONING

In savory recipes, *salt* refers to flakes of sea salt, such as Maldon; in sweet recipes and baking, it's usually best to use fine sea salt to distribute it evenly and subtly. *Pepper* refers to freshly ground black peppercorns. *Season* means adding sea salt flakes and freshly ground black pepper, to taste.

SPOON MEASURES

All spoon measurements should be level, unless stated otherwise.

WEIGHT/MASS/VOLUME

I use scales to weigh ingredients in grams and kilograms and have not tested these recipes using cup measurements. Conversion into cups has been provided by the publisher for this edition without retesting; where possible, follow the weight measures for best results, especially for baking.

Acknowledgments

COOKBOOKS ARE TEAM EFFORTS AND this is no exception. It is the product of incredible hard work by a group of wonderful women I feel lucky to know.

Thank you to Matthew and the team at The Experiment. To Rowan at Square Peg for your conviction, and Susannah, Natalie and the rest of the team for your added enthusiasm. I am so grateful you wanted to make this book. Thank you Claudia at Greene & Heaton for getting the ball rolling! And Eleanor and Cate at Pearson Lyle for your patience and continued friendship while I wrote.

Charlotte, your elegant design looks incredible and we are all so grateful for your hard work. Lucy, thank you for all your time and patience; I can't imagine a better, or wiser, editor.

Emma, Lizzie and Tabitha always bring such joy and talent to a shoot. Thank you for your tireless hard work creating the beautiful images and the laughs we had. You wear those aprons so well, badgers.

Special thanks to you Emma, for the Forest House and its magical light. To Isla, for amazing help with the shoot recipes and to Poppy for such thorough and enthusiastic testing help. Thanks to my family, and to Chris, chief nonvegetarian-taste-tester, for patiently tolerating my endless testing and writing. x

Index

About the Author

ALICE HART—a graduate of Leiths School of Food and Wine and a longtime and accomplished food writer, food stylist, chef, and cookbook author—is a master at crafting seasonal vegetarian recipes, inspired by her travels around the world, that celebrate produce and other whole foods, as well as spices and herbs by the handful. The author of three previous cookbooks, her recipes and writing have appeared in *The New York Times* and many other outlets. Hart lives in the vegetarian-friendly seaside city of Brighton, in the UK.